VINTAGE BOOKS

A DIVISION OF RANDOM HOUSE, INC.

NEW YORK

altared

Bridezillas, Bewilderment,

Big Love, Breakups, and

What Women Really Think

About Contemporary

Weddings

edited by

colleen curran

Grateful acknowledgment is made to the following for permission to reprint previously published material:

Hal Leonard Corporation: Excerpt from "You Decorated My Life" words and music by Debbie Hupp and Bob Morrison, copyright © 1978 by Temi Combine, Inc. All rights controlled by Music City Music, Inc. and administered by EMI April Music, Inc. All rights reserved. International copyright secured. Reprinted by permission of Hal Leonard Corporation.

Henry Holt and Company, LLC: Excerpt from "The Road Not Taken" from *The Poetry of Robert Frost*, edited by Edward Connery Lathem, copyright © 1969 by Henry Holt and Company. Reprinted by permission of Henry Holt and Company, LLC.

Credits for the contributors, which constitute an extension of the copyright page, can be found on pages 367–368.

Library of Congress Cataloging-in-Publication Data
Altared : bridezillas, bewilderment, big love, breakups, and what women really think about contemporary weddings / edited by Colleen Curran.
   p. cm.
   ISBN: 978-0-307-27763-3
   1. Weddings—Anecdotes. 2. Weddings—Planning.
   3. Weddings—Humor. I. Curran, Colleen.
   HQ745.A357 2007
   395.2'2—dc22
   2006038706

Book design by Stephanie Huntwork

www.vintagebooks.com

Printed in the United States of America
10 9 8 7 6 5 4 3 2

CONTENTS

family & budget

getting hitched

for better or for worse?

introduction

colleen curran

♥

When I started working on this book, I had been engaged for three years with no intention of setting a date, sending out invitations, finding a dress, or any of the other responsibilities that go into planning a wedding. My fiancé and I had been dating for seven years. We bought a house together. We started talking about kids. Once, he described me to friends as his "life partner." I just looked at him and asked, "Is there something wrong with us?"

When strangers, coworkers, or family friends noticed my engagement ring, they'd ask, "When's the big day?"

I'd always smile and say, "Spring." I said we were getting married in the spring for three years. Spring sounded so far away, so full of promise, so out there over the rainbow where we would live happily ever after together, end without end, amen. The spring was always out there. We could get married any day.

As many of the contributors in this collection write, I never saw myself as a bride. It was an issue of identity for me. I felt like if I became a fiancée, if I became a bride, I would lose an important part of myself. The part that I'd spent all this time trying to cultivate—the independent *me* part. The strong, single woman me. I was twenty-eight years old. My life was finally starting to come together. I was just starting to get published. I was finishing my first novel. I had a busy full-time job as an editor. Now I was supposed to drop everything and plan a wedding?

I loved my fiancé, Francis. Had fallen for him the first time I saw him on my first day of graduate school. He was tall and strong. Funny and smart. He was an English major, for Christ's sake. We could talk about books. We could talk about art. I bought a house with him; obviously, I wasn't afraid of commitment. So what was my problem?

I wasn't sure, exactly. But I knew it had to do with anything bridal. During those three years, I ventured into a few bridal gown boutiques but always felt so out of place, I'd chicken out, turn tail, and run before I even tried on a dress. At the bookstore, I'd dash by the bridal magazines, scanning the covers—"How to Make Your Perfect Day Perfect!" and "101 Amazing Cakes!"—while holding my breath. A friend passed along her much-loved and dog-eared copy of *The Anti-Bride Guide*, which I could barely even crack. Even *The Anti-Bride Guide* was asking questions and demanding answers. What kind of ceremony did I want to have? Where did I want to have it? Barn or backyard? What did I want to wear? Gown or tube top? There were so many choices. And none of the choices felt right.

The overt message in the bridal industry is that your wedding is the most important day of your life. Over and over again, in the pages of the glossy magazines, in the bridal shops that sell trinkets and monogrammed napkins, the message is: "It doesn't get better than this, ladies!" Hence the time, effort, and sheer truckloads of cash that go into planning a wedding. I struggled with the idea that if I became a bride, it meant I was going to become the kind of woman who obsessed over seating arrangements, hairstyles, dyed shoes, caterers, and floral arrangements. I'd stop being the strong, independent, career-minded woman that I'd always wanted to be. Every time I thought about planning my wedding, I felt like I was crossing a line, moving over into enemy territory, where I would lose my time, my identity, and myself.

The bridal industry is big business today. There are 2.4 million couples getting married in the United States every year. More than $72 billion is spent in the United States annually on weddings. As contributor Catherine Ingrassia reports in "Diana, Martha, and Me," the average cost of a wedding in America is roughly $26,800. Most women spend six months to a year planning their wedding, with or without the aid of a wedding planner. I had a hard time making peace with this information. Especially when I felt very strongly that the symbols of the modern white wedding—the white dress, the veil, the father giving away the bride—don't translate to modern life.

The traditional white wedding isn't going out of style

any time soon. And yet there are new traditions, new ceremonies to symbolize the commitment of two people to a life together—from couples getting hitched in a drive-through ceremony to same-sex marriage (which at the time of this writing, is still not legally recognized in most U.S. states, except for Massachusetts). And despite the big numbers spent on weddings, the modern wedding is changing. For example, today, many brides pick and choose which elements of the wedding they want to employ, from foregoing the veil to ditching the retinue of bridesmaids. Others get married by friends ordained over the Internet. And even more couples decide to scrap the tradition of making the bride's parents pay for the wedding and instead decide to foot the bill themselves.

As I thought more about planning my own wedding, it became clear that the modern wedding, like any ceremony embraced by an ever-changing culture, is shifting, changing to fit the times. The modern wedding is new ground. And I wanted to figure out how to navigate that territory. How to make it work for me. I wanted to know, how do other women deal with it?

I began contacting other women writers, writers whose work I admire, writers with bright minds and sharp wits, to ask them about their weddings. How did they deal with their weddings? What happened? Did they elope? Did they have big splashy affairs? How did they make their weddings work for them?

And respond they did.

I heard from a few writers who got married in their

twenties, more who got married in their thirties, and several who got married (for the first or third time) in their fifties and beyond. I heard from brides who got hitched on a shoestring budget to brides who "brought on the pouf and circumstance" (in their own words). And for the first time, I started to hear voices that rang true, that made sense to me, more than anything else I had read in bridal magazines or on TheKnot.com. I heard from women like Elizabeth Crane, who thought that $1,000 was a ridiculous amount to spend on a couture dress that she would wear for approximately eight hours. Instead, she went looking for a home-made dress at a price she could live with. I heard from women like Jacquelyn Mitchard, who writes about what it was like to be widowed, with no expectation of falling in love again, but how she fell head over heels for her sexy, young carpenter and decided to marry again. I heard from writers like Farah L. Miller, who had to deal with divorced parents who refused to get along at her wedding. I heard from single women like Meghan Daum, who writes about what it was like to attend a wedding after yet another painful breakup and Curtis Sittenfeld, who writes about her vow to attend every wedding to which she was invited. I heard from Ruth Davis Konigsberg, who writes about what it was like to be pregnant at her own wedding; while Anne Carle writes about her backyard wedding in "Weddings Aren't Just for Straight People Anymore." Not all the essays are about living happily ever after, because real life is not a fairy tale. For example, in "The Best-Laid Plans," Jennifer Armstrong writes that despite her obsessive planning for the big day, she realized that she wasn't ready to get married and called off her wedding. And then I heard from others, like Dani Shapiro who writes in the sharply observed "Happily Ever After" that the wedding is merely one day in a woman's life, that the real celebration is the many days of sharing a life together that come after the wedding.

Here are essays that explore with candor and wit the importance of the modern wedding, how it is changing today, how these women dealt with those changes and pulled off weddings that worked for them: whether their weddings were traditional, nontraditional, or a combination of both. Here are women telling the truth about what the big day is *really* like.

As I worked on this book, I learned that planning your wedding can be fun and exciting (as well as frustrating and crazy-making). I discovered that you can throw a wedding on your own terms. That the wedding isn't about running through a series of motions that don't mean anything to you. I learned that the wedding is meaningful. That it is important—like any ritual or ceremony that we decide to embrace. It just depends on how much meaning you want to give to it.

This past spring, I finally got married. And for a short time while I was planning the wedding, I did become the kind of woman who spent too much time worrying over the font on invitations and monogrammed matchbook covers. But for once, I was glad to have that time. I had finished my novel; the hours at my job had eased up; there was time. Planning my wedding was a time to focus on something that wasn't just about me and my single girl plans: It was about taking the time to focus on my family, my friends, and most important, it was about my husband and our life together.

In May, I got married in my side yard, among three rosebushes, flowering day lilies, and blue hydrangeas. We were married by an Episcopalian minister who spit on us a little as he pronounced us man and wife. We were surrounded by friends and family who had driven miles or flown across the country to celebrate with us. I truly felt crushed by love, as Julianna Baggott writes in her essay "The Child Bride (and Groom)." We danced, we drank, we were surrounded by love, a love that keeps going for us.

I hope this book does the same for you. That it opens the conversation about the state of the modern wedding. That it shows you can throw a wedding on your own terms and not lose your identity. That it explores, as Lara Vapnyar writes in her essay "The Girl, the Dress, and the Leap," the many exciting, frightening, and thrilling ways that the modern wedding with all its trappings isn't really about finding the perfect wedding dress or getting the perfect font on a monogrammed matchbook cover. It's about being ready to take a leap of faith—being ready to say, "I do."

taking
the
vow

the
child bride
(and groom)

julianna baggott

♥

THE BEGINNING

I was only twenty-three years old when I got married. Dave was twenty-six. By today's standards of arrested adult development, regression, and ever-rising life expectancy rates, I was a child, and maybe Dave was, too. In any case, that's what it felt like and, with each anniversary we celebrate, we seem to have been younger and younger way back when we got married.

I met my husband, Dave, in grad school at the very first party of the year. A month later, we were on a road trip together. We pulled off I-95 to have sex in a Red Roof Inn, midday. This is astonishing only in that we were so damn

poor. Sex at a Red Roof Inn was a huge luxury. There, perhaps inspired by the grandeur, lounging under the orange
comforter, he told me that he wanted to spill his guts.

I said, "Okay."

He said, "I really like you."

Now this didn't strike me as spilled guts. We'd been
inseparable since we first met. He'd just taken me to a family reunion and, on the way, he'd met my parents. We'd
pretty much covered the liking, even the *really* liking. I said,
"I don't think that constitutes having spilled your guts."

"How about this?" He paused and then said, "I'm in love
with you and I want to spend the rest of my life with you."

Now this, *this* was spilled guts. It was completely coura-
geous and elegant—even amid the Red Roof Inn décor
with its paintings bolted to the walls. I took it as a proposal.
I said, "Yes," as in *I accept*, as in *I do*. "I love you too."

I should stop right here and say that everything from
here on out in this essay is foofaraw. This is the essential
moment that Dave and I consider to be the start of our marriage—not the wedding itself. Embedded in every marriage, there is a true moment when your hearts sign on for
good. It doesn't necessarily happen when the guy mows
Will you marry me? into your lawn or trains a puppy to
bring you a velvet box. It doesn't necessarily happen in the
white hoop gown or because some exhausted justice of the
peace says so. It usually happens in some quiet moment, one
that often goes unregistered. It can happen while you're
brushing your teeth together or sitting in a broken-down
car in the rain. Some unplanned, unscripted moment.

But when people ask about your wedding day, they want a grand story. Not something that ends with stealing mini hotel soaps and shampoo bottles from a Red Roof Inn.

And so we make up another story. We create a grand affair.

A GENERATIONAL FOOTNOTE

We announced our engagement two months after the Red Roof Inn affair, and it's surprising now how unsurprised everyone was. It seemed like such a normal thing to do at the time—to fall in love, get engaged in three months, and get married in less than a year—at age twenty-three. And yet now, a decade and a half later, this seems like a terrible idea—a choice that only the destitute would make in a time of crisis.

But this was all happening right on the cusp of a new generation of women. The generation that had gone before us and tested the you-can-have-it-all notion had come back and written up a sobering memo: Balancing family and work was much harder than they'd thought.

My friends evidently were digesting the news. They started in on careers first. Their marriages, if they came at all, came late. Many have just gotten married in the last two to three years and now in their late thirties are starting to have their first children.

All that needs to be said here is this: I missed the memo completely. Was I out drinking? Was I too distracted writing poems on cocktail napkins? Was I already in a Red Roof Inn having sex off I-95? Hard to say.

THE PREPARATION

I had no real wedding plans in mind. I'd never dreamed about my wedding day. I knew girls were supposed to. I knew women were likely to have planned it many times over before the day actually arrived. But I hadn't. I was in graduate school. I loved graduate school. I'd still be there if they'd have let me stay on. Dave felt the same way. We were only interested in the ceremony's readings and in writing our vows—we were in graduate school for such things. Basically, we wanted in on the word action, but everything else, well, we didn't much care.

When people would say, "Your big day is coming up," I'd cringe. I didn't want to shove myself into the gown and get dolled up. I didn't want to have to accept the heavy weight of marital advice—from the blissful hand graspers to the depressives explaining, through gusty sighs, that marriage constitutes a life sentence of hard labor. I wanted bigger days to look forward to—maybe quieter but bigger in their own ways.

Our rings are a good example of our lack of interest. My great-grandfather had found a diamond brooch in a lump of tar while cleaning out a ladies' room some decades earlier, and the diamonds had found their way into a number of rings throughout the family. We used some of these from a ring that my grandmother had given me, then got a plain white gold band and a gold ring for Dave, both purchased through the strip-mall chain Van Scoy. The total cost: $239.99.

My mother was going to make my gown, but in the first store we visited to look for ideas, I found a dress on sale. I said, "Close enough." It cost $79.99.

My parents, who have four kids, have a system for weddings. They give each of us a set figure. One: You can elope and take it all in a lump sum. Two: Use all of it and then some of your own to throw a huge bash. Or, three: Our choice, throw a low-budget affair and pocket as much of the leftover as possible.

As I mentioned above, we were in grad school for poetry and fiction. This was, quite possibly, going to be the largest chunk of change we'd ever see in our entire lives.

We chose to have the wedding in my childhood church. It is one of the ugliest churches in America. When they do the photography art book of ugly churches, you'll find it right up front on page two—if not the cover.

It's a squat cinder-block number with a few stained-glass triangles in the concrete facade. The plastic chairs are mismatched—various shades of green, orange, and yellow. The art in the church was done solely by parishioners. The Stations of the Cross were abstract—black felt spiderlike things on purple felt backgrounds. The Jesus on the Cross was, well, how do I put this? Big-boned? Heavyset? He was fat. His loincloth was skimpy, and, because he was lifted high above us, you felt pervy when you raised your eyes to him—as if you were trying to catch a glimpse up his skirt.

The church was quite elegant, however, in comparison to the place we chose for the reception: the Sangerbund.

It's a German beer hall. This wasn't a nostalgic choice about our forebears and our mother country: Neither Dave nor I is German. Neither was it a style choice. Germans aren't known for their gracious hospitality, décor, or food quality. They are known for their beer quality, however, and this seemed to outweigh the other factors at the time.

That and the price. The Sangerbund was, by far, the cheapest per square foot and per meal. The meal would be something sauerkraut-ish, heavy on the gravy. And it would be served by women in lace-up tops—à la St. Pauli Girl— except the women would all be quite stout and aged.

Perfecto!

THE BLURRY DAY ITSELF

Because weddings are sociological in scope, not psychological, I had the sense throughout it all that Dave and I barely existed. We were already married, in our own way, at the Red Roof Inn off I-95. This was the communal manifestation. This was an adaptation of some sort, something that was only loosely based on us.

I'll spare you the battling bridesmaids and my brother-in-law's last minute decision not to sing our wedding song because he doesn't like to sing except when there's a real focus on him, and the beauty shop that gave one of my bridesmaids a satellite dish hairdo, and get right to the event itself.

Dave and I were kept in the church basement right before the wedding in two separate rooms, like holding pens. There was a door between us. I opened it and saw him across the room. He was wearing a rented tuxedo and a red bow tie and cummerbund. He was pacing, hands in his pockets. I whispered his name and he looked up.

"Hi," I said.

"Hi."

"I'm getting married," I said.

"Me, too!" he said, as if this were the strangest thing. And it did seem like a giant coincidence. Sometimes, still, one of us will say, "I love you" and the other will say it back—but in total amazement. "I love you too!" And sometimes we'll admit to how odd it is. "What are the chances? I love you and you love me."

I didn't tear up at this point. I wasn't yet sentimental about Dave. We were both too new to each other. This was more like a weird movie we'd both been chosen to star in. Soon enough it would be over and the paparazzi would ease up and we'd be back to our normal lives. This was something to endure.

And so when people asked me if I thought I was going to cry at the wedding, I'd shrug. "I don't know." I can be so unsentimental in so many ways. The traditional wedding— with all of its awwwing and honeyed adoration and cloying sweetness and condescension—well, I couldn't stomach it. I wasn't the type to go soft at flowers and candy. Pity the boyfriend who bought me a stuffed animal for a birthday gift.

But I didn't realize that the wedding wasn't only about becoming something new. It was also about leaving some other part of myself behind.

And so my father was the one who started me crying. And he'll always get me. I can't even begin to talk about him here. My God, this man's sweetness and brilliance and his philosophies on life . . . I can't begin. Here's a quick description: He has, more than once, walked a stranger's baby up and down the aisle of an airplane so that the single mother, traveling alone, could rest a minute.

He took my arm. We walked into the church and everyone stood up. It was this, too, that got me—this standing up, the formality of it, the respectfulness. The fact that people had come from such distances to be here for this.

I lost it. I bawled. People had to pass me tissues at the altar. There was a lot of snot. It was ugly.

But the priest, a true intellectual, a man of great wit and humility, gave an inspired homily. And although I can't begin to understand how they fit together, I remember he quoted Anthony Burgess (*A Clockwork Orange*) and Erma Bombeck and plenty in between. He calmed me down. Dave and I said our homemade vows, which, for all of our wanting in on the words, ended up being very traditional and simple and vowlike.

Then it was over. We were married.

And we were loved unsparingly. In fact, we were pressed with so much love that we felt like flowers being flattened—wedding-dress bustle and all—into a precious-memories book.

From here on out, we got lucky. There were some wedding guests who needed a careful eye, but everyone was on their best behavior. A brief accounting:

Dave's people were also a source of prewedding anxiety. My parental in-laws-to-be, especially. There are three of them—Dave's mother, Dave's father, and Dave's father's wife. I hadn't yet figured out the meaning of the cliché about marrying the whole family. That would take years to decode. And because the in-laws were, by and large, WASPs, their passive aggression was so subtle that I just thought they were all sweet as pie.

I was nervous about my oldest sister. Kate is nine years older than I am and was living in New York, working as a director/producer, and unmarried. She had, in fact, just broken things off with a man she was about to move in with. The Triple Asshole, my mother had dubbed him. Kate's happiness was of great concern, and there was a strict rule against making any allusions to *The Taming of the Shrew* in front of her. She did show up (fresh from an impromptu fling in Mexico). At the reception, she took to introducing Dave to people as such: "This is Dave. Julie's *first* husband." This was funny, of course. And every time she did it, I actually felt relieved. (My sister is unwieldy and wonderful and bitchy and hilarious and incredibly generous and kind and vicious, etc. . . .)

Even the conflicting groups—the nuns and college bud-
dies—seemed harmonious. My mother relied on nuns
throughout her life, and so more than a few showed up. One
was in full regalia—the all-white habit with the enormous
halolike wimple. We wanted them to be comfortable while
at the same time we wanted our drunken friends to have
fun—inoffensive fun.

A word on the young wedding. When you get married
young, your friends are young, too. They aren't yet worrying about a merger. They aren't having to dodge in and out
to breast-feed or check in with the sitter. They aren't yet
tied to their husbands and wives. The young wedding has a
greater possibility of being a big, messy, sexy free-for-all.
Dave and I still hear bits and pieces of what happened later
that night.

Which brings me to later that night . . . Dave and I left
the wedding as soon as we could. Someone had hunted
down my grandfather's Cadillac convertible, which had
been sold after he died, and had sweet-talked the people
into lending it so that it would be a surprise for us, just to
drive around on our wedding day. And it was—a huge surprise, like having my grandfather there with us. We drove it
to New Castle, where we had a room at the David Finny
Inn. There was a celebration of Old Towne going on with
fireworks. We found a window in a hallway that led to a tar
roof. We climbed out the window and stood there—me in
my wedding gown and him in his tux—among the hum-
ming air conditioners and watched the fireworks. The fire-

works seemed personal. We took them personally—a celebration for just the two of us.

We were new then, our lives stretched out before us. Our families had let us go. Our children had yet to find us. For this very short time, it would be just the two of us—just us two kids. It was a honeymoon, and we were eventually honeymoonish. But before all of that began, I should tell that I remember this vividly: We opened the guests' envelopes filled with checks and money. I don't know which of us tossed a handful into the air first or climbed onto the bed and started jumping. But we both ended up there—throwing the money into the air while jumping on the bed, throwing and laughing and jumping, until we ran out of breath.

the wedding vow

curtis sittenfeld

♥

I grew up in a family of wedding junkies. One of my earliest memories is of waking around four in the morning on July 29, 1981, to watch Lady Diana and Prince Charles exchange vows. This was shortly before my sixth birthday, and my family crowded in front of the tiny television in the cabin in rural Minnesota where we were on vacation. Mostly what I recall is the sprawl of Diana's train (twenty-five feet of taffeta and lace), the general grandeur of the proceedings, and the sense that if ever there was an event worth waking up in the middle of the night for, this was it.

A few years later, when my parents were planning to attend the wedding of family friends in our hometown of Cincinnati, Ohio, a message was relayed the Saturday morning before the ceremony: The groom, who was in his early twenties and had charmed my older sister, Tiernan, and me with his friendliness and goofy energy, had just learned that the two of us were not invited to the wedding and he'd called himself to say he wanted us there. This development was treated by all Sittenfelds with as much urgency and reverence as if the president of the United States had requested a private audience with us. Dresses! Shoes! White gloves! Chop-chop! (And, yes—as little girls, Tiernan and I really did, on special occasions, wear white gloves.)

At the weddings we didn't accompany our parents to, our father would wrap slices of cake in cocktail napkins, slip them in his jacket pocket, and give them to us the next morning, the white icing slightly smeared, the edge of a pink or purple sugared rose still visible. I've heard that some children sleep with a slice of wedding cake under their pillow, believing they'll dream that night of the person they're meant to marry. For my family, the magic and mysticism of the wedding cake resided more in how it tasted. We're all enthusiastic eaters, and we considered creamy, buttery wedding cake to be about as good as it got.

During adolescence, weddings continued to hold a special place in my imagination. At my boarding school, they regularly occurred in the campus chapel, and I plotted with another girl in my dorm—though we never had the nerve to go through with it—to crash one. It wasn't that we had visions, à la Vince Vaughn and Owen Wilson, of knocking back free drinks and seducing guests; we just imagined the ceremony would be really romantic, and it would be fun to see the bride's dress. Meanwhile, for years, my younger sister, Jo, and I played the same game when we were killing time on car trips or jogs: *If you got married tomorrow, who would your bridesmaids be? And you can't say more than ten.* Sometimes, secondarily, we'd also pick grooms.

I suspect it was my excessive reverence for all things matrimonial that led to my own wedding vow, which, unlike most wedding vows, involved no one besides myself: When I was twenty-two, I made a pledge that I'd attend every wedding I was invited to. Like a religious zealot whose moral failures only make her more determined to stay the course, my own vow came about because of a slipup of sorts. I failed to attend the first wedding of my peers, and then I repented by going to every other wedding for the next seven years—no matter how far away, how expensive, or how tenuous my relationship to the couple.

The wedding I *didn't* go to took place the summer I graduated from college. I was interning at a newspaper in North Carolina, my friends were getting married in Southern California, my then-boss didn't want me to take time off (I often worked on the weekends), and I had grown apart from the friends I'd once shared with the bride and groom. Plus it was going to be a Mormon wedding, so it wasn't even like the awkwardness could be smoothed over with booze. All of which is to say, my reasons for not showing up make perfect sense to me now—and yet I didn't let myself get away with such excuses again for years to come.

After the fact, it weighed on me that I hadn't gone. I once again ended up living in the same city as the couple, and when they showed me pictures from the big day, I felt pangs of remorse. Besides being a huge personal milestone, I told myself, weddings are an act of optimism, a time when people come together for happy rather than unhappy reasons. And I hadn't been there. Thus was born my wedding vow.

I made the vow in 1997, and over the next seven years, I'd guess that I attended twenty weddings: the four-day Pakistani-Indian extravaganza in Florida where I, too, came away with henna-decorated palms; the backyard affair in New Hampshire where the bride was barefoot, with blue toenails; the ceremony between two of my former college TAs, where the photographer was moved to give a toast with his mouth full; the autumn wedding where the bride was pregnant; the wedding where I slept in a college dorm; the wedding where I slept in a cabin at a camp; the wedding on the beach where I couldn't hear the vows; the wedding on an outdoor stage where I couldn't hear the vows; the wedding by the lake where I couldn't hear the vows. (And I'm not, as far as I know, deaf, so as a bit of friendly advice—if you're springing for the salmon dinner and the tulle veil, you might want to spring for a microphone, too.)

Had I not made my vow, I still would have gone to a lot of these weddings. Even so, not having to stop and think about it gave life a certain clarity. I never did those social math equations in which you take your affection for your friends, plus the juicy possibility of hooking up with another guest, minus the expense of a plane ticket and hotel room, minus the time suckage/shlepping factor, and all of it either does or doesn't equal a positive number. For me, it was a positive number—a positive answer—from the beginning. In fact, it's recently occurred to me that I may have accepted wedding invitations the bride and groom sent with the assumption that I'd decline. I picture the couple tallying their guest numbers and getting to the names they're on the fence about. "Hey, what about Curtis— should we invite her?" the groom asks. "Well, we're in Seattle, and she's in Boston," the bride replies. "Plus, I haven't laid eyes on her for seven years. So I'm sure she won't come, but what the hell? If we send her an invitation, at least maybe she'll give us that Waring Professional Belgian Waffle Iron off the registry." Naturally, this scene is followed by me pulling the oversized ivory envelope from my mailbox and dashing upstairs to book my plane ticket immediately.

Even when attending a particular wedding really didn't make logistical sense, I'd simply employ the nuptial version of heroic measures. In 2003, I was living in Washington, D.C., and working as a part-time English teacher, and I'd agreed to cochaperone a group of high school students traveling to New Mexico on a Sunday morning in July. Then I learned my friends Alan and Christine were getting married in Rhode Island the Saturday night before. A conflict? Hardly! What I'd do, I decided, was attend Alan and Christine's afternoon wedding, go to their reception for about an hour (you know—long enough for me to get the reception's flavor, and for them to feel the beneficence of my presence), return my rental car to the Providence airport, fly from Providence to Baltimore Washington International Airport, spend Saturday night at an airport hotel, and meet the students and the other chaperone in the morning before our plane departed for Albuquerque.

This is pretty much how things proceeded and it was a lovely wedding—it was genuinely moving to see the couple's families together, and the reception was at a mansion overlooking the glittery Atlantic Ocean. Then, after my allotted hour at the reception, I got lost on my way back to the airport and ended up frantically filling the gas tank of the rental car while trying to change out of my wedding shoes and wondering if I was going to miss my plane—and it was hard not to wonder, *What am I doing?*

At just about every wedding I went to, there were two moments that occurred. Moment A was the one in which I'd think, *This is so touching. Truly, these displays of familial and romantic love restore my faith in humanity. God bless the universe!* Moment B, which happened with increasing frequency, was the opposite: *Who are these people, and why exactly am I here among them?* The sheer number of weddings I attended also made me see how repetitive they are, and it made me wary of the most elaborate and expensive ones—no matter how much trouble you go to or how much money you spend, it still only lasts a weekend.

I'm pretty sure my wedding-vow-induced wedding cynicism peaked during a wedding that occurred two weeks before I moved cross-country. Distracted with packing up my apartment (or, more accurately, distracted by my all-consuming avoidance of packing), I didn't realize until just a few days beforehand that I was uncertain about the details of the rehearsal dinner. I e-mailed a friend who also would be a guest, and he e-mailed back informing me, as delicately as possible, that while there was in fact a rehearsal dinner, it appeared that I was not invited. *Wait a second*, I thought. *I'm flying to this wedding right in the middle of all*

my moving chaos, and I didn't even make the rehearsal din-
ner cut? I considered not going—if I were to fake strep
throat, I wondered, would the ideal day to hoarsely call the
bride be Thursday or Friday?—and this was the first time it
occurred to me that the net effect of the wedding weekend
would have been the same, but I'd have enjoyed myself
much more, if I'd just said no, then stood in my apartment,
burned five hundred dollars, and hung out at home.

Ultimately, of course, I did go to that wedding, and I
had multiple Moment As and Moment Bs. And then at
the very end of the night, literally while I was standing in
the driveway waiting for the van taking guests back to the
hotel, I began bantering with a guy I knew only dimly. A
few days later, back at home, I e-mailed him, and the
exchange turned into some of the best e-mailing of my
life, eventually punctuated by two weekend visits. Sometimes after receiving one of Driveway Guy's smart, funny,
and thoroughly entertaining e-mails, I'd think, *I can't
believe I almost didn't go to that wedding! Because then this
thrilling new relationship in which I will surely find long-
term love would never have happened! Long live my wedding
vow!* Pretty soon, however, it became obvious that Driveway Guy and I got along much better over the computer
than in person—the awkwardness of our first weekend
together was surpassed only by the awkwardness of our second one—and then I didn't know *what* to think. That
attending the wedding where we'd struck up the conversation had been pointless? That my wedding vow itself was
pointless? That I had completely forgotten the reason I'd

made the vow in the first place and become a matrimonial mercenary?

The game I used to play with my sister notwithstanding, these days I myself would never want to have ten bridesmaids. In fact, when it comes time to plan my own wedding (which I see as neither imminent nor terribly distant—I now live with my boyfriend of two and a half years) I hope to make it as low-key as possible. I've even floated the idea of eloping, which neither my boyfriend nor my family likes. Barring that, I'd want it to be informal and small—a fifty-person gathering one afternoon in a park, say, or a backyard. Presumably, this would mean not inviting some of the people whose weddings I myself traveled so far for, those brides and grooms whose vows I teared up at, whose champagne I drank and whose cousins I flirted with. And while once I imagined that not being invited to a wedding would surely, for anyone, be a grievous disappointment and insult, I guess it's a mark of how much the wedding vow changed my view that I now suspect plenty of people I know would see such exclusion as a relief.

In the end, when I finally didn't show up for a wedding, it was less a decision I made than one fate made for me. My friend Katharine, a former coworker, was marrying her fiancé Jim in San Francisco over Labor Day weekend of 2004. I was living in Washington, D.C., and on the morning I was to fly west, I got an ocular migraine, which meant I was seeing greenish spots that made it difficult to do anything except lie down and close my eyes. After a few hours, the migraine subsided enough that I decided I could take a cab to the airport. Missing the wedding, after all, was not an option.

But as we crossed the Potomac, I felt increasingly queasy. (Perhaps this was my karmic punishment for considering faking sick two years earlier.) By the time we'd reached the airport, I'd broken into a clammy sweat, and throwing up did not seem beyond the realm of possibility. As someone who'd once fainted on a plane—an experience that's both melodramatic and truly disgusting—I knew it would be foolish to board a cross-country flight. Which meant I wasn't going to the wedding. Which meant, at long last, I'd broken my vow.

Later in the day, back at my apartment, when I called the bride to apologize, I couldn't help thinking of how at receptions in the past, I'd always noticed the handful of table assignment cards that weren't retrieved. I'd wonder, *Who flakes on coming to a wedding at the last minute?*

I definitely felt uncomfortable about my own last-minute flake-out, and sad to miss celebrating with Katharine and Jim. But ending my perfect attendance streak, however involuntarily, also turned out to be liberating. Unlike when I was twenty-two, I learned I could, at twenty-nine, miss a wedding, feel bad . . . and then move on. In fact, to truly beat myself up about it was kind of arrogant—surely, the wedding had proceeded just fine without me. In fact, it was quite possible that the bride and groom had noticed my absence exactly zero times. I also realized that it probably wasn't a coincidence I'd gotten the ocular migraine when I had—the week preceding Katharine and Jim's wedding had been one in which I helped my boyfriend move from D.C. to Philadelphia, I attended several days' worth of back-to-school faculty meetings, and I had multiple deadlines for freelance articles. A normal person might have recognized from the start that declining to attend the wedding would not reflect a lack of affection for Katharine. But I'd been so hell-bent on keeping my vow that I'd stopped seeing the forest for the trees. I'd forgotten that weddings are a lot of fun largely because when you're at one, you're in the mood to enjoy yourself. If you can't or won't enjoy yourself, well, you probably shouldn't go. With this hard-won lesson in mind, I've skipped a handful of weddings in the last few years. Miraculously, the world has continued to spin on its axis.

When I look back, I don't regret making my vow, but because it made me more of a wedding cynic, I'm not sure I'd recommend it, either. Or maybe it's that I became a cynic because I'd been such a wedding sucker to start with; I'd been one of those people who makes it into her twenties still thinking of weddings as magical occasions sprinkled with fairy dust. If you never in the first place believe such a thing, then you'd never experience the disappointment of realizing you were wrong—or the excitement, in certain moments at certain weddings, of being completely right.

diana, martha,
and me

catherine ingrassia

The first time I saw Martha Stewart's *Weddings*, I was standing in a Chicago Kroch's & Brentano's bookstore in 1987 entranced by Martha's smile and the towering wedding cake beside her. A graduate student who couldn't even afford to buy the $50 book, I leafed through the oversize volume imagining how I could someday fashion my own wedding with the same WASPy patina of privilege and effortlessly worn elegance. The pages characterized a wedding as "monumental," "the richest . . . of all the events in the course of a human life," "the most magical, most fanciful event conceivable"—lofty terms for a basic union. Though I had just met the man who would become my husband, weddings were not necessarily on my mind. Nevertheless the preoccupation with that ritual and the seeming inevitability of *someday* getting married made the book very seductive. A few years earlier, I, like 750 million other people, had indulged my fascination with the wedding of Prince Charles and Lady Diana in July 1981, watching all three networks on three different televisions simultaneously (just in case one of them got a different angle of "the dress"). It was a wedding to which we all could aspire.

Stewart's book and Princess Diana's wedding became touchstones for an entire generation of women and created specific expectations that still influence weddings. Never before in the history of the world has more time, energy, and money been spent on weddings. Today, the average American wedding costs $26,800 (more than half the median household income), a price that has increased by 400 percent over the last twenty years. At the same time that we spend upward of $125 billion a year on weddings, we have a 50 percent divorce rate, the highest among Western countries. How can we reconcile this ceremonial expenditure and this institutional failure? What do weddings mean in a culture in which 90 percent of the people will ultimately marry, but more than half of those marriages will end in divorce?

As an academic with a focus on women's literature and history, my own relationship with weddings was complicated. The first wedding I was in (and the first I remember with any detail) was my aunt's in 1974. A large, formal Italian wedding befitting both the youngest child and the only daughter in the family, the entire experience, from the size of the engagement ring (two carats) to the venues for the ceremony (Catholic church) and the reception (country club), imprinted on my young brain what a "real" wedding was supposed to look like. What impressed me most, perhaps, was the Italian wedding cake: five towering layers of cannoli cake, each supported by a battalion of white porcelain cupids with an illuminated green fountain in the first layer. (Inexplicably, I still have one of the porcelain cupids.) The ivory dress, adorned with seed pearls, was preserved, and the pictures of the wedding hung on my paternal grandmother's wall for nearly twenty years.

Despite my early fascination with my aunt's wedding, I got married in pink. I saw the Demetrios dress in a magazine, tried it on at the same Italian bridal shop where my aunt had purchased her dress, and never looked back. I had a sapphire, not a diamond, engagement ring, I never considered changing my name (nor did my husband consider asking me to), and I ended up with a wedding that was a bit of a religious and cultural pastiche. I really wanted to be married in a Catholic church, a desire thwarted by the fact that I wasn't actually Catholic. In 1990, my husband and I were married in an unadorned Unitarian church under a chuppah, with "Ave Maria" playing as a tacit nod to Catholicism. The wedding and the reception (complete with sit-down dinner for 150), for which my parents paid for everything, were grand. But, like the weddings of many people who get married in their twenties, it was really my parents' party, not mine. I never created an album of wedding pictures, never hung the "wedding shot" on the wall, and, I think, never really felt ownership over the experience.

As women marry later—the average age for the bride is twenty-seven, twenty-nine for the groom—the bridal couple increasingly assumes the financial responsibilities for the event. Currently, nearly a third of couples pay for their own weddings, and less than 25 percent of brides have parents who pay for everything. Couples go into debt to throw a wedding and fall victim to the power of the wedding industry, which repeatedly tells them the importance of the event and its centrality to their own lives. Yet how important is it, and what meaning do we invest in the traditions associated with it?

The original ceremony of marriage has rather humble beginnings. While the first marriages were basically a form of kidnapping (an act that instituted the practice of groomsmen to help the groom keep the bride's irate family at bay), most unions between a man and a woman created alliances between two groups. The exchange of a valuable object— the bride, money, livestock—solidified that relationship. The term "wedding" itself originally meant "to pledge, wager, or stake"—with a very specific reference to the financial vow made. A bride was, if not purchased, then offered as an item in exchange. The husband and his family, in essence, bought the bride and the property (dowry or goods) she brought with her. In fact, in the eighteenth century, British newspapers published the amount of a woman's dowry with the wedding announcement. When a father gave away his daughter, he contractually entered into a financial union, not a romantic one, and as a result the chastity of the bride was of paramount importance to ensure an appropriate line of inheritance.

Many people assume that the white dress, now standard in most American weddings, symbolically represented the bride's virginity and was always a central part of wedding customs. Actually, that's a retroactive (and erroneous) myth.

Though white gowns were occasionally worn by brides in the fifteenth and sixteenth centuries, the white dress did not become a wedding tradition until after Queen Victoria's 1840 wedding, which, like Princess Diana's, had a profound influence on wedding practices and popular traditions. The original wearing of white coincided with a class-based desire to make the wedding an opportunity for public displays of wealth. White is an incredibly impractical fabric to sew or wear, and a white dress would have been owned only by those who wouldn't risk getting it dirty.

During this period, even fabulously rich brides—including Queen Victoria—typically had their wedding dresses remade as evening gowns. In the nineteenth century, the average American woman got married in her best dress or had a dress made that would then become her best dress. Blue (associated with constancy and virginity) and yellow were favorite colors for wedding gowns, although many a bride (especially on the frontier) would have been married in black, since it was a more practical color. The inevitable obsolescence that now characterizes wedding dresses would have been unheard of in earlier times. So would the average amount of $800 spent on a dress today.

Many other popular "traditions" of the American wedding are a product of marketing and commercialism. The diamond engagement ring? De Beers Diamonds, which was founded by Cecil Rhodes in 1888 and became the world's largest diamond mining company, organized a marketing campaign that equated the diamond with engagement rings, culminating in the 1948 tagline "A diamond is forever." Wedding veils? Roman brides typically wore brightly colored veils to ward off evil spirits (not to demonstrate modesty), but the practice of wearing a veil did not emerge again until the late nineteenth century with the cultural preoccupation for feminine modesty and decorum. White, multilayer wedding cakes? While the symbolic breaking of bread had long been part of a wedding ceremony, the many frosted white layers that now signal "weddings" were not even technologically possible until the beginning of the twentieth century. The development of white sugar paste frosting (1888) and the ability to tier the layers with pillars (1902) created the precursor of the modern wedding cake.

Should it matter to us that these popular traditions are relatively new? As a culture we make meaning of weddings through white dresses, wedding cakes, and veils; they're the lens through which we read romantic unions. So, like all traditions, they're as real as we make them—which is to say, very real indeed. That reality became apparent to me when I finally got my copy of Martha Stewart's *Weddings*. I recently found a used copy on the Internet for $3.54. I thought that it would strike me as outmoded, some sort of time capsule providing a window into a moment that had passed. Rather the opposite was true. Though happily married for sixteen years, I still found the images as appealing as I had years before—perhaps more so because they provided a vehicle for remembering my own wedding and anticipating my daughter's wedding. (Okay, she's only seven, but a mother can plan ahead. . . .) It may be the same reason that the people who most often cry at weddings are

married; witnessing the act of public intimacy that characterizes all marriage ceremonies and hearing the vows that,
in any form, promise the same thing remind us of the powerful commitment we've made to another person and to
ourselves. The familiarity of the white dress and the cake
help us—as individuals and as a culture—find comfort in
rituals and process the change a wedding represents. As we
celebrate unions together, the ceremony, whether simple or
elaborate, provides a sense of order and continuity. When
our wedding echoes those of our mothers and grandmothers and perhaps anticipates our daughters', it reminds us of
the community of generations that surrounds us. It also
helps anchor us. Though perhaps some of us work to bal-
ance our professional and personal roles in a time when
women's lives are more complicated, we can be secure in
our knowledge of what it means to be a bride. So, upon
reflection, I've decided that Martha had it right. A wedding
is an incredibly rich, magical, and monumental event that
allows you to transport yourself into a story that is at once
familiar and also completely unique.

the
dress

one day

Getting Married on a Budget
Later in Life in a Dress My Deceased
Mother Made Me, DIY Style

elizabeth crane

I was, in many ways, like every other little girl growing up in the sixties and seventies. "One day," I thought, "I will have a beautiful wedding and it will be the best day of my life." We were in the era of Gloria Steinem, but we were the children of women who were still finding their way through feminism. Our mothers may have had careers, but they married young; they got divorced but they got married again; they went to work but they still put dinner on the table. I understood early on that marriage, at the very least, shared the top spot on the list of goals. I got it at school and at the movies and on TV and in every women's magazine around our house, even the *Cosmo* that was in my hot little hands at an entirely age-inappropriate juncture, which may not necessarily have urged marriage but sure as hell didn't want me to be alone. A happy ending was one with a man in it, and it was years before I thought to question this.

I had many plans for this wedding of the century. They changed over the years, but included any number of dress styles from sleek to poufmongous; locations from the beach on Fire Island to my grandparents' house in Iowa. The grooms were always sort of secondary. Sometimes they were classmates or colleagues, sometimes they were JFK Jr., sometimes Robert Downey Jr. They were, of course, perfect, whoever they were, but the wedding was the thing.

Somewhere along the line this changed, and I suspect it came in the "I'm in my thirties and I'm not married yet what does it all mean?" era. I became clear about the statistics on marriage, and that as a child of divorce I had perhaps some long-latent negative associations with the institution, but also came to accept the fact that I couldn't marry just anyone, that what I wanted was more than a wedding. I wanted a meaningful commitment that had a chance of lasting. I wanted "picky" to not be a bad word. (Can you tell I heard this a lot? Enough to question whether or not it was true? And finally concluding that it was? And that it was possible that some people, like 50 percent, to quote one commonly heard statistic, were maybe not picky enough? And ultimately to conclude: *Right on, I'm picky!*) This seemed to go hand in hand with realizing I wasn't just anyone, and that just anyone wouldn't marry me anyway. It's been my experience that it is still difficult in our culture to make decisions like holding off on marriage, or (gasp!)

choosing not to marry at all, or like, let's say, being an artist—anything that strays even slightly to the left of center. Being single for as long as I was in this setting was quite often painful, and though I'd always believed that sharing your life with a partner would be a wonderful thing, in the event that I did not find that person (and evidence suggested strongly to me that I might not), I hoped to be fulfilled and productive and satisfied and useful (and not lonely) regardless of whether I found a mate. Although I was on a slow track to personal and creative success (suffice it to say this is a word I've always had trouble with, but that I've come to understand can and must be defined individually), I met that goal beyond my wildest dreams. Lo and behold, as soon as that happened, who finally came along but The One.

And let me say too that although we recently celebrated our first anniversary, I am still convinced, in some ways, that I will only know what marriage really means ten years down the road. I know that I'm as in it now as I'll ever be, which is not nothing. In fact, it's more than just something. Although I fail on a regular basis, I work hard on being in the moment, as the Zen/Kabbalists/movie stars/self-helpy people say, and so if you follow the logic, I will certainly never be more legally bound to Ben than I am today, but because it's still so new, my perspective on it is perhaps not as complex as it will be in the future, after we have even more experiences shared as this unit-thing. I agreed, under God and in front of my friends and family, to stick with this dude, and that's my plan. What I mean is, it doesn't seem enough to me to say that I'm legally bound to this person and leave it at that. Or even to say it's a committed relationship. Certainly, I believe that marriage should be defined by each couple making the choice to get married. You wanna have key parties with your neighbors? OK, great, but that's not gonna work for me. What I'm talking about is far more nebulous. What our marriage is now is what I wanted marriage to be. We're equal. Spiritually, mentally, and emotionally equal. Finances couldn't interest me less. I mean, insofar as I like having some, yes, but not in terms of our equality. That said, our entire three years together have been what I truly dreamed of, beyond the white dress fantasies. We don't agree on every last thing, but we communicate fairly easily, and when we don't, we try harder. (When one of us walks away in a huff, we eventually come back together laughing, because it's so out of character for both of us.) We have a lot of similar interests, but I also have similar interests with some random person who reads *Us Weekly* magazine, so that's only a part of it. We have fun, but I have fun with a lot of people. We make up silly songs, which I occasionally do with a few other people, and we get naked, which I do with no other people ever, unless it involves a paper gown, at which time I promise you I do not enjoy it. We are two very unexamined-life-isn't-worth-living-to-a-ridiculous-degree-prone people, always working through the next thing life brings, even though we haven't weathered any big crises yet (although frankly, we both came to the table having weathered enough trauma for any two people, and I'm hoping we've already had our share).

Perhaps that's what I'm waiting for, though, for the ultimate definition, which is wrongheaded of me, I'm sure. I
want to prove that we can weather a storm together. But
you know, if at all possible, without the storm. Here's the
best thing, I think. This marriage makes me feel that it's
OK to be me. Not that I ever had a choice, but God knows I
tried, for the sake of many other relationships, to be any
number of people who weren't me, always failing miserably. I was finally about as close as I'd ever been to being me,
and glad to be me, shortly before I met Ben. (Caveat: If you
are or were my friend, then you most likely did know me. If
I dated you, not so much.) At the same time, this relationship has helped me come to understand that everything
isn't about me, anymore, and that apparently it never was
anyway (what?), which is frankly a huge fucking relief. If
anything I'm more me now, because of Ben.

Meeting the right person only confirmed what I had con-
cluded somewhere along the way, that a wedding is only one
day. You want it to be a wonderful, memorable day, but you
don't want to look back and say, "That was the best day of
my life," the implication being that all that followed wasn't,
and I have been to some wonderful weddings that ended in
divorce. Ours was wonderful and memorable, perhaps more
so because we had to do it on sort of a tight budget, requiring
more than a bit of creativity. (The words "tight budget"
here defined as "Martha Stewart at the dollar store meets a
hundred people in our postage stamp of a backyard.")

For starters, I had some ideas about what kind of wedding dress I wanted, but I did not want to spend, well, what

nice wedding dresses cost. I wanted something sexy enough to thrill my groom but not freak out anyone I was related to, something elegant but uniquely me. Something striking but not super-bridey, something that would rock my groom's universe but not expose anything my parents didn't need to see, something simple and tea-length with a few special details (on this I was flexible; I love all manner of detail), something that, decades from now, wouldn't scream 11:00 to 11:05 a.m., September 18, 2004, but would be somehow current and timeless and completely me at the same time, something that turns out not to exist in any variation of the color white. It didn't seem like too much to ask. I scouted around one day and came close to putting a deposit down on a very simple, custom-fitted three-quarter-length dress for maybe $400, but in the end it was too simple. Eventually I heard about a designer sample sale at a fancy Michigan Avenue shop (you know, the kind that's upstairs?) and tried on probably two dozen dresses of every variety. One even had lace pants underneath. Let me tell you a little about this process, because it's interesting in that way that lifestyles, like let's say those of the rich and famous, that are foreign to me are interesting. You make an appointment. This, I realize now, probably should have told me it wasn't going to work out. I have an appointment book and sometimes I even write things down in it, but I don't often look at it. In any case, I actually showed up for the appointment and tried on a lot of dresses designed by names you hear at the Oscars, and I quickly imagined myself posing with my head over my shoulder and saying something like, "Badgley Mischka," or the one I gave some serious thought to, "Richard Tyler." The price range is fairly reasonable for the quality, considering these are dresses that are normally upward of $6,000. Very few dresses in this place were over $1,500, and most I looked at were $1,000 or under. It was nothing like my dream dress: pink it was, actually, a pink so pale you could only detect it in certain lights, satin, and mega-princessy, with a fitted bodice and a large skirt, spared from cake-topper territory by its perfect simplicity, magnificent cut, and the absolute yumminess of the satin. It had a scooped-out open neckline and a deep V in the back, unique because one side layered over the other to create the V, and the skirt had giant box pleats, which allowed for fullness without any uninvited poufiness. The price on the tag was $1,000, which is without a doubt on the low end these days, especially for a Richard Tyler dress, which the saleswoman felt the need to keep reminding me. I will probably never be the sort of person who can decide to spend $1,000 on the spot for anything that isn't potentially lifesaving, and since I couldn't convince myself that this dress was going to do that for me, I left the store, not completely sure I wouldn't come back the next day hoping it hadn't sold, but unable to drop the bills without at least sleeping on it. I kept coming back to: It's one day. All brides want to feel beautiful on their wedding day, but I wasn't convinced I couldn't achieve this for less than a grand. I looked at it for a good long while and finally told them I'd think about it.

The appalled saleswomen (who outnumbered me by

three) said, "Oh no, you must take it today; we can't possibly hold it for eight hours," as though I'd asked them to loan me their grandchildren for an overnight. I knew it was the only one they had, but I tried to explain that this was a lot of money for me and that I couldn't just drop that kind of cash without thinking about it, and this was before I found out there'd be an additional $500 fee for alterations. (I still have no idea why it costs this much to sew a hem, even a big one, but it does.) In accordance with my entire wedding philosophy (and I should say I didn't exactly know I had one until this moment, but very simply it comes down to the "one day" thing. I can't justify the idea of amassing any kind of debt for, er, a party, albeit a special one), I just couldn't see spending that much money on something I was going to wear exactly once and that constituted a significant fraction of our budget. The single most expensive item of clothing I've ever bought was a shearling coat that I stalked at Barneys until it went on sale for half price, and it was still a lot of money, but it was in my budget, and it was at least justifiable knowing I'd wear it for ten years. At this point I got irritated and went home saying I'd take my chances and bemoaning the vast conspiracy of the evil wedding industry that convinces unsuspecting women their lives will be unfulfilled without an ice sculpture shaped like a bride and groom and a twenty-piece marching band.

A few months before the wedding, I still didn't have a dress. But on the way home from the swank upstairs store, I remembered something. I remembered that I wanted my mom to make my wedding dress. Naturally, the fact that she passed away several years before I met my husband seemed at first like it might pose a problem. (That and the fact that at the time I was still in the dating era I like to call the Marginally Disgruntled Postal Worker/Unmedicated Bipolar Drug Addict Years.) When my all-around super-awesome future husband Ben proposed, it was bittersweet for both of us on that front; both his parents were also long gone. Still, if anyone could pull this off from beyond the grave, it's my mom. No lie. Ask anyone. She was always a high achiever.

My mother, like many of her generation, out of a combination of thrift and tradition, filled much of her available free time with a variety of needlework projects that included knitting, reupholstery, and needlepoint. She sewed many of my childhood clothes, made a wardrobe to match for my best doll, Bibsy, and created couture gowns for my Barbies, and although she taught me the basics of sewing, my abilities are limited to curtains, A-line skirts, and the like. Anything as complicated as a sleeve or a pleat would end up being handed back to her with a pitiful look and a plea for damage control. Being an incredible perfectionist was her blessing and her burden, but in this area it was always a blessing to me. (Well, except for that period in seventh and eighth grade when even the best handmade clothing did not seem cool. At that time it was Huk-A-Poo or die.)

Fortunately, I also remembered that I never throw anything away. If you have any similar inclinations and/or tendencies to keep anything that enters your house, do not read on unless you have some person in your life to whom you want to say, "See, I told you I should have kept that broken fan from Uncle Jehosephat," as what follows is about the best possible argument ever for this case, which, generally speaking, leads only to piles of newspapers, chipped red pots and pans that belonged to your stepgrandmother, and about a million buttons, snaps, and spools of uselessly dried-out (but lovely) thread that belonged to all of your grandmothers. My mother and father both carried this gene and passed it down, and now in addition to all the stuff I've been never throwing away, I have all the stuff my mother never threw away, and will someday have the collection of five hundred videotapes my father currently refuses to throw away. The fact that Ben (like-minded saver of things) and I had recently moved into a place with a huge attic was only a bonus for us as people who enjoy saving anything and everything "just in case" and don't mind walking in between stacks and stacks of boxes both full and empty (you know, for the next time we move).

Getting back to the point: In the late 1980s I'd been a bridesmaid in another super-schmancy wedding in which we were allowed to wear whatever we wanted as long as it was white. I couldn't afford anything remotely like whatever the other bridesmaids were going to come up with, so I figured my best option was to have my mom make me a dress. She'd come through for me on several occasions, like my high school graduation, when I had to have this silk Calvin Klein slip dress that cost $400, an outrageous sum for 1979. She found the exact pattern and made it for me for about forty bucks. For my friend's wedding, I picked out what was then a very stylish, mostly very simple Vogue pattern, a sleek, floor-length, off-the-shoulder column dress with three-quarter sleeves made more eighties-like by the presence of a wide, wide collar (if this collar were a trailer, it'd be a double-wide), and went down to the fabric district, where I found a beautiful satin brocade for less than sixty bucks. The dress had been a big hit at that wedding (and I've always taken a special pride in saying, "My mom made it," especially at an event where everyone else's clothes cost a lot), but had been crumpled up in a bag in a trunk for, well, the ensuing fifteen years. Among other things I have also never thrown away, besides the dress, was a good half yard of the leftover fabric to play with. I knew before I got home that I had my dress. It would need some tweaking, but I suddenly remembered my mom saying, "You can wear this again someday if you just take off the collar, maybe shorten it up." I made a few calls and found a local designer named Valerie, who seemed to be the right one for the job. I had heard about a dress she wore to a Björk concert made out of a sleeping bag.

The collar gave us nearly another yard of fabric, some of which Val used to build a mini-train. She took off the sleeves and used velvet and satin ribbons for the straps, which met at a V in the back and trailed down below that. She added some sort of haphazard layers of pleated tulle underneath the train (funky part #1), and I added some of my stepgrandmother's rhinestone pins (funky part #2, and might I add, see?), two on the straps in front, one at the bottom of the V, and two more to pin up the train for the reception, revealing more of the tulle for a sort of Carmen Miranda—in-the-twenty-first-century sort of thing (funky part #3). Val seemed to be impressed that I could still zip it up fifteen years later, but it was a just-barely sort of zipping up. Fortunately, my mom had the foresight to leave inch-plus seams all around (standard being ¾ inches), anticipating, if not the inevitability, at least the possibility that it could be let out in the future.

The result was so much better than the former dress of my dreams, and with all due deference to Richard Tyler, better than that, too. Plus the complete outfit, including shoes and earrings, still cost less than the fancy store's damned hem. It was the perfect blend of classic and new, but best of all, I got to fulfill my dream of wearing a wedding dress my mother made. I felt beautiful and so grateful to have found such a vital way to bring my mother into the day, and to feel her presence in a very tangible way. My husband said I looked "SO HOT!" about a dozen times, which is for sure the reaction I was going for and made me feel like a million bucks.

The actual day of my wedding was pretty sweet. My dad and stepmom very generously offered to pay for it—and okay, we went a bit over budget, but if I told you the actual dollar amount you might say it couldn't be done. Flowers alone can cost what we paid for our entire shebang. I want to be up front about having blatantly ripped off my dear friends Sue and Frank, whose wedding was one I will always remember as being in the top five most creative and poignant weddings ever, in spite of the rain. Ben and I had sun. And 72 degrees. We might have special ordered it, but we didn't.

What I Stole From Sue and Frank:

- their minister
- creative decorating
- handmade invitations
- creative music
- participation of friends and relatives (including Sue and Frank)
- actual film vs. video
- sewing at least some of the bridal party's clothes

To qualify some of the things on this list, David, their minister (ordained in the Universal Church of Life), is also a mutual friend, and I could also have had Frank marry us but I temporarily spaced that he was also ordained, and if I'd had Frank marry us then our wedding would have been less Sue and Frank–like and we and our guests wouldn't have gotten Sue and Frank's Top Ten Reasons to Get Married and Stay Married. David got everyone to yell "YES!" that they were in favor of our wedding, and it only went up from there. Since we had the ceremony in our tiny backyard, I hung strings of pearly-white paper from the trees, and my cousins and friends decorated whatever they could with tulle, flowers, and candles. We purchased all of our flowers from Trader Joe's, and Lisa, one of my bridesmaids, spent the entire day before the wedding arranging the multicolored bouquets featuring many hydrangeas in the mismatched ninety-cent vases I'd collected from thrift shops in previous weeks and tied with tulle, and damned if those arrangements weren't as beautiful as any I've ever seen, and I once went to the wedding of an actual florist, a schmancy one, who outmatched Lisa only in sheer numbers.

Eager to avoid putting my bridal party in anything heinous and allow them room for their own personalities while still trying to have some sort of coherence, I sewed an entire dress for Ruby, our flower girl, and simple wraparound skirts for the women (as well as ring pillows of the same vintage reproduction cotton), with which they could choose their own top. It was hard not to feel connected to my mom while I was at the sewing machine that summer. I had heard many stories of important events in her life that she'd made her own clothes for: prom, concerts, her own wedding trousseau. In the end, sewing for my bridal party was another opportunity for me to feel her presence in a tangible way. Although my elderly machine wasn't my mom's own, it had been in the family, as has my entire vast thread, button, and notion collection, and for me it's kind of impossible to avoid feeling the complex maternal history attached to these physical things, not just to my mom but to her mother before her, who also spent time teaching me the basics of the sewing arts. Our friends Tom and Piper played drum and concertina, which I have to confess I wasn't certain about until I walked down the aisle, and was blown away by how perfectly us it was. Another friend, Anne, sang a song during the ceremony, accompanied by her husband, Chafe, on guitar, and she chose a song by Nick Drake that, well, gahh. It was about finding love after a long time. If there was previously some hope that I might not weep during the ceremony, it was gone about thirty seconds into the song. Seeing Chafe looking down at his guitar just smiling and knowing he was smiling both because his wife is awesome and also because they were so super-happy for us just put me over the edge. Ben's sister Amy honored all the people who couldn't be there, my friend Bob spoke about how depressed I used to be back in New York and now I have everything I've ever wanted, and Lois (my stepmom) read a beautiful poem. Ben and I wrote our own vows but also read traditional ones. The most money was spent on food, and we almost didn't have a cake, but at the last minute found someone to do it and I gave her a picture and we got a totally Martha Stewart–looking cake that also tasted really, really good (not so much on our anniversary, though, after a year of being in the freezer).

For many years, I doubted I'd ever get married. I'd fantasized about the wedding, but as a child of divorce, I waited perhaps longer than some, more interested in finding the right person than settling down for the sake of it. Plus in my twenties I was too tied up being miserable, in my thirties I was too busy recuperating from the damage I did in my twenties, so it wasn't until I was forty that I was like, "I'd marry me! Where's the guy?" When I met Ben, I knew the wait was worth it, except for the part about Mom being gone. The wedding was everything I wanted—family and friends gathered to celebrate our commitment. Doing it on a budget took a little more time and effort on the part of the bride and groom, but I never lost sight of the idea that it was one day out of our lives together. I know for sure that if we'd served coffee and Ho Hos to the same bunch of folks, with a boom box and a mix tape, I'd have been just as happy. Maybe when we renew our vows . . . And you know, now that I've written a few pages, I think I know what marriage is now, a year and a half in. It's everything that's us.

the girl, the dress, and the leap

lara vapnyar

♥

I bought my wedding dress in a tiny shop on one of the
damp, gloomy streets of old St. Petersburg. The woman at
the counter put down my name, the name of the dress
(Princess 4), the price (the equivalent of $16), and asked
for my phone number. "Two three eight," I said, "then
seven two . . . no . . . seven eight . . . no . . . fifty eight." The
woman raised her eyes at me. I started to cry. She got up,
came out from behind her counter, and smothered me in a
big sweaty hug.

Through the tears and frequent hiccups, I told her that
I'd moved to St. Petersburg only a couple of weeks ago, and
that I hadn't memorized my phone number yet, that I
didn't know anybody in St. Petersburg except for my fiancé
and my future in-laws, that all my relatives and friends
lived in Moscow, that my mother wouldn't see my wedding
dress until the wedding, that my best friend didn't even

know that I was getting married, and that just a week before I didn't know that I would be getting married myself. The woman assumed that I was pregnant, and I didn't try to dissuade her, because the real story was too complicated.

About a year before, my uncle, who lived in New York, had offered to help my mother and me emigrate to the United States. It was 1992, a time when the Soviet Union was about to collapse, the uncertain future wasn't too promising, and everybody who had a chance to emigrate was eager to do so (people who didn't have a chance were even more eager). Neither I nor my mother was completely sure if we wanted to move to the United States, but everybody said that only an idiot could pass up this opportunity, and so we agreed. My uncle filed the application for us, but since we knew that it would take a very long time for the documents to get processed, and there was no guarantee that we'd ultimately get a visa, we decided not to talk about it until we got a response.

For the last week of the summer break I went to St. Petersburg, where I stayed with some family friends in their centuries-old building that didn't have an elevator. I met Dema, my future husband, on the staircase. He was climbing up; I was skipping down. He couldn't see me, because somebody had screwed out the lightbulb the day before, but he said that he liked the cheerful sounds of my steps. We spent the three remaining days of my vacation walking the streets of St. Petersburg, ignoring the beautiful sights, talking about physics, calligraphy, popular psychology, and the rare animal named Przewalski's horse after the man who discovered it. In November, Dema came to Moscow and we spent another three days together, ignoring the beautiful sights of Moscow this time. When apart, we sent each other letters. My letters were detailed and pretentious (Why on earth did I write that my favorite writer was Joyce, when I couldn't move past the first couple of sentences of *Ulysses*?). Dema's letters were honest and wonderful and full of grammatical mistakes. In December, when he came to Moscow for the second time, we decided that it was best to ignore the beautiful sights without leaving the apartment. On the last of the three days Dema asked me to marry him. I said, "Yes!" I don't know if he had seriously pondered what it meant to be married or explored the idea of something being for the rest of his life. I certainly hadn't. What we had was here and now, and it was mind-blowing. I couldn't imagine my life without it or beyond it. At that time I strongly believed in leaps of faith. Everything wonderful required a leap, and the greater and more impossible the leap was, the greater the happiness was to be achieved in the case of success. It didn't occur to me to imagine what happened if a leap resulted in a fall.

We ran out to a subway kiosk, bought a bottle of champagne, and opened it as soon as we came home, without waiting for it to chill. Then, feeling shaky and slightly nauseous after a glass of warm champagne, I told Dema about our papers making their uneasy journey through U.S.

Immigration offices even as we spoke. "Are you thinking of leaving?" he asked. I said that I would never leave without him. Nothing else mattered.

We decided that I'd go to St. Petersburg to spend my two-months-long winter break there. When the break was over, I planned to return to Moscow and stay there three more months until my graduation, and after that I would either move to St. Petersburg permanently and look for a job there, or Dema would find a job in Moscow and move in with me. Neither of us cared for the official ceremony of a big wedding. We didn't see why we'd need the marriage certificate, a mere piece of paper certifying that we belonged together. We knew that we belonged together. Nor did we see the point in the idea of a stranger prodding us to say some big words in front of a big audience. His vows were implied in his proposal; mine, in my acceptance. Neither of us particularly cared about the sprawling feast, where the guests would get so drunk by the middle of it that they'd forget what they were celebrating. And that revolting money question with the parents of the groom arguing with the parents of the bride over who spent more, and who gave more gifts or more expensive gifts, and who had more guests and whose guests ate more! Weddings had always seemed to me a sure way to kick romance out of the marriage. The only thing that I kind of wanted was a wedding dress. A magical white gown, an ethereal headdress, flowers. The only chance I'd ever get to feel truly beautiful. The only chance for my husband to see and remember me that way. I told this to Dema. He laughed. He said: "Women are so silly, they think that the dress or the hair makes all the difference." He didn't get it. It was the first time I became annoyed with him—not for long, though. We hadn't yet developed a capacity to become really mad at each other.

"We're getting married!" I said to my mother. She slumped onto the couch and started to cry, but she more or less calmed down when I said that we weren't going to make it official. I think she saw this as a cue not to take the whole affair seriously.

My first days in St. Petersburg felt like a child's game. I was playing the part of a young married woman. I went shopping with a big checkered bag, I bought bread, I bought onions, I bought rice and buckwheat, I bought meat—I'd never bought meat before. I called my mother several times a day to ask how to stew meat or clean buckwheat. I made sure to have dinner on the table by the time Dema came home from work, even though he didn't seem to care. I went to lunch with my new in-laws. I bought myself a wallet, because I thought that keeping money in a crumpled wad in the pocket of my jeans like I used to do was unfitting for a married woman. I bought myself a nightgown, because I thought that pajamas were just as unfitting. Everything was exciting and new and not completely serious.

The seriousness struck one morning, when my mother called to say that she got a letter from the INS. The U.S. Embassy scheduled the interview with immigration officials for us. She said that if we failed to appear, we couldn't apply ever again. And that my uncle would be so angry that he wouldn't bother applying anyway. We weren't sure if we wanted to emigrate, but we were afraid of losing the opportunity to do so irrevocably.

That night Dema and I had the first serious conversation of our marriage. We discussed our plans for the future and whether the United States was a good place to realize them. Our goals turned out to be simple, clear, and blissfully alike. We wanted to:

1. be together
2. have exciting and meaningful jobs
3. see foreign countries
4. possibly have children one day

It looked like all of those things should be obtainable in the United States, and so we decided to try to go there. The prospect of emigration frightened me amazingly little, probably because I concentrated not on departing, but on arriving. I didn't think of the place I had to leave, of all the things that were dear and important to me that I would lose forever. I thought of the new place, and new life, and all the new and exciting experiences that were stored for me there. In short, I thought of emigration like the great adventure, much like my marriage. I had jumped into marriage without thinking and it was working fine, and there was no reason to suppose that the emigration wouldn't. And as with marriage, the idea of it being permanent somehow escaped me. In addition, I thought that I knew what emigration was all about. I'd just emigrated from Moscow to St. Petersburg.

Every morning after Dema left for work I would choose a different route to walk toward the center, marveling at how the architecture was nothing like Moscow's, taking in all the wonderful foreign details, from the way the streetcars were painted to the way people dressed. Even the Russian language wasn't the same in St. Petersburg. People used other, more interesting, words for bread, rye bread, and newspaper stand, and had subtle, appealing accents. Immigration to St. Petersburg was beautiful; there was no reason to think that immigration to New York wouldn't be. I sat down and wrote a long letter to fax to my uncle, in which I begged him to find out if it was possible to include Dema in our immigration application.

My uncle handled the matter much like the son-in-law in a popular Russian joke of those times. In the joke, a woman asked her son-in-law to arrange that she be buried in the Red Square Wall along with the top Communist Party officials. If he was a good son-in-law, she said, he would find a way to pull it off. And so the next day, he came home, tired, but happy, slumped into a chair, wiped the sweat off his forehead, and said: "I did it, Mother. The funeral is tomorrow." My uncle told a similar thing to my mother. "I did it," he said to her on the phone. "I pulled all the needed strings. They will include Dema in the application, but only if they register their marriage and send me a copy of the marriage certificate within two weeks." My mother was crying so hard when she told me all this that she had to hang up in order not to waste the expensive long-distance call. She felt that she, my uncle, and the nasty U.S.

immigration were all pushing me to marry somebody I hardly knew. "But, Mom," I said, "it doesn't matter. We're already as good as married." As for marrying somebody I hardly knew, I thought that I knew enough of Dema. Love was not science like physics or biology. Love was more like art. You saw a painting and you knew whether it worked right away; you didn't have to stare at it for years.

There was a law that required a period of at least thirty days between the filing of the application and the actual registration of the marriage, but everybody said that there were plenty of marriage-registration officials who would give us a green light in exchange for a reasonable sum of money plus flowers or a box of chocolates (to make it look less like a bribe and more like an expression of gratitude and respect). It turned out that our friends were too optimistic. The officials didn't accept bribes from just anybody, but only from the people they trusted. We asked all our friends if they had any connections and visited a lot of marriage-registration places in person, trying to persuade the wary officials that we were honest and trustworthy bribe-bringing citizens. All in vain. The week was coming to an end and we had almost lost hope, when Dema's camping buddy remembered that he knew some guy in the St. Petersburg Police Department who used to be chummy with the director of one of the Wedding Palaces. I don't know what kind of relationship he had had with the director, but we didn't even have to give her money, just a big box of chocolates. The director blushed at the box, murmured that we didn't have to do it, and shyly put it away in one of her desk drawers. She said that she could squeeze us in for the two p.m. slot the following Thursday and offered to take us on a tour of the palace.

For some reason I'd assumed that the palace would be some pompous Soviet-style monstrosity, all marble and gold, velvet and mirrors, crystal candelabras over busts of Lenin, and oil portraits of Yeltsin. And there was indeed plenty of marble and gold, and a red velvet carpet and crystal candelabra, but everything was tasteful and beautiful, with quiet classical music playing in the background, evoking the atmosphere of nineteenth-century ballrooms rather than Communist Party assemblies. Before the Revolution, the building used to belong to some famous Russian count or prince, and they must have kept or re-created the original furnishing. The place looked just like I'd envisioned the room where Natasha from *War and Peace* danced at her first ball. I saw a wedding party in the hall. The bride was standing by the tall gilded doors waiting for the cue to enter. She was wearing a long white dress just like Natasha's, and she looked just as anxious and hopeful, her fingers squeezing a small bouquet, her feet treading the deep velvet of the carpet. "She stood with her slender arms hanging down," Tolstoy wrote about Natasha, "her scarcely defined bosom rising and falling regularly, and with bated breath and glittering, frightened eyes gazed straight before her, evidently prepared for the height of joy or misery." I identified with Natasha's readiness to make a leap, and with her belief that whatever happened to her would be the height of either joy or misery, not something bland in between these two states. If a magician asked me to choose one scene from all world literature where I would want to be transported, it would've been Natasha's first ball from *War and Peace*. And a simple twist of fate gave me a chance to get as close to this fantasy as I ever would. On Thursday, it would be me mounting the brightly illuminated stairs. My feet would be treading the lush red carpet. My reflection in the long white dress would be gracing the majestic gilded mirrors. I felt exultant, I felt vigorous, I felt ecstatic, until I realized that I didn't have the dress.

That night Dema and I had the first serious fight of our marriage. He refused to understand why it was absolutely necessary to have a long white dress. We never planned to have a big wedding, did we? We just needed the marriage certificate, didn't we? He didn't see anything wrong with the only festive outfit I had brought with me and had just worn to his birthday party. The outfit consisted of a dark green silk blouse, black belt, black leggings, and lavender pumps. Yes, he read *War and Peace*. No, he didn't remember Natasha's first ball. He might've skipped that chapter. He might have skipped the Peace sections and only read about War. It was the first time we turned away from each other in bed. I spent the rest of the night crying and wondering if I was making a mistake. What kind of a person could skip Peace in *War and Peace*? Everybody skipped War! Did I really know Dema? Did I really want to marry him? Did I really want to emigrate? I thought of the strange and scary double doors in St. Petersburg's subway, of the people frowning at me when I asked for directions, of the sharp northern wind thrashing my flimsy Moscow coat. And this was Russia, my own country, where people spoke my own language even if they used the wrong words for bread, rye bread, and newspaper stand. Moving to the United States suddenly seemed terrifying, as did marriage. How could I assume that my marriage would be a happy one? Had I ever witnessed happy marriages? Didn't I know that living together always became either boring or ugly with time? What gave me reason to believe that Dema and I would outwit the statistics and stay deliriously happy for the rest of our lives? The fact that we didn't really know each other? I remember lying in bed on my back, clutching the blanket, staring at the ceiling in horror, until the image of myself in a long white dress worked itself into my mind. The dress was light and translucent, like a wispy cloud, covered with delicate embroidery, sprinkled with tiny diamonds that reflected the candlelight. I was demure and radiant, walking up the marble staircase to the serene music in the background. The dress was my good-luck charm, my guardian angel, my key to happiness. I fell asleep with a hopeful half smile on my face.

And so it went on for days afterward. Every time I would become seized by fear and doubts—and as the wedding date neared it would happen increasingly often—the vision of my wedding dress would relieve the anxiety, but every time I would happily plunge into the world of my dreams, the reality of not having the dress would infallibly yank me out and make me feel the fear and the doubts with renewed strength.

"You really have to have the dress, don't you?" Dema asked one day. He had just sold his collection of miniature car models to buy two thin and simple wedding rings. He gave me the leftover money, the equivalent of twenty dollars, and asked if that was enough for a dress.

I spent the following couple of days trying to find out what twenty dollars could do for an aspiring Natasha Rostova. Twenty dollars wasn't enough to buy a sparkling imported dress in one of the subway kiosks. Nor was it enough for ordering a dress from one of the big wedding dress shops (and there wasn't enough time to wait until they made it). Twenty dollars was enough for borrowing one of the bland, yellowed, too large, and too long dresses from the Wedding Palace's rental shop. And twenty dollars was more than enough to buy a white blouse, a beige skirt, and cream-colored pumps in a department store. The bad thing was that each of those items could single-handedly ruin my *War and Peace* fantasy and simultaneously my chance at happiness.

I was walking home from the department store, stooping to protect myself from the wind, clutching the collar of my coat to keep it tight, feeling cold, sad, and angry, angry at the saleswoman at the department store, at the St. Petersburg weather, at the ugliness of the damp run-down buildings along the canals, at my uncle, at U.S. Immigration, at the brides who had beautiful dresses, at Dema, at Tolstoy, when I saw a couple of wedding dresses in the window of a tiny shop. They didn't look anything like the high-waist, Empire-style dress that Natasha would wear, but they looked both elegant and inexpensive, and so I rang the bell. The woman who ran the shop told me that they usually made wedding dresses to order, but there were a few ready models I could try. All the dresses had different names: Princess, Sleeping Beauty, Svetlana, Nadezhda, Spring, Summer, and some came in different versions—there were Princesses 1, 2, 3, and 4, Svetlana 1 and 2, and six Summers. That didn't mean that they differed according to their names. They all looked alike, all made out of cheap tulle over heavy linen, all decorated with tiny beads, buttons, and appliqué. Svetlana 1 didn't look more like Svetlana 2 than, say, Summer or Spring. I liked Princess 4 because it had tiny iridescent metal disks instead of beads; I thought there was something magical about the rosy glow they sent over the appliqué leaves and flowers next to them. Two other reasons why I liked Princess 4 the most were that it fit, and that it cost only $16. "You'll be okay," the woman at the counter said to me after I stopped crying and blowing my nose into her embroidered handkerchief. She packed the dress, the headdress, and the gloves together, wrapped them in coarse brown paper, tied the package with a string, and gave it to me. I said, "Thank you."

My wedding dress was light and translucent, like a wispy cloud, covered with delicate embroidery, sprinkled with tiny mother-of-pearl flowers, with a modest yet exquisite headdress made as if out of a bouquet of lilies of the valley and forget-me-nots. I looked quietly radiant as I stood by the tall gilded doors waiting for the cue to enter. Nothing of the sort appears in my wedding photographs. In the photographs, there is a skinny, tense-looking, very young girl. Her dark hair is messy; long strands are falling all over her face and neck. Her headdress is made out of paper and wired tulle. Her dress is shapeless and stiff and bunched up on the bottom so that the tips of her lavender pumps show. The roses in her hands have ridiculously long stems, three straight green lines stretching across her body, and the pale pink buds are about to fall apart.

None of it matters. The girl is ready to take a leap.

back in black

lisa carver

♥

For me, getting married has always been like throwing up. I do it as alone as possible, feeling sick, drastic, and doomed. My first one was before a justice of the peace in Philadelphia. I was nineteen years old, marrying a thirty-five-year-old Frenchman so nervous his fingers had swollen up and the ring didn't fit (earlier, he'd passed out at the blood test). I wore my work apron from Kelly & Cohen's Diner. We did it between shifts. We did it not for the green card, but for our twin, tremulous hearts that somehow reached through age, country, and political differences to touch each other.

We moved to Paris. He was a composer and a real, live communist. I decided I was a capitalist. I felt that because I loved him so much, and knew myself so little, I would have to make myself his enemy, his opposite, or else be swallowed whole. For the next two years, my obsession with him grew, and my need to see myself as separate from him grew with it, until finally all there was to do was leave—not only him, but his country as well, and the music and theater and the whole way of life we had created together.

When I first met Robbie, I was mesmerized by what he was not. He did not hate and fight God and state and the patriarch. He was neither dirty nor ugly nor paranoid nor brave. Attractive, reliable, upper-middle-class, Robbie was inexplicable to me. When he asked me to marry him, I felt like a Mayan girl at the lip of a volcano, about to be sacrificed to appease the gods and protect the village. I knew I would marry this man for what I thought he could give my son, who was four years old—stability, faithfulness, normalcy. Things that I and his natural father could not give. I would have said yes to Robbie anyway, even without my son, because I believe in the Butthole Surfers song, the one that goes, "It's better to regret what you have done than what you haven't." To know better, to avoid a mistake, is not high on my list of qualities to aspire to. The chances are that any path I take—to marry or not—is going to turn out to be the wrong one, and in the end I'd rather be a kamikaze of love and marriage than merely AWOL.

Robbie and I got married on a tiny, rocky island in upstate New York in a storm at dusk. My best friend, a thousand miles away, was pissed off at me for yet again not inviting her to my wedding. I shivered in the pelting rain and felt pissed off at the groom for looking solemn and right. Nothing else was right: no white dress, no guests, no flowers, no doves, no butterflies set free out of season in the wrong location just to look good and die. I find something rude about appropriateness. Having been raised with chaos and abandonment, that's the only life that looks real to me. Order of any kind—tradition, a planned life, even a neat room—strikes me as suspicious. Somebody has imposed their will on the natural state. I am of the Edward Gorey school of thought. He let things be as they truly were so much so that he didn't even mow his lawn or trim his hedges. I made no arrangements. While the red-faced minister droned on at our wedding, the poor birdie-looking professional witness in patterned fake silk (the minister's neighbor) slid slowly down the muddy side of the hill until finally she disappeared from view.

I guess I thought (though I didn't really *think*) that by being all haphazard and isolated and gloomy, by doing the wedding ceremony all wrong, I was unjinxing the marriage, or at least freeing it up to be what it wanted, and freeing myself from becoming "a married woman." And it worked. Both of my marriages were open. I felt like a rebel, but I still liked that I was a *legitimately* loved rebel. When I fooled around with someone else, I didn't take off my wedding ring. I was vaguely dissatisfied with the arrangement, but I expected to be.

And then my son's nanny got married.

Her name is Karen. She is a lovely person. She looks like Britney Spears (pre–Kevin Federline). She's so nice she doesn't even have anything bad to say about President Bush. She still sends thank-you cards. She was marrying a fireman, and she prepared for the ceremony for over a year. She registered with Linens n Things. She meticulously went through her Kenny Rogers albums to find just the right song. She showed up for work hungover the day after her bridal party. (I never had a bridal party. I never registered. I picked no songs, apparently preferring uncomfortable silence.) In a complete philosophical turnaround, I felt amazed and touched by someone's respect for the rules. This was not sentimentality or conformity; Karen used traditions to guide her in being considerate. Like when she let her little sister coordinate the bridesmaids' dresses instead of her mom, even though her mom would have done a better job, because her sister wanted to feel like a grown-up woman capable of ordering and dying shoes lilac in time for the wedding. On the day Karen found out the cranberries that were to be sprinkled on the autumn-themed centerpieces had not ripened due to a freak cold spell, she broke down and cried. And having gone through the whole process with her, that didn't seem a stupid reaction to me at all. I was about ready to cry myself.

Karen did everything a thousand degrees different from me. When she heard through the grapevine that a stripper had been at her fiancé's bachelor party, she was horrified. She fumed and felt jealous, yet said nothing, giving her fireman his sleazy last-days-of-freedom space. Me, I'd taken Robbie to a strip joint myself. Partly because I'm, uh, liberated, but partly because I didn't know how to let him be, to do something like that apart from me. I had no sense of community and would have felt threatened if he'd had one. My favorite book as a child was *Lamont, The Lonely Monster*. When I compared myself to Karen, I realized how terribly lonely I really was. While partly it was biological and inescapable, partly it was a choice I'd made and kept making. To be alone on my wedding days and in all my days. To withstand any and all expectations. To be proud and scared until the day I die. After thirty-five years of being sure about the superiority of my position, suddenly I wasn't.

Even though I knew beforehand what her dress looked like, I was stunned when I saw Karen walk through the church doors in it. With her twelve-hour-attended-to hair and French-manicured nails, she was a real bride. She was really leaving us. Her life would now be with this Malibu Ken fireman standing up at the altar, too wooden-jawed to be real. But he *was* real, because when the priest told him to, he kissed our Karen and took her for his own. And she took him, in front of everybody, with dramatic language and surrounded by the sweet-smelling flowers flown in from Hawaii, and they actually looked happy about it.

At the reception, the mood turned merry, and Karen's twelve months of attention to detail became even more apparent: the careful seating arrangement; the tearful and sincere little sister's speech; the ribald and masculine best man's speech (which I think also produced a tear or two); the jocular disc jockey who kept things rolling. And then there were the classic mess ups that happen whenever you corral 140 people into one room, no matter how meticulous your pre-thinking: the little kid (mine, actually) who stuck her finger in the wedding cake; the confusion of the old people about drink tickets; and navigating the thin line between strangers about what is funny and what is gauche.

"Everyone who has been married less than one day, exit

the dance floor," said the DJ. The bride and her groom blushingly went to their seats.

"Okay," he said. "Now everyone who has been married less than one year."

Other, also blushing, couples left.

"Five years!"

As this group exited, no one was blushing. In fact they seemed a little cranky. I was so proud of my husband and me, in our finery, for still standing. At that moment, I was in love with marriage and weddings and habits and beliefs worn soft with use.

Finally only the two oldest people in the world were left, a couple of shrunken apples who had been married fifty-five years. The DJ called the newlyweds back up to dance with the oldieweds, and their youth made a nice contrast with the other couple's age, just like life. Tradition buoyed the bride and groom. You could see flickers of doubt—or I thought I did—in their faces; they were lost, and then found again, falling into the motions made by thousands or millions who had gone before them.

When I kissed Karen good-bye, I felt not good enough for her. I felt like a dark, slinky shadow of doing-everything-wrong. I'd always been proud of that about myself, but now dark just looked . . . well, *dark*, next to her shining rightness.

Robbie and I talked about it on the couch that night. "I'm glad that I am outside culture," I claimed, "and I make a good living observing it. I wouldn't want to be inside. It's just that they all looked so toasty in there today. Inside history."

He said he felt the same. "I know they must have problems too, but . . ."

"But they won't be problems of their own design. They'll be shared problems, just like today was a shared victory: hope over cynicism. I think I may be cynical! I never thought that before. I think I considered myself a revolutionary, but I'm . . . I'm lonely!"

"You have me," he said.

It was the first conversation we'd had in a very long time. I think we were able to converse instead of argue because we both knew, without exactly knowing we knew, that this was the end. There was nothing to struggle against or toward anymore. Struggle was the only way we knew how to be with each other. I always wanted to dig closer and closer to him, to get a good foot- and handhold on him, on the problem. I wanted to win. Sex was a physical manifestation of the struggle: hips pushing and grinding to get closer to this person who remained a mystery and an aggravation, feeling constantly, for seven years, like I was *just about to* solve the problem. But the solution, like our witness on the storm-muddied island hill on which we were married, kept slipping further and further out of range. Somewhere in the soft glow of Karen's unoriginal but joyful wedding, it became clear how miserably we two loners were failing in our attempts to imitate the healthy people. That's what we argued about all the time. Not about money or sex, fixable problems if you just go on *Dr. Phil.* We argued because we were mad that we were arguing. What we argued about was what we were arguing about, and you can never bring that to any conclusion because there's no beginning or middle. All you can do, when you see it, is to disengage your hooks from each other's bones, turn away, and start walking.

Both times, I'd married to escape loneliness. Both times, I ended the marriage to escape a different kind of loneliness.

Eventually, I lost the house. I lost my in-laws, whom I'd adored. I lost my multiline discount on car insurance. My children felt lost. My divorce dismantled every structure that getting married had put up over our heads to protect us.

Before all that happened, while still married, I was talking on the computer (yes, I know, I'm totally sleazy) with a fellow across the country in even worse straits than I was about to fall into. He was already divorced, his instruments were in hock, one guy wanted to kill him, he'd been in jail five days for gun possession . . . which he'd possessed due to the guy who wanted to kill him. He no longer possessed the gun, or anything really. He left it behind in the town that was home to the guy who wanted to kill him, along with his ex-wife, who, for unrelated reasons, also wanted to kill him, and the pawnshop with his stuff in it. Now he lived in an empty apartment in the desert with only a mattress, a computer, some ramen, and one half-eaten can of strangely stinky nuts. He got a job in a club but was fired for reasons too complicated for me to understand, but which I imagine must have had something to do with whatever made the other guy and the ex-wife want to kill him. The same thing that made me, Lamont, the Lonely Monster, want to join my life to his ragged, wide-open one. He was the antithesis of everything I'd tried so hard to turn myself and my life into with my marriage to Robbie. It felt like coming home.

When we got together, there was nothing for me to hide or change or try defensively to explain. We were happy and the kids were happy. I didn't ask him to get a job and behave; he just did. He didn't ask me to not ask things of him; I just didn't. It was nice. I know it looks bad. But I also know my six years that looked good held so much secret tension that my son ended up spending some time in a mental hospital; my husband, who had never been to jail or fired from a job or even come close to putting anything in hock, tried once or twice to punch holes in our walls; and I spent some months I'll never get back on Zoloft.

That sick, drastic, and doomed mood in which I got married the first two times was also the way I felt about marriage itself. Why? All the usual reasons: My father left me; there are double standards for women in this world; in some places wives are even burned alive for cheating or disobedience. And then there was my own tendency to make the man my everything, which I fought by making him in some ways nothing. The feminist in me cringed at the words to the Kenny Rogers song playing at Karen's wedding: "Like a rhyme with no reason in an unfinished song/There was no harmony; life meant nothin' to me, till you came along." And yet that was my dream, wasn't it? That's what I secretly wanted from marriage.

I was terrified of being married, but being scared of something makes me run to it, not from it. I have a recurring nightmare where a tidal wave hovers over my head and instead of trying to reach the shore, I dive under it. As if I would ever come out on the other side of something so overwhelming. But it's the only hope I have.

I don't know how it is that with this grizzled ex-con divorcé from the desert, it's just easy. I recall that Al Green lyric, which I previously thought of as inane: "Being in love means feeling good about someone." The more you like someone, the nicer you treat them, and then the nicer they treat you, and then the more you like them. It sounds pretty dumb, but it's true. Everything is just easy when it's easy. Not that he doesn't irritate me, but you know, I irritate myself, and I don't hold it against me. I just forget how infuriating he is as soon as my mood passes, instead of remembering and counting and measuring what this person has done to me and what he owes me, and always looking for new ways to explain his deficit to him in a way he'll understand. Food tastes better when you haven't fought or silently seethed about who cooks more often. My intestinal health has surely improved with this guy. The kids like me being happy because they get yelled at less, and because they like me and wish good things for me.

I don't want to have sex with other people anymore.

He never asked me to marry him; it was just assumed. I think the kids brought it up: "When are you going to marry our mom?" I don't remember how we decided there would be a ton of people at this wedding or that we would just put the bill to feed them on the credit card because what the hell. I know that one day he said he missed his crowd in San Diego and that's how we figured out we'd do the ceremony in San Diego. We decided to have lots of daisies because that's my favorite flower. Then I decided I didn't want any daisies at my wedding. I'd rather happen upon them, not hire someone to grow them just to cut them down for me. I'm not an entirely different person. My third wedding will still have some elements (or anti-elements, really) from my first two. But I'll mean them differently. This time, my wedding ring is black; my wedding dress is, too. Not like Bauhaus, but like my hero Laura Ingalls Wilder, who wrote *Little House on the Prairie*. Her mother told her not to. She said, "Marry in black, you'll be back." And maybe I will be, again. I'm different, but I'm still me.

I don't feel bad at all that this will be my third marriage. Sometimes you have to try out both coasts before you decide Ohio is the place for you. Nothing against the previous neighborhoods, or against moving in general.

Life *is* hard. But sometimes it isn't at all, not at all. Even an anxiety-ridden, lonely monster won't spend her entire life under a rock, all curled up and hissing. Sometimes she'll uncurl and bask in a spot of sun.

plans
&
preparations

there went the bride

carina chocano

♥

When I was thirty-three, my younger brother got married in a little town outside Madrid. A few days later, my then-boyfriend of three years and I retired to our Barcelona hotel room to fight. Like most things that would have been fun if we hadn't tried to do them together, the trip had completely curdled. It was obvious that we were over, so I did the only logical thing. I brought up the subject of our relationship. Why was it so difficult? Why was it so bad? And why, seriously, why weren't we getting married?

Embarrassing as it was to admit even to myself, I was feeling besieged by the 360-degree turn the popular culture had taken in matters wedding- and marriage-related. In the ten years since I'd graduated from college, it seemed a cottage industry had sprung up around freaking single women out. One minute, it was 1993 and my generation was going to collectively boycott marriage; the next it was 1997 and Bridget Jones was in the middle of a full-blown panic attack. A year later, the *Sex and the City* girls started freaking out in quadruple, and then nobody was safe.

Naturally, my then-boyfriend responded by going on the offensive. That's how it was with us—we fought in the round. We were lobbing recriminations back and forth at high volume, when, out of nowhere, he popped a corker:

"I was planning a surprise wedding for you in December, but now you can just forget it. You blew it."

For a moment, I was speechless.

"A surprise wedding?"

"Uh-huh."

"And you were going to surprise—me?"

"Yup."

Pause.

"What was I going to wear?"

It wasn't a rhetorical question. I honestly wanted to know. In a way, the idea of being driven to a mystery location, having a veil slapped on my head, and being led down the aisle in a daze as my family yelled, "Surprise!" seemed as viable an idea as any. Because when I thought about my wedding, I drew a complete blank. That's not to say the idea of getting married didn't appeal to me. In theory, it did. What I couldn't bring myself to do was imagine myself as a bride. Occasionally, with some effort, I'd muster a hazy, mysterious image—like, there I'd be, standing in a field somewhere, wearing a white sundress and holding a small bouquet of wilted daisies. Then I'd realize that I'd mentally scrambled an old boyfriend's Southern upbringing with an Estée Lauder ad and inserted myself in the picture. Obviously, I felt like a moron.

The truth is that, even in my early twenties, I felt too

old for the optimism that the part seemed to require, too self-conscious for the self-involvement, too broke for the expense, too jaded, in general, to put myself at the center of a tradition so thoroughly hijacked by commercial interests it made the contemporary consumerist Christmas look like a ritual of self-abnegation. Part of me wished I could project myself into the part of the blissfully self-obsessed, confidently demanding, insanely overspent-but-it's-my-wedding sort of bride (I guess I've always believed there must be bliss in this kind of entitled unself-awareness), but it was the same part of me that wished, with doomed and plaintive futility, that I was still a kid, worried about how I'd avoid it all, but feeling like time was on my side.

Even though I grew up on three different continents, the view was always essentially the same. We lived in a succession of nice, quiet, leafy neighborhoods filled with executive husbands, nonworking wives, and ample domestic help. Some of the wives golfed, some played tennis, some volunteered at hospitals or charities, some, like my mom, took to managing the household with military precision. Although—or, possibly, because—she had help, she was able to expand the parameters of a well-run, well-organized household to accommodate activities such as periodically removing the silver from its chamois bags, polishing it, and putting it back into the cupboards, where it remained until the next cleaning. Doorknobs were divested of fingerprints on a weekly basis. The leaves of the ficus tree plants were dusted individually. Sofa cushions were to be fluffed the moment your butt left the seat under penalty of nagging.

Sometimes, we'd have Sunday lunch in the dining room, my mom would lift the lid from a porcelain soup tureen, the steam would curl up, and I would have trouble breathing.

As I got older, I attributed the failure of my bridal imagination to factors that I knew to be neither novel nor particularly interesting, but that in the aggregate comprised quite a ball of wax: late-divorcing, incredibly acrimonious parents; the midlife bankruptcy of said parents; the concurrent, unrelated yet not unremarked ascension of a younger brother to disconcerting wealth; and an undergraduate education specifically designed to make it impossible to navigate the real world without first deconstructing it to pieces. Plus, my postcollegiate career had not only proved nonremunerative, but also afforded few opportunities to socialize with the sort of people who don't split the check with you at dinner and then try to charge you a dollar extra for the Diet Coke you ordered because they just had water.

I wasn't the kind of girl who grew up dreaming about her wedding. I grew up dreaming about my divorce. Not that I thought of it that way, exactly, but the future life I imagined for myself as a kid looked nothing like the lives of the wives that I saw around me. What it resembled— though this didn't dawn on me until I was twenty-seven, my mom had just left my dad, and I picked up my first *Elle Décor* at the airport on my way to visit her at Christmas— was one of those glossy photo paeans to the sophisticated Paris/London apartments of middle-aged art dealers and fragrance company executives who, having emerged from the other end of marriage, were finally free to paint the walls lilac and relax.

Three years after the Barcelona incident, I met my soon-to-be-husband, and a couple of years after that, we got engaged. The engagement came as a surprise, as did our fast and almost discussion-free commitment to throwing a wedding. We set the date right away, and suddenly I was staring down an eight-month time frame within which to plan a destination wedding for one hundred guests. I was happy and excited, but I still dreaded the thought of the wedding.

For women of my generation, women in their mid- to late-thirties, the big, white wedding had somehow (but when exactly?) come to represent a sort of over-the-top, hair-trigger reaction to all the ambivalence, cynicism, and doubt that came before it. If you spend, as I and most of my friends have, the entirety of your twenties and a good part of your thirties in frustrating relationships, then the wedding, when it comes, presents a unique problem. Do you go quietly (and discreetly) after all that bitching? Or do you swallow a decade and a half's worth of words and throw down?

Every aspect of celebrating a marriage seemed to me to be distorted by consumerism and status anxiety, divorced from its original meaning. What did it mean to wear white and be given away? Didn't the falseness of both of those gestures, given that the overwhelming majority of married couples I know lived together before marriage, tip the performance into irony? The solution, of course, was to depart from convention and tradition—but somehow, I was never able to get behind the bride-wore-hot-pink scenarios, either. It takes a certain kind of person to resist the pressures and seductions of a wedding industry estimated to be worth somewhere in the vicinity of $40 billion. And as I would find out, I'm not that sort of person.

The first move I made toward "tradition" came as I was standing at the Sav-On Drugstore on Franklin and Western—the kind of place that makes you feel like you've just shuffled in off the street in a dirty bathrobe, muttering, no matter what you're actually wearing. I was waiting in line to pay for batteries and Advil, when it occurred to me that it might be a good idea to buy a bridal magazine or two. At first, it was hard even to choose a magazine. A *Martha Stewart Weddings* cover was devoted to huge diamond rings. Several others were dedicated almost exclusively to wedding gowns, and I'd already decided I wouldn't be wearing one. All I wanted—or all I thought I wanted—was some basic instruction on exactly how many pieces of paper an invitation should contain, and what those pieces of paper should say. Maybe a couple tips on decorating. That was it.

Not long afterward, I went shopping for "something to wear to my wedding" with a similar bride-phobic friend whose wedding would coincide with the fourth month of her pregnancy. Having soldiered through something like ten relationships between us in our thirteen years as friends, we were happy but disoriented, as though we'd suddenly emerged from ten years in the jungle into a very shiny mall. We bought party dresses, a hot pink chiffon frock for her and a bubble-skirted champagne-colored one for me. My friend even refused to try on anything in white, intent on staying as far away as possible from what we had come to think of as the "bride costume."

When I tried my bubble dress on again at home, however, I started to lose my nerve. As divorced from reality and cobbled-together from no longer extant traditions as the whole white wedding thing seemed, the idea of going completely nontraditional seemed rife with pitfalls, too. What if instead of original and stylish I just looked like I'd thrown something on as an afterthought? Did I want to commit to being the disappointing bride? I exchanged the bubble dress for a slightly "bridier" tea-length dress in ivory. Then, two days before her wedding, my friend called me in despair. "I look like a fat girl in a nightgown!" she wailed. Twenty minutes later, I met her at a nearby bridal salon, and she walked out of there in possession of a long, white strapless gown with a full, floor-length skirt. I returned the tea-length dress and ordered a long linen one from J. Crew. It looked like a wedding dress, without any of the flattering rib-crushing properties. So a month later, I sent that back and bought a long, strapless silk dress with a mermaid skirt and a sweetheart neckline. I told another friend about the whole saga. She said, "Honey, you're a hair away from Vera Wang."

Soon, and without my knowing exactly what had happened or how, the dress obsession had metastasized to all aspects of the wedding planning. I pored over magazines, trying to find images that I could recognize as somehow belonging to us. As much as part of me dreaded the idea of staging an elaborate, possibly alienating spectacle, I was secretly thrilled at all the aesthetic possibilities. Here, finally, was an excuse to spend money like I'd never spent money before! And it was guilt-free spending, too. Like it or not (and usually I don't), the last decade or so has been a banner one for the systematic replacement of life with "lifestyle," and the fact is that the cheesy, corny wedding is—at least as far as the media is concerned—a thing of the past. Before I knew it, I was spending all of my free time thinking about wedding favors and invitations, centerpieces and bridal registries, cakes and photographers. One by one my inhibitions fell away. And slowly but surely, our wedding took on all the characteristics of a Martha Stewart photo spread. In my head. The more excited I got (about the signature cocktails, the mariachis, the postceremony parade—yes, the parade), the more frequently I was beset by sudden panic attacks. What, in God's name, was I doing and why? I'd imagine myself walking down the aisle in my pretty, but let's face it, completely absurd gown, and be suddenly filled with overwhelming shame. I'd fallen for all of it, like a sucker.

One weekend, when I was flu-ridden and flying on a 102-degree fever, I spent a weekend watching a show on the Style channel called *Whose Wedding Is It Anyway?* It's a show about brides and wedding planners rushing around and conquering jitters as they approach their special day— a day that to an alien observer would look more like a coronation than a public declaration of commitment between two people. More than anything, the bride-and-planner dynamic recalled the dynamic between a princess and a lady-in-waiting whose job it is to make sure that protocol is complied with. In one episode, the planner and bride kept a mopey groom locked up in the best man's hotel room, biding their time away from the postceremony cocktail, so that they could make the all-important grand entrance at the reception. Over the course of two days, I must have heard the word "princess" a thousand times. But the word could not have been farther away from its meaning. The average American woman couldn't pick an actual princess, with the exception of everyone's favorite celebrity princess, Diana, out of a lineup at gunpoint. They were not dreaming of the special day when they could mock-assume the responsibilities of the figurehead of parliamentary monarchy and visit AIDS hospices, in other words. What they wanted was to enact the "fairy-tale princess" role of Walt Disney's imagination, to fulfill a childhood fantasy that may or may not have been actually theirs. It certainly wasn't mine.

One afternoon, my fiancé and I sat down to "figure out" our ceremony. Neither one of us is religious, so we knew we wouldn't be getting married in a church. For a while we thought we'd have a civil ceremony, but in Mexico, the process would have required blood tests, chest X-rays, professional translations, notaries, and reams of paperwork. In the end, we decided that we would have a friend marry us by the power vested in him by the Internet. Since Mexico doesn't recognize the Universal Life Church, we'll actually be getting married at City Hall in Los Angeles shortly before we go. In other words, our wedding will take place before our "wedding."

Our "wedding," then, will be a reenactment of a sort, and we look forward to it every day. It will also be the biggest, nicest, most fun party we ever throw. Or maybe it won't be, exactly. Because we're not in Mexico to obsess about the flowers and the lanterns and the tablecloths—all the fretting is being conducted now via phone and e-mail—we won't have as much control over the event as we might have had if we'd planned it at home. It might rain, as it has on that date for the past three years running. (We forgot to look into the weather before booking the date.) I might, as I get ready to walk down the aisle on my mom's arm, be overcome with embarrassment. I might capitulate to the small-town makeup artist and wind up looking more like Baby Jane than like myself. If it were possible for me to return the silk gown, which it's not, I might do it and start all over again at Level 1, the cocktail dress. Maybe I'd then cycle through five more dresses and wind up with a ten-foot-long train and a veil.

The truth is that, two months before the event, I'm still alternating among excitement, horror, and genuine surprise at how it was exactly that we wound up here instead of eloping and taking off for Thailand for a month. But what has changed is that the idea of the wedding itself has, for me, taken the place that marriage once occupied in my imagination. What I mean is, I now see the wedding, and not the marriage, as the possibly great, possibly regrettable transitional stage in my life. But when it's over, we'll be married, a condition that now looks to me a lot like those pretty rooms that seemed like such a happy reflection of their inhabitants—a warm, enveloping place where I'll finally get to feel like myself again.

my bridal meltdown

rory evans

Having spent the bulk of my twenties and early thirties
alone in my apartment, I had no idea what it would be like
to live with someone. Especially someone I was about to
marry.

Jamie and I started dating when he was living in western Pennsylvania, a very cushy 475 miles away from me.
After a two-year teaching post ended, he, his cat, and his
hockey equipment moved in with me. And it was soon
thereafter that I realized I was always in a toxic mood. We
had gotten engaged before he moved in. I assumed our new
living situation would be like our relationship: a seamless
and happy fit. But I had never accounted for how hard it
was going to be to get used to the sound of him whistling or
slurping coffee or chewing food. It was the first time I'd
lived with a boyfriend, much less a fiancé, and how I missed
all the privacy I'd taken for granted—the evenings of sitting in the middle of the living room floor, trimming my

toenails and talking to my friend Rachel about absolutely nothing for an hour an a half, the mornings of waking up, showering, and falling back asleep on the sofa. We live in a duplex apartment—the living room directly over the bedroom—and I remember sitting in bed, eyes bugged out, aghast at the sound of Jamie's stocking-feet footfalls as he walked between the sofa and the bathroom. "Stop pounding!" I snapped, as if I expected him to grow dainty little gossamer wings and flutter to the toilet, as if I expected him to disappear.

Adding to my unhappiness was his underemployment. In a summer of irrational fears and anger, this amplified my lifelong Yankee dread of someday waking up flat broke. At the time, mine was the only paycheck, and Jamie spent his days on the fool's errand known as looking for a tenure-track position in the humanities. And doing lots of fix-it-build-it projects around the apartment. (And, of course, desperately seeking shelter when caught in the sudden squalls of my bad moods.)

I wrongly thought that since there were two of us, I would have to work doubly hard and make twice as much money. I also had the large bill of our wedding to reckon with. Honestly, the wedding planning itself sparked very little grief, because the event would be so casual, and the venue was more or less a one-stop shop. I just didn't have it in me to chew and gnash over small decisions like which wine would be best with dinner (beer goes with cheeseburgers, right?). I trusted my mom to do whatever she thought best.

It was the paying for it that I was so stressed out about and kept me busy with an insane amount of overtime assignments, which, of course, just bred further resentment of this sweet, unsuspecting man who had thought he was moving in with someone loving and friendly and fun. I am ashamed to think of how many times I slammed doors that summer with the conversation-ending "One of us has to work!" As I stretched myself ever thinner, taking on various freelance assignments on top of my part-time editing job, I would mentally offset some aspect of the wedding—like, this 600-word Q&A with Yoko Ono would pay for the open bar. (*Kampai,* Yoko, BTW.) Every night before falling asleep and every morning before getting up—when I should have been looking to my left at a man who is the kind of handsome I still don't think I deserve—I'd lie in bed and do a mental inventory of all the things I had to get done before the wedding: story for X, story for Y, story for Z, revise story for X. Write memo for Tom. Send ideas to Linda. Oh, and find the time and supplies to make four hundred clothespin self-portrait cake toppers.

Let me explain: The idea came to me very early on in our engagement, and was inspired by a streetwalker-looking doll my little sister made when she was in first grade. She rolled a peg clothespin in lime green satin, wrapped a cotton ball around its shoulders, glued some orange yarn on its head, and drew a floozy, pretty-lady face on it. (It is, to this day, the coolest thing I think my sister has ever made, in her lifetime of making cool things.) I decided to make bride and groom self-portraits out of clothespins, in arts-and-crafts replicas of the very clothes we planned on wearing, and I would then place one on top of each of the two hundred cupcakes we'd overordered for the one hundred guests at our cookout wedding.

Almost every night as I walked home from the subway, I would stand at the very edge of the sidewalk on the corner of Lafayette and Astor Place and think: "If I could just get hit by a bus, I wouldn't have to deal with any of this." I didn't want to die, but I did want a valid excuse for blowing off all the work that was making me so miserable (and so miserable for Jamie to be around). I fantasized about lounging in a hospital bed and watching gobs of vapid daytime television. Then an actual bus would come whooshing past, snap me out of my reverie, and I'd head home to have dinner, then do a few hours of work.

Stress manifests itself in the body in lots of ways. Some people lose tons of weight. I wasn't so lucky: Instead, my right eye started twitching and I broke out in eczema. Oddly, even though stress triggered the big patches of red, itchy bumps on my arms, wrists, knees, calves, neck, and—in the final weeks before the wedding—my eyelids, scratching at them was my greatest comfort. It bears mentioning: I'm sufficiently low-maintenance that I really wasn't worried that my eczema would "ruin" my wedding day look. (It's a tad difficult for someone wearing a white tank top and white jean skirt to get all princessy over a splotchy red rash.)

Besides, I actively did not want it to get better, since then I wouldn't know how to channel my anxiety. When I got called into my boss's office, I'd sit in the chair on the other side of her desk and, to quell my nerves, automatically reach for my knee and start scratching. I would stand in front of the open refrigerator, wondering what we'd have for dinner, and scratch at my inner elbows. Jamie would holler from across the room, "Stop scratching!" If I were sitting next to him on the sofa and mindlessly scratching, he would forcibly remove my hand from my rash. At night, in bed, when I was watching *Law & Order* and thought he was asleep, I'd reach for my elbows and wrists and dig right in. Invariably, in half sleep, he'd grit his teeth and whisper, "Stop it." One weekend, about three weeks before the wedding, Jamie went to Buffalo to go sailing with his friend Scott so I could work full tilt, uninterrupted, on the last few projects I had due. Yes, I was happy to have the privacy so I could just focus (no chewing noises!) and work. But more than anything, I remember being so thrilled that I could go lie down in our cool, dark bedroom and scratch with impunity.

I know none of this stuff—the itching, the hit-by-bus fantasies—sounds glamorous or bridal or even very mature. It couldn't be just me, right? As I flipped through the bridal magazines at the newsstand (I had a wedding to pay for and wasn't about to shell out five bucks for a stack of advertisements), I saw that the overarching theme is "getting ready for your wedding is the time of your life! It doesn't get more thrilling or creative than this!" But I found it hard to understand that any overextended bride was buying any of it. I sometimes look back and think I crammed a marriage-worth of strife and worry into just a few prenuptial months. I like to think I know myself better than to say that maybe I was testing Jamie right down to his marrow: You think you want to be with me? Even when I have too much work? Even when I'm a foul beast? Even after I tell you you're *breathing too loud*? I also like to think I know myself better than to say that maybe I was so miserable because, after I'd gotten what I'd thought I'd always wanted—someone cute, kind, and funny to love and love me back—I wasn't so sure I really wanted the responsibility of caring for it all the time. I've watched some of those Bridezilla wedding shows on the lady-cable channels and been utterly gobsmacked at how upset and apoplectic some of the brides get about the botching of small details—the wrong color Jordan almonds, a veil length that's off by an eighth of an inch. But then I think maybe there's a conservation of matter—that every bride has to worry and pick and be miserable a certain amount; it's just up to her what the fuss is. And that the fuss, no matter what shape it's in—be it a missing fake pearl from a tacky thigh garter or slamming a door when you have too much work—is just a displacement or expression of the fear of being with someone else for the rest of your life.

Eight days before my wedding, I handed in the last of my assignments. Miraculously, I'd finished all my stressful work (and had the blooms of eczema to prove it!). Now I just needed to make four hundred self-portrait clothespin cake toppers. On a Friday morning, I went to the art store to buy supplies. By that point in the summer, Jamie had started a job as a cabinetmaker, so he joked that both of us would be spending our day working with wood. When he got home at six o'clock, I'd been painting, gluing, and assembling for almost eight hours straight, with about forty self-portraits to show for it. For the Rorys, I painted on a little white tank top, wrapped and glued a white piece of eyelet for the skirt, Magic Markered hair, eyes, and mouth, glued a piece of tulle on top, then glued and snipped on coffee-stirrer arms. For the Jamies, I painted blue shorts and a pink polo shirt, brushed the head with glue then dunked it into "dirty blond" yarn fuzz, markered the eyes and mouth, glued on arms that had been painted with pink sleeves, and then—in what our (gay) friend David approvingly refers to as "the height of faggot nonsense"—used a green fine-point Sharpie to draw the world's tiniest alligator onto the shirt.

Jamie surveyed my progress. Then he sat right down to help me. He decided that in a sea of four hundred, some of them had to look a little different, so he made one guy have a red thong and a crazy curly thatch of chest hair. On another, he drew a painstakingly detailed pair of tighty whities. By the end of the night, we had close to one hundred, packed them up, and got ready to drive to my parents' in Massachusetts the next day. We spent the rest of that rainy weekend with my mom, at her dining room table, putting together the rest of our cake toppers. Jamie went into my mom's cellar workshop and sawed the head of one of the pins in half, and then glued the resultant half-sphere onto the "stomach" of another pin, making a pregnant bride with a shamrock tattoo on her forearm and a white tank top that didn't cover her bump. In a feat of fine art unlike anything I'll ever see again, he individually glued one-inch strands of satiny embroidered floss onto the back of one pin's "head" to make a mullet for a hillbilly groom (with pink wife beater and fringy, shorty-short denim cutoffs).

He, my mom, and I were in a creative fugue state unlike anything hinted at by the bridal magazines. My mom's table was covered with self-portraits-in-progress as well as tissue-paper-lined boxes of the finished products. At one point, my dad traipsed through the room, sort of shook his head, and said to my mom, "Alice, you and your projects"— not quite derisively but not quite affectionately either.

I flashed my eyes over to Jamie, in fear that he'd take my dad's comment as some sort of dismissal or insult or emasculating insinuation. Jamie, I was happy to see, was too caught up in the faggot nonsense of faithfully re-creating a comb-over to notice. Of course, at that moment, I had to appreciate his indulgence, his readiness to offer his time, keen motor skills, and even keener sense of humor to what I knew in my heart to be a rather inane endeavor. If being married meant more of this, then I was finally and completely ready.

A week later, we got married in outfits that matched the clothespins. The big reveal of the entire event came when people entered the lodge's large, screened-in porch for dinner and saw the tower of cupcakes with their self-portrait clothespin cake toppers—audible gasps and hearty ooohs and aahs. There followed the supremely satisfying exchange (several times) of "Where did you get them?" and "We made them together!" In the weeks following the wedding, our friends e-mailed digital pictures of the cake toppers in various locales. Our friend Heidi planted hers in the soil of her hanging fern, over her kitchen sink. Scott, who got the mullet-head, had his presiding over the living room from the mantel. My friend Curtis wrote to say that she had soaked them together in a teacup to get the frosting off their legs, and that it was the sexiest thing that had ever happened in her kitchen.

Our own set we store in a glass spice jar, with their (our?) feet bound with the thin green satin ribbon I wore that day as a belt. Every time I look at it, I feel irrationally happy. It's the same feeling I get most of the time when I'm in bed watching *Law & Order* and look to my left and watch Jamie when he's asleep. Even in wakefulness, I usually feel like this—a certain, hazy kind of happiness. Even if I'm still getting used to the noises Jamie makes when he's chewing.

the best-laid wedding plans

How I Called Off My Wedding

jennifer armstrong

I stood on a pedestal, thick white satin hugging every curve of my butt without scrunching, falling precisely to the tops of my silver-sandaled feet without bunching. The top seam of my strapless gown skimmed the top of my breasts, and my bare skin peeked seductively through the lace-up back to my exact specifications. I don't mind saying it, because I'd picked this dress myself, I'd had the seamstress rework it until it was basically couture, and I'd endured five fittings to get here: I was a vision of perfection.

The gal on the pedestal next to mine, drowning in pouf and lace, caught my eye in the mirror and sparkled like we shared a delicious secret. "What's your date?" she asked, all aglow. My first reaction: *Should she really be asking me about dating? I'm engaged, after all.*

And then I caught my reflection in the mirror again, remembered why I was here. Panic set in. Let's see, it was late July. What would make sense? Not August. That was too soon. "September."

"OhmyGod, me too! When?"

"Uh, the second weekend." Total gaffe: Any bride has memorized not only her own date, but the exact date of every Saturday within at least four weeks of hers.

"Oh, mine's the eighteenth, so a week later."

An embarrassed flush spread from the top of my dress, up my neck, to my cheeks. I'd put my wedding on September 11. Not impossible, but . . . unlikely, a mere three years after the terrorist attacks. The shop fell silent then, save for the occasional tussling of tulle. Who knows if she was onto me, but that was beside the point. When I stood there lying to a total stranger, it seemed all too obvious, the symbolism cinching my lungs like the seamstress yanking the strings of that lace-up back: I wasn't being honest with myself or my fiancé. We'd had a date, nearly a year before, and we'd been postponing ever since. Actually, *I*'d been postponing. And I wasn't sure I'd ever stop.

The truth about my feelings showed up in the wedding planning—whether I was barreling forward with the goal-orientation of an Olympic athlete, oblivious to anything except getting to the finish line; dreaming of a destination wedding that would take us far away from our everyday reality; or convincing myself that a cool New York wedding would make us into the happy urban couple I wanted us to be. But the fact is that I got so caught up in the planning itself that I couldn't see that every one of those phases was telling me something very important about my relationship.

Facing my indecision proved the biggest struggle of my life. When doubts first began whispering through my head, they didn't make sense to me. I'd spent so long loving my fiancé—more than a decade, since we met in college. I had found a man who shared my love of Shakespeare and Elton John, who was taller than me but not too tall for me to kiss, who was smart (a nonnegotiable requirement) and funny in the exact right way (puns and sarcasm are both essential). He balanced my remedial financial skills with budgetary obsession and was so organized he made me feel wonderfully free-spirited (though anyone can see from my meticulous day planner that I am not). I was so sure we belonged together that I followed him from Northwestern University in my hometown of Chicago to Southern California (where he was stationed as a navy officer), back to Chicago (so he could go to grad school at Northwestern), and finally to a New Jersey suburb of New York—where he got a job at Mercedes-Benz, and I could finally chase my national-magazine dreams after years of local newspaper reporting. And I did just that, landing a gig at *Entertainment Weekly*—which required that I start as an assistant, but my diligent spirit was prepared to do what it took. We bought a condo in Jersey. Dan proposed. Everything seemed on track.

So how could I feel like it didn't quite fit? I had methodically plotted a perfect wedding that I didn't want, the same way I'd carefully constructed a perfect life I was beginning to realize I didn't want. The evidence was there in the preliminary wedding preparations when a strangely errant desire immediately surfaced: It seemed I wanted a small, casual affair, with just our closest friends and family—not the princess-bride wedding I'd always imagined having. Instead, I envisioned an evening party, essentially, kicked off with some vows followed by a yummy dinner and *maybe* a little dancing.

Then I even found the dress. My mom and I were walking through a mall in suburban Chicago when I was home for Christmas. This gorgeous little thing shimmered at me from a shop window: silvery white, with a halter top, plunging back, and swishy skirt that fell just below the knee. Sort of a Marilyn Monroe number, with less plunge in front and more dip in back (*perfect*, since my curves are more modest than Marilyn's and my back is one of my better features).

I stopped in the middle of the mall when I saw it, and I gasped enough that my mom reacted as if I were suffering a grave illness. "I'm fine, Mom," I assured her. "It's just . . . that's the dress."

"It's pretty. Are you guys doing something for New Year's?"

"No, that's my wedding dress."

I *never* expected what came next. Not from my mom. My mom is cool, laid-back, and, more than anything, all about letting her kids make their own decisions (e.g., mistakes). The woman let me move to Southern California right after college into an apartment that I'd never seen, with a job at a far-flung newspaper that was paying me $320 a week, and never issued one word of doubt or warning. But weddings, I learned, do funny things to people beyond the bride. "You would wear *that* to your wedding?" she said. "How would you wear a veil with that?"

"Um, I'm not wearing a veil."

"You *have* to wear a veil. You need a wedding gown and a veil."

She looked so indignant, was so emphatic, that, at the time, I thought maybe I *did* need a gown and a veil. The only person I liked to please more than my boss or my fiancé was my mom, after all.

I never saw that dress again. But later that week, on a proper search for a proper dress in proper bridal stores, I found the one I'd tailor to perfection: a strapless, pure white column dress with a reasonable little train and silvery beading along the top. I got a veil trimmed with a little sparkle to match the beading. The silver bits reminded me of the shiny Marilyn dress I'd passed by—my (tiny, imperceptible) nod to the bride I'd wanted to be.

I'd fancied myself a modern woman who knew what she wanted and wasn't afraid to get it. But I was slowly starting to see that the only thing I wasn't afraid to get was a wedding dress that everyone else would think was gorgeous and, thank God, appropriate. And as for what I wanted, that was nothing more than a sparkle along my bustline. The wedding planning consumed me. So much, in fact, that when I look back at that time, even Dan hardly enters my memories. I was on autopilot, preparing for something I had been waiting for all my life. Whether I wanted it wasn't up for discussion.

In my mind, I was doing it *for* him. For *us.* I had dreamed of this day for so long, but I refuse to use the excuse that I was brainwashed, like all other girls, since childhood. I wasn't dumb—I had the wherewithal to figure out I didn't *need* a wedding to be a modern successful girl. But I was a searing romantic. Always had been, for as long as I'd liked boys. And it was *because* I liked boys so damn much. I'd always believed in true love, because I was always in love, period. This one had simply outlasted the others and made it to the finish line. This was it, and I was so ready. We'd been through a lot together, from all the time spent apart during his navy years' interminable deployments to several rounds of breakups and reconciliations during our mid-twenties. But we'd been through a lot together *mostly by being apart.* And being apart, especially when one of you is on a navy ship in a uniform, gives a relationship the feel of something for the ages. Destiny skulks around a lot. *Meant to be* sounds like a phrase coined just for you.

This was why I was really psyched about this wedding. It would serve as the climax to an epic romantic saga. What had I been thinking, looking at that cocktail dress, staking out mere restaurants for the occasion? Thank God I'd gotten the gown, the marbled Chicago Historical Society with the sweeping spiral staircase for me to walk down, the cake with the raspberry ganache. A day to celebrate the miracle that was us—the triumph of true love over adversity! I couldn't wait to say our vows before our family and friends—the ones who'd questioned our many reconciliations, who'd wondered if we were too young when we'd met, who'd raised skeptical eyebrows when I passed over perfectly good other men to remain fixated on Dan.

It crossed my mind, briefly, that one of the reasons I wanted this ceremony was to prove to all of them not that love conquered all, but that Dan loved me, that *I* conquered love. But, no. I loved him, too. Of course I did. Why else would I have kept this going for so many years if I didn't?

Wedding magazines stacked up on our coffee table, the useful pages (about invitations and favors and place cards, areas I hadn't yet tackled) dog-eared, later to be torn out and fastened into a binder with colored tabs and a personalized checklist I'd typed out myself by combining the pointers in several leading bridal publications.

It is amazing how wrapped up in minutiae one can get when one is avoiding bigger issues, like the fact that one's fiancé has started talking about kids right at the time that one has realized one might avoid them forever. Or the fact that one's fiancé wants to move farther into New Jersey just as one has been overcome with the desire to move into Manhattan at any cost. Or the fact that one has just gotten promoted at one's dream job, so one is actually writing feature stories for a national entertainment magazine, and one is thinking about writing a book and pursuing new dreams, not settling down with a dog and kids and a yard. Because one spends more time in the city with one's new group of invigorating, creative, writerly friends than one does at home in Jersey with one's fiancé.

And I defy you to find anything that manufactures obsession with minutiae more efficiently than the bridal industry. The wedding biz is an insidious ally to the bride who's determined to ignore her feelings, doing the same job the institution of marriage does for couples who are afraid to think too much: It structures gut feelings out of the picture, gives us steps to follow so that we feel like we're moving forward with a momentous decision when all we're doing is obsessing to the point of near mental illness over invitation fonts and frosting flavors.

Even on nights when I found myself with perilously little wedding planning to do—the cake was now ordered, the invitations chosen if not officially purchased—I could scrounge up something to worry about as I sat on the sofa with my binder. I could spend hours, for instance, compiling beauty tips from bridal magazines, even though they were the same beauty tips I'd read a trillion times in women's magazines (apply two coats of mascara; blot your lipstick) with the bonus implication that this was your one big day ever! What you looked like would never matter as much again! So why not shell out a few grand on a laser treatment, get the extra-expensive foundation primer that doesn't seem to do much, spring for the hair extensions?

One thought began to haunt my days and nights: What if I got a zit that day? I was fairly prone to them. *What if one showed up that day? WHAT WOULD I DO?*

I never did come up with an answer. I simply lived in dread.

This OCD phase went on for months, my greatest pleasure in life checking off another wedding-planning step. Then came my bachelorette party.

Now, I don't mean to disparage it: My friends worked hard on it, and I'd approved all the plans months earlier. We were holding it in June during a visit home sans fiancé—the wedding wasn't for another five months, but we wouldn't have time for it then. When I got to my party, I couldn't help feeling that I was at the wrong place. It was as if a stranger had been the one to approve those plans. A stranger with a nearly-100-percent-checked-off wedding-planning list. A stranger who was totally okay with an afternoon bachelorette party that involved a lot of Pampered Chef kitchen gear (complete with special bridal apron), white wine spritzers, and do-it-yourself mani-pedis.

Though it wasn't even so much the party itself—most of it was like an old-school slumber party, except we were grown-ups so we paid a massage therapist to show up for some rubdowns, which I must admit were great. What got me was the way everyone oohed and aahed when I opened gifts like bath towels and the way people wouldn't stop asking me about the goddamn wedding, like it was the only thing in my life.

And then it dawned on me: That's because I'd asked for bath towels on my registry, and because the goddamn wedding was the only thing in my life.

I'd asked for it all, and I wasn't sure I wanted any of it.

When I returned to New York, I stopped obsessing over my wedding-planning binder. Hell, I stopped looking at it, period. Weekly reminder e-mails from the wedding Web site TheKnot.com (telling me exactly how long it was until my wedding date and which essential tasks that meant I should be doing) dinged my in-box, and I deleted them with only a cursory glance. I was well ahead of schedule anyway, I told myself. I deserved a break. Until, of course, the reminders started to mention things I hadn't done, like finalize the caterer's menu or choose favors. I deleted those, too, as if that would delete them from my brain.

Then the bills started pouring in—we owed the rest of the $5,000 for the reception space, $300 for the cake, and a several-thousand-dollar amount for the caterer (exact total to be determined when I actually committed to a menu). Dan, the one with the checkbook, stayed on top of these things, unfortunately. I couldn't stay in denial, couldn't put them off. Those three zeroes on the end of the check to the Chicago Historical Society knocked me dizzy as I put it in an envelope, sealed it, and mailed it under the watchful eye of my fiancé. The cake bill, I couldn't help noticing, would buy me a couple of good pairs of jeans, an exceptional pair of shoes, or several trips to a couples counselor (especially one covered by insurance). The caterer remained the one realm where I had total power—*I* was in charge of finalizing menus, so *I* could decide not to.

I ignored the caterer's calls, and, incidentally, we tried a string of marriage counselors in addition to ordering the cake. All we got was an old woman who asked us if we were achieving orgasm (listen, lady, if there's something to achieve, I achieve it) and a man who had the nerve to tell us we were getting old (Dan was now thirty-one; I was twenty-nine), so we might as well settle for each other and make things work.

And then we gave up on the counseling. We had a wedding to plan—there was no time to keep up these awkward first dates with ineffective therapists.

Time was, after all, of the essence at this point. We had to order invitations. TheKnot.com had been saying so for weeks. It was pretty insistent about this. Even worse, the personal e-mails from the nice man at the invitation store were saying so. And they were pretty insistent, too. The last one went something like, "If you don't confirm your order by this weekend, WE WILL NOT HAVE THEM ON TIME. Unless you've changed your date, in which case, please let me know." He was a soft-spoken, painfully polite man, not someone who would use all caps willy-nilly. He meant business.

And so it was that I decided to sit down with Dan that crucial invitation-ordering weekend (not a second before) and say, "We should have a destination wedding, I think."

"We should," he agreed. I was shocked at how easily this went.

So shocked, in fact, that I said, "Or maybe we should just have the wedding like we planned."

"No," he said, "we should have the destination wedding."

"You're right."

"Really?" he said. "Maybe we should just have the wedding like we planned."

"No," I said. "Destination wedding." I was so confused; who wanted what here? No matter, I thought. I had won, hadn't I? "No more of this silly froufrou stuff we didn't want," I said, genuinely excited about this new plan. "Just us, our families, and a few friends, on an island."

"Where?"

"I don't know, the Bahamas. We've never been there. It's like a fresh start."

"The Bahamas it is."

And so we ran from the invitation man, from TheKnot .com, from the remaining preparations and the elaborate planning I'd already done, from the thousands of dollars in deposits we'd put down. From the fact that we both knew *I didn't want this wedding.* We dashed off a letter to all the folks we'd sent save-the-date cards, telling them to use the date now for whatever they wished but to get ready for a damn good time in the Bahamas . . . someday . . . soon.

I told my parents, who were incredibly supportive and understanding, because that is their thing—I was relieved to find the mom I always knew receiving the news, rather than her crazy wedding-gown-and-veil-fixated personality. Dan told his parents on the phone and reported that the news had gone down eerily smoothly. I suspect both sets of parents knew something had been amiss for a while, and had been married long enough themselves to know there was nothing *they* could do to fix it.

Months passed, brochures were collected, budgets were made, questions were batted away with "we're working on it." A destination wedding was not had. It was not even planned.

Then I went to that final dress fitting, and came out with yet another plan: We would get married in Manhattan. We were now moving into the city from New Jersey. We had purchased a condo on the Upper West Side at my insistence, as part of our fresh start, our attempt to bring my diverging identities of Dan's Fiancée and New York Writer Girl together. Clearly, this was my problem when I was lying to my fellow bride in the dress shop: I had not yet reconciled my identities. But this new wedding plan, by God, might just do the trick.

What better way to celebrate this new life together than to get married in a small park, then hold an intimate gathering at a classy restaurant? Why, New York was full of parks and restaurants! How hadn't we thought of this before? We would declare our new identity to the world: Here we are, Urban Power Couple! Surely this was what I wanted. I loved Nora Ephron movies, after all.

But that was just the problem: No matter what wedding I thought up, I seemed to be simply recycling some ready-made fantasy sequence. I was positive I wanted a life in New York—that was the one thing I'd figured out in this mess—so I was trying to make my wedding a part of that. But as it turned out, I couldn't find much time in my New York life to research those parks and restaurants. I threw out a Google search here, an e-mail there, but when I didn't get immediate responses, the planning ground to a halt yet again. I printed out a few restaurant reviews, but never got around to visiting the places.

Dan, incidentally, said he'd go anywhere, at any time, and pay anything I needed to get this thing done. He even went so far as to pick an October date (nearly a year after our original date) and write it on the calendar, which his mom found out and helpfully mentioned in her Christmas newsletter to friends and family, which happens to include my parents, who went nuts to hear there was a wedding date they didn't know about.

That incensed me, but what bugged me even more was Dan's total capitulation to my demands. I know that seems irrational—ask for what you want, then get pissed when you get it. But suspicion clouded my every thought as he suddenly reversed his earlier wishes to have kids soon, to get a house with a yard and a dog, to have a wife who'd take his last name. Every time he gave in, I didn't think, "Yay!" I thought, "Really?"

He reminded me of myself, a few years back, when I would say or do anything to stop him from talking about us breaking up to see other people. When I would wish he'd be more affectionate or wonder about our future or just hope we'd go out to dinner instead of staying in to watch *Star Trek: The Next Generation* ... but I would swallow those thoughts, hold my breath, smile, and enjoy Captain Picard's latest adventure for fear of tripping a discussion that would lead to our demise.

I hated myself then, and thinking of it now made me hate him, despite all of my love for him.

In the end, getting away from that former me, in all her forms, became the priority. She would never know who she was or what she wanted—she would only ever know how to be what everyone else wanted. And the path away from her happened to lead the wrong way down the aisle. So that is where I went.

. . .

Calling off your wedding sounds big. I would use it sometimes (and still do) to give people a thrilling little snapshot
of me: Instead of being Dan's Fiancée, I am now the
Woman Who Called Off Her Wedding. It makes me seem
brave and independent and modern. And I like that better
than being the girl who did everything she was told.

But the act itself felt more like a billion tiny, excruciating steps—the exact opposite of those brainless, satisfying
steps to planning a wedding—every one of which required
me to stop, catch my breath, have a sob, look around, find no
one there to comfort me, and then do it all over again.
Telling my parents, packing up my stuff, moving out of the
condo into a low-rent studio in the East Village, explaining
the situation to everyone . . . months of exhaustion. Throwing away my wedding binder for good? My one big moment
of relief.

One task sticks in my head as virtually impossible—
and I mean *physically* impossible: taking off my beautiful
1.5-carat solitaire-and-white-gold engagement ring, the one
I had once literally quivered with excitement to show off,
and handing it to my ex-fiancé as I left the condo. Another
task *remains* impossible: taking my wedding dress out of
the closet and figuring out what to do with it. It hasn't left
its black garment bag since that final dress fitting.

What if that dress is right, I am wrong, and I could've
had a life as beautiful as my gown portends? I realize I'll

never know, really. But I do know that I'll never wear that dress, in that form, at any wedding. I also know, as it turns out, that I don't reject marriage wholesale, because part of me is still that romantic who believes in a kind of true love. The kind of love that's truer because both people know themselves, each other, and how insane a proposition marriage is—because they know the artifice of weddings and the institution itself are built to tell us what to want every step of the way. The more you're thinking about hors d'oeuvres, the less you're thinking about your own and your partner's unwieldy life appetites; the more you're thinking about satin and tulle, the less you're thinking about losing your own identity to this union; the more you're thinking about the reception space, the less you're thinking about where you and your partner are in life, where you're going together, and whether you want to be any of those places.

I'm also starting—slowly, carefully, mindfully—to envision the wedding I might have someday: an intimate crowd, for sure, that includes my wonderfully supportive family and those amazing writer-crowd people who have become the best friends of my life; a cozy, quiet, cool reception space, probably in New York, definitely with kick-ass food and wine; vows that say something along the lines of, "You're the best friend I have, you've seen me at my craziest and still seem to like me, and you inspire me to be a better person, so, hey, let's give this ridiculous marriage thing a go."

Oh, and the dress? I have this little silvery white, Marilyn Monroe number in mind. And I'm confident I'll find a way to get exactly what I want.

etiquette
&
registry

manners
and the
marrying girl

elise mac adam

♥

When I got engaged, I was excited to get married. I loved my fiancé, but something strange happened. I began to have wedding nightmares. My night sweats had nothing to do with second thoughts or waning passion. My dreams stemmed from the sinking feeling that I wasn't the kind of girl who could pull off a wedding. In the dark I would obsess over family dynamics, thinking of the many ways I could offend or alienate my dearest friends and family members at my upcoming nuptials.

Would my friends hate me if I didn't invite any children? Would I fail the Mrs. or Ms. test when addressing invitations to people I didn't know and get accused either of being conservative or inflicting my liberal politics on people? Was it rude to accept generous offers of assistance? Or was I supposed to gently demur? How could I decline when I needed help quite urgently?

Then I remembered Miss Manners and her Gentle Reader, the salutation which she had used since her first etiquette column was published in 1978.

There was salvation. Rules, the more rigid the better, would rescue me. Faced with two families and the threat of embarrassment, I embraced the rules and mowed through my engagement like a visiting diplomat. I was a nervous student, consulting books while I composed invitations, planned the food (in spite of the fact that we served Italian food, and etiquette books tend to offer menus that can only be described as New England Civilized), and negotiated guest list intricacies. I set out to be as rigorous as possible. I didn't care if my rigidity seemed eccentric. Paying attention to rules that no one else would notice felt virtuous, like running extra miles or forgoing an ice-cream sandwich.

It was a crutch, sure, and it only took a few weeks to learn that adopting stiff policies was going to make me utterly insufferable if I didn't bend—without giving in to decadence, of course. Learn, then, from my near follies.

LESSON LEARNED #1: INVITATIONS—DON'T WRITE THEM ALONE

How hard is it to compose an invitation? It's a happy missive, usually greeted with smiles. In an urge to embrace everyone equally, I set about composing something all-inclusive, naming all parents. I submitted a few versions to my then-fiancé, my future mother-in-law, and my mother for approval and sighed with relief. Everything I wrote was satisfyingly traditional, verging on bland. What possible issues could there be?

Famous last words. My future mother-in-law preferred that she and her husband's names appear in the strict construction that only uses the husband's first name. My mother was quite emphatic that I use her whole name.

Such small details on a piece of stationery that only the most extreme nostalgia maniacs don't throw away, but so important. I examined scads of etiquette books and came up with solutions that included putting each set of parents' names in the format each preferred (symmetry be damned). I tried to unearth novel solutions (as if novelty would have helped), and I got more and more anxious, fretting about displeasing my fiancé's family and wounding my own.

And then my future mother-in-law, with one swift stroke, pulled the plug on my angst. "I like the traditional way best, with just the bride's parents' names. Those others just look so cluttered. The old-fashioned way just seems nicest. Don't you think?" There is nothing memorable about my wedding invitation (except perhaps the gray ink), but I can't think about it without being grateful to my mother-in-law's preferences and the peace I found in so-called stodgy tradition.

LESSON LEARNED #2: COMPULSIVENESS DOESN'T ENHANCE THE THANK-YOU NOTE

My etiquette love occasionally took masochistic turns. I couldn't stop measuring myself against a rigid standard and quickly became demonized over things like thank-you notes. Of course they had to be written, but I had to turn them around in twenty-four hours or else I'd wake up composing them before my alarm started blasting. In at least one instance I wrote a note before I had even figured out what the present was: "Thank you so much for the toucans. I can't wait to use them."

Even my friend, beside whom I always fall short when it comes to efficiency, was forced to comment. "My parents got your note before they even knew the present had been sent. Are you getting enough rest?"

Not really. But I couldn't put on the brakes. Etiquette had me in its stranglehold. If I wrote the notes, and wrote them quickly with some degree of charm and inventiveness, I would forestall the threat of alienating anyone. Even putting stamps on my thank-you notes made me feel so pure and accomplished for having written them that I was almost at a loss when I didn't have to scratch one off. Fortunately, other tasks bubbled up to give me the opportunity to feel virtuous, or at least distracted.

LESSON LEARNED #3:
SEATING PLANS ARE WORTH
THE SUFFERING

The exquisite agony of thank-you-note writing was matched only by the pain of the seating plan. Reviled by many as annoyingly fascistic and parade-dampening, the seating plan exemplifies etiquette's invisible powers. Happy are the nuptials where there are no guests who could possibly be at odds with each other or capable of being insulting. At my wedding, we had a few cases of more than simple distaste, one long-settled but still bitter divorce, and one pointed "everyone would be happier if you kept these two apart" scenario. (I also had to put a fair amount of work into diluting what threatened to become the Dud Table.)

Creating a seating plan for eighty people is like an excruciatingly long LSAT problem: "Sam won't sit next to Myrtle and Sheila can't sit next to anyone wearing black. If there are ten people at each table, who will be on Sam's left?"

It took a week of heavy contemplation to finalize the seating (after which, naturally, a few people couldn't come, and the musical chairs sound track started all over again). I knew well enough to separate the divorced couple and to seat the members of a failed fix-up at different tables. But when I presented my plans to my future mother-in-law, stories of small resentments among people practically unknown to me poured out, and balancing tables for maximum peace and entertainment proved tricky with all of the additional restrictions. All this work still didn't ward off all strangeness. One guest showed up without his wife (she was in India), so I seated him near an old female friend of his. This led to an interesting moment in which another guest attacked him for publicly flaunting what she assumed was an affair. In the end, I was so thrilled to have seated everyone, I didn't even care that some couples rearranged things so that they could be closer to their spouses. It may have been naughty, but it was out of my control.

LESSON LEARNED #4: SOMETIMES TRADITIONS HAVE TO BE LEFT BEHIND

Even though my obsession with comportment bordered on the obsessive-compulsive, don't think my relationship with etiquette was all hearts and pearls. Pre-wedding, my apartment became an etiquette farm. I couldn't stop collecting books on manners. If something stumped me, I had a tendency to leave a pile of texts lying open to key pages and sadly prone to the eager jaws of our young cairn terrier, who would shred them. (A 1924 volume of Lillian Eichler was a particularly tragic casualty.)

Paradoxically, the more one tries to be "by the book" (any book, all books), the more one will second-guess oneself. Consider the ubiquitous response cards that you stuff into invitations, hoping your guests will check a box or jot a note and let you know whether or not to expect them. They are, as it turns out, far from traditional, because back when these bits of behavior first calcified, prospective guests knew that the only thing to do with an invitation was to send back a handwritten note saying whether or not they'd be attending. I got stuck. Should I count on my guests knowing to get back to me themselves? That would be the absolutely most correct thing to do and I was nothing if not accurate. But in the modern world, you have to demand a reply or no one will say anything, and response cards only go so far anyway. I sent mine out and still had to do a round of uncomfortable phone calls, asking people what their plans were for a certain Saturday in January. It doesn't matter how gentle you are, dear Reader, some guests are going to need a poke.

LESSON LEARNED #5: YOU CAN'T ALWAYS GET WHAT YOU WANT, BUT YOU CAN REGISTER FOR IT

And there's still no doing everything right (or "right," since etiquette is sometimes relative). Because it isn't traditional, and my childhood favorite, Miss Manners, says it's appalling, I decided not to register. Which was worse, refusing to register and annoying everyone or violating a code of manners that only a few people even know exists?

When everyone from my oldest friend's parents to my mother-in-law's cousin insisted on registry information, I had to bend my rules again. In a fit of capitalist optimism, my fiancé and I signed up for useful kitchen items that promised to renovate my culinary skills. This wasn't good enough. There were protests that kitchen items were too practical. I added some flatware. Complaints came in that my choices weren't complete. In the end, most people gave the presents they felt like giving, but, in hindsight, given the fact that our terrier nipped my in-laws' poodle while we were cutting the wedding cake, it would have been wise to have registered for some (more) obedience lessons.

LESSON LEARNED #6:
INVITATIONS CAN BE MAILED
A LITTLE LATE

My mother, a woman whose reluctance to make decisions should qualify her for a government job, realized a little late in the game that she wanted to invite a few more people. Like a jerk, I balked because those invitations would be going out late and this lateness would be seen as insulting.

I was terrified of the Killer B-list. Etiquette texts caution against it. And the B-list does seem mean, as if one has to wait for the more important people to bow out before one can fill tables with some also-rans. Of course, this wasn't the case at all. I didn't have severe space limitations; I just had a mother who got inclusive at the last minute.

But with weddings, appearances are often more memorable than substance (which is why guests will remember your wedding dress better than your tenderly written vows), and I was torn. Which risk was more perilous: offending the late invitees with a postmark too close to the RSVP date or denying my mother her friends?

For my mother, I shut up and mailed all of her invitations. Everyone came. No one noticed—or if they did they didn't snark.

LESSON LEARNED #7:
GIVE UP . . . A LITTLE

I didn't pick my wedding dress. I had ideas, of course. I was planning to order something fabulous in pink from California. The appeal of getting something custom-made without having to leave my house had considerable appeal and seemed consistent with my family history.

My mother didn't choose her own wedding outfit. One of her father's patients created something for her: a Jackie-O-ish pink suit with gold buttons (no pillbox hat, but probably only because the whole event took place indoors in a high-rise on Manhattan's East End Avenue). My mother never had warm things to say about her suit, but she didn't seem to mind missing out on having to make that decision, and it seemed reasonable that she wouldn't have much to say about my choice.

But when she heard about my mail-order plans, my mother got strange. She wouldn't admit to feeling sad or left out, but something was wrong. I guiltily took her to a bridal store that was having a sale, and within minutes she popped up with a dress and a beaming saleswoman to hold it up to me. So much for thinking pink. My mother's selection was whitish, low-backed, scoop-necked, A-line, exquisite, and traditional. She was happy. How could I argue?

Etiquette is really about making everyone comfortable, and bending is occasionally wise, if not necessary. My dress wasn't nearly as important to me as it was to my mother. I didn't have to give in, but I did. And doing so was like having a get-out-of-jail free card in my back pocket. That one moment of generosity would buy me a chance to dig in my heels when I really needed it.

LESSON LEARNED #8:
ETIQUETTE CAN'T DO EVERYTHING

These moments made me realize that even etiquette has its practical limits. Living by the book (hell, living with the dog who ate the book) was creating impossible standards. And so I had to learn to read etiquette not as a fundamentalist with the Ten Commandments, but as a Supreme Court justice with some of the vaguer amendments.

"Strange" is the word that really says it all about modern weddings. After being rigorously taught about fighting to "have it all" and being pumped full of nuptial pornography in the form of can-do magazines and movie-star photo spreads, even the woman who never thought about her wedding dress and who always rolled her eyes at Pachelbel's

Canon can find herself in a panic. It isn't that she doesn't want to get married. She just doesn't know what to do—because nothing, nothing feels natural.

How could it? All eyes are on the bride. Everyone's ready to compare her wedding to the scads of nuptials they've already attended, and she must take the feelings of two families into account, unless she is one of the very lucky few whose parents and future in-laws will be happy with anything, or nothing at all. (Where are these folks and what meds are they on?) Etiquette offers a snug structure that guides the confused and gives strong, firm answers to the most beleaguering problems. It's an unlikely life preserver in the harrowing seas of tulle.

For several years I've been writing about etiquette for the Web site Indiebride.com—answering plaintive queries almost daily. A lot of questions are standard: abused bridesmaids; couples who don't want to invite children; brides afraid of the spotlight; and people wondering if it's all right to ask for cash on invitations. (Nope!) Often, readers confuse etiquette advice with therapy, and either seek help on more fundamental problems or try to use it to get away with murder. Etiquette can tell you how to finesse the moment and avoid social upset, but it can't change the basics. You can't fire a bridesmaid because you don't like her figure, and if your father despises your fiancé, you'll still have to navigate that ugliness, after the pigeons have eaten up all the rice.

Etiquette is great at dictating the "how" of things. The books all come with charts and lists galore: bridesmaids' duties, items to include on registries, rehearsal protocol . . .

you understand. But none of the tomes on my shelves—and some of them have been hanging around for hundreds of years—encourage you to think about the "whether" of things and reject elements that don't suit you. "Traditional" is not synonymous with "necessary." Etiquette should sculpt your plans, not dictate them. You can learn all about bridesmaids, but no one ever says you don't have to have them. And you really don't.

For my part, nuptial tranquillity came to me, finally, when I rejected the traditions that simply weren't for me:

No bridesmaids

No shower

No aisle

No veil

No being given away

No father/daughter dance

No name change

No cake smash

No tossing (of bouquet, rice, garter, anything)

The photographs show a traditional wedding. I'm a bride in white(ish) with a tuxedoed husband. Everyone's smiling. The flowers my mother-in-law chose are gorgeous and only one centerpiece caught on fire. Underneath the charm were tremors of bad behavior, but all I knew was that the band was playing every song I wanted to hear and I was married to the man I had loved for so long.

Etiquette saved and tormented me, but it taught me perspective and showed me how to live in two families at once. It was good practice for the future. Now we are three (four, with the etiquette-book-eating terrier), and wedding etiquette is really a practice run for parenting etiquette, which more people should learn.

Unsolicited advice goes entirely against the tenets of good manners. So while you didn't ask for them, here are seven bits of etiquette advice that should make your nuptials, and even more quotidian moments, less fraught:

1. Pick a few nonnegotiables, elements that have to go your way, and don't budge on them. Since you're asking, I wanted to be married by a judge and would accept no substitutes when it came to music. I was married by Uncle Bob and serenaded by Little Jack Melody and his Young Turks, all the way up from Texas.

2. Be willing to compromise on everything else. My mother picked my dress for me and I can't fault her taste. There will always be time for pink.

3. Feed every guest and every vendor. Everyone needs to eat.

4. Don't ask for presents or money in your invitation. It looks either weird or mercenary.

5. If you don't get a present from someone, it's just as well. That's one thank-you note you don't have to write.

6. Weddings should offer more pleasure than pain. Stir the pot only if you have to. It was unwise, for instance,

of my brother to tell my mother two days before my wedding that he thought her dress was too big. She has agonized over it ever since and memorably tried to fob it off on me as maternity evening wear.

7. Lapses in manners make for good stories. Let them happen, commit them to memory, and feel free to enjoy them (with the names changed to protect the guilty) at dinner parties for the rest of your life.

the registry
strikes back

janelle brown

♥

My fiancé and I stood among the appliances stacked high
on the shelves, totems to culinary efficiency, their gleaming
stainless-steel surfaces still unsullied by greasy fingerprints.
In the next aisle over, the glassware sparkled in the early
morning sun. The room smelled like vanilla: comforting,
sweet, the scent of home (ours! together!). It was Registry
Sunday at Crate & Barrel, and we, after years of agonizing
over other couples' registries, were finally about to begin
our own. Endless possibilities lay before us: the children
we'd have, the homes we'd live in, the omelettes we'd cook
in top-of-the-line anodized-aluminum nonstick skillets.

Drunk. We were drunk with options. Or perhaps that
was just the mimosas, made from freshly squeezed orange
juice—the stylish silver juicer only $23.95, that the sales-
man was only too happy to demonstrate—clutched in our
increasingly overwhelmed hands. Or was it a sugar high

from the waffles, which a friendly saleswoman had just handed us, still hot from the waffle maker (on sale, $39.99!) and drowning in gourmet syrup?

Greg and I caught each other's eyes as the solicitous saleswoman chattered on about the waffle maker's heating elements and indicator lights. "Should we . . . ?" I asked, the scanning gun twitching in my sticky palm.

"Do we really need . . . ?" he asked, staring at his reflection in the appliance, his eyes slightly bugging out. Maple syrup glistened on his lips.

Reader, we didn't. But we did register for the juicer. We pointed the scanning gun and hit bleep.

To see wedding commercialism at its most crass and canny, visit Crate & Barrel on a Registry Sunday. In the early hours of the morning, before the store opens to the public, the newly affianced are invited to a "private" browsing session where they can peruse the store's goods and start a registry. Couples are greeted with a brunch buffet (produced on the spot, using, of course, Crate & Barrel appliances) and a goodie bag (ours included a hideous pair of heart-shaped champagne glasses, a box of Marimekko thank-you cards, and a registry guide reminding us that no couple was complete without both formal and informal table settings). At Registry Sunday, a personal shopping adviser offers instructions. And then, like hunters on opening day, the couples are let loose upon the store, scanning guns in hand.

Long before I got engaged, I knew that when the time came, I would register. A registry is, at its heart, utterly pragmatic. People give gifts at weddings, which meant that we would be receiving dozens, if not hundreds of gifts. A registry would make things easy. It would eliminate the guesswork, the unwanted gifts, the overlapping presents, and to ensure that we wouldn't end up with a kitchen full of near-identical appetizer trays or floral tea cozies sent from Idaho by Aunt Edna.

When I signed up for the Crate & Barrel Registry Sunday, I did so knowing full well that registries are big business to department stores and houseware chains (they were, in fact, conceived by one: Marshall Field's, Chicago, 1924), which is why those same stores were luring us with waffles and discounts and personal shoppers. The romantic mythos of the registry—that, together, friends and family are setting up the new couple with all that they'll need for their life together—had been kept alive not just by tradition, but by industry.

But until I had the scanning gun in hand, I was not aware of the extent to which a registry is both a challenge and a temptation: a dangerous cocktail of outdated marriage conventions, fantasy projection, and contemporary consumption culture that is difficult for even the most abstemious bride (which I was not) to avoid intoxicating herself with.

Deciding to do a registry at all had been a feat of compromise for us. My fiancé, a formerly impoverished ascetic whose life possessions easily fit into the payload of his ancient truck, had only recently recognized the merits of buying anything frivolous at all; whereas I, a decided aesthete, had been known to spend my weekends hanging out in home decor stores just for fun, reading the Design Within Reach catalog as if it were a magazine. Something about the idea of registering sat uneasily with us. Blatantly asking for specific presents felt acquisitional and opportunistic.

"It's like presenting a shopping list to our friends and saying, 'Gimme,' " observed my still-reticent fiancé, when I told him about our date with Crate & Barrel.

But that, said our friends and family, was what weddings were all about: the one time in your life when you ask and shall receive, in abundance.

"Register for a honeymoon," said one friend.

"Register for home electronics," said another.

My mother, a firm traditionalist, would think of no such thing. Registries were for crystal and china, for silver and cutlery—for, she said, "The things that you'll own for the rest of your life." I had listened to her disparaging remarks about the registries of other couples whose weddings she had attended; couples who had registered for wooden spoons and pepper grinders, useful but decidedly unglamorous household objects with trifling price tags. "Who really wants to give a wooden spoon for a gift?" my mother would complain.

Maybe I didn't feel compelled to stack my cupboards with silver, but I saw her point. In twenty years, that wooden spoon would be moldering in a dump somewhere, but a silver bowl would last forever. It was a principle, I convinced Greg, that we should use for our registry. If people were going to go to the trouble and expense to buy us gifts, we should make sure their gift would be appreciated and used for years to come.

So we finally agreed. We would register, modestly and reasonably, at only two stores: Zinc Details, a favorite specialty design boutique in San Francisco, and Crate & Barrel. We would register only for items we truly loved or needed, objects that were beautiful and eternal. We would not descend into shopping madness, in which we registered for a hundred things we didn't need and wouldn't ever use— panini presses and steak knife sets—simply because they appeared in one of those registry guides published by bridal magazines or because a department store clerk suggested we wouldn't be complete without it.

No, we would be rational. We would have taste and originality. We would not be greedy.

So what had happened at Crate & Barrel?

Frankly, we had been seduced. The sober plan of registering for a few key items—glassware, flatware, some utilitarian appliances—evaporated the minute we stepped into the barrage. It is rare, after all, that you are let loose in a store and allowed to indulge your every homemaking fantasy. That cocktail set? Bleep! It's practically yours. The turquoise vase? Bleep! It's already on your dining room table. It's all so ephemeral—each electronic beep simply adding a line on a list somewhere, with no money exchanged, no box to be carried home—that the question soon becomes not "Why?" but "Why not?"

We walked out of Crate & Barrel that Sunday dizzy, not quite sure what had hit us, and in possession of a registry packed with frivolous kitchen gadgetry: espresso makers, juicers, ice-cream machines, woks. Jittery on freshly brewed cappuccino, I could almost convince myself that we really did need that juicer. Think how much fuller, how much healthier, our lives would be if we could just start each day with a glass of freshly squeezed orange juice! But Greg looked vaguely ill.

ROSENTHAL LOFT PLACE SETTING, $86, FROM FITZSU

Part two of our plan was to register at Zinc Details, a stylish boutique in San Francisco that carried only high-end artisan wares such as vintage Japanese lacquerware, imported cashmere blankets, and furniture by local designers. This would reaffirm our initial registry goals of registering for unique, beautiful objects that we would keep forever. But the registry was in-store only, which meant that our friends in Los Angeles (where we had recently moved) wouldn't be able to shop there; which, in turn, seemed to necessitate that we register at the equivalent shop in Los Angeles, a boutique called Fitzsu.

This brought our grand registry total to three stores; which, all things considered, was still hovering around normal. We killed another two weekend days poring through the two boutiques, picking out German table settings, Finnish glassware, and enough Italian decorative bowls to cover every flat surface in our home. These, we assured ourselves, were the kinds of beautiful objects that would really last forever, each a piece of art in itself; the sort of things we would never buy for ourselves.

Even Greg was starting to enjoy the process. "Don't you think we should register for both soup plates and bowls?" he asked, caressing the "modern" yet "timeless" striped china we had carefully selected. "I mean, they do look nice together. And what about the matching espresso cups? Just in case we get that espresso maker . . ."

"But see," I explained, finally putting those lost weekends in home design stores to good use. "You want a different color . . . to add contrast to the table." We were starting to sound like Martha Stewart clones, and I secretly found it exhilarating. Who knew my Spartan fiancé could enjoy this as much as I did?

The modest bride is supposed to pretend that gifts are irrelevant to getting married, a nice gesture but secondary to the whole love-and-commitment part of the wedding, but the truth was that I loved the gifts. I loved hearing the doorbell ring, loved seeing the poor UPS deliveryman juggling a half dozen boxes, each the size of an oven, loved the explosion of Styrofoam peanuts. Even though I knew what was coming, I still experienced a frisson of excitement each time I ripped open the wrapping paper to discover an item I'd coveted (bleep!) in the store.

Thrillingly, the objects piling up in our living room were ours—not mine, or his—but gifts for us together, Janelle & Greg, the first we'd ever received as a couple. Each object was a glimpse into the life we were going to have together—

a life where we served roasts on silver platters to exactly twelve guests (instead of barbecue on paper plates to thirty). A life where we would need crystal goblets for both red and white wine (wine that that wouldn't come with Charles Shaw labels) and one where we lived in a house that would have abundant shelving to display the uselessly gorgeous decorative bowls we'd registered for. Instead of being the perpetual guests at my parents' table at Thanksgiving, we would be hosting the meal ourselves, on our own imported German plates, with our own children and (looking long-term) grandchildren lined up and down the table.

But that fantasy life was not here now and would not be for a long time. The gifts were, for the most part, going straight into the closet, where they remained sheathed in their boxes. In our care to pick out only beautiful objects that would last us forever, we had somehow ended up with an avalanche of presents better suited to a middle-aged yuppie couple with two kids living in a six-thousand-square-foot loft in Tribeca. Who really, really liked freshly squeezed juice.

If this was who Janelle & Greg were, then I had never met them.

CALVIN KLEIN IZMIR DUVET COVER, $225, FROM MACY'S

We realized what we'd missed when we looked at the registry of friends who were getting married just a few months before we were. They had registered at Macy's, and where our registry was full of "forever" objects and Crate & Barrel kitchen geegaws, their registry was decidedly practical: towels, sheets, luggage. Sonic toothbrushes. Toiletry cases.

"Luggage?" brightened Greg, growing enamored with the process. "We can register for that?!"

And, despite a nervous feeling that we were, just possibly, overindulging, back we headed to the shopping mall, to register for more practical items at Macy's.

Back in my mother's day, the registry was a trousseau for the woman newly emerged from her pubescent pupae. Everything she (and, by association, her husband) would need to fit her (and, by association, his) first home with the complete accoutrements of homemaking and entertaining. In 1969, when my mother was married, this made sense. She had never lived on her own before and had not even a dinner fork to her name. But I—like most of my friends— waited until I was thirty-one to get married, and by that time I'd already accumulated an entire house full of stuff. What would once have gone into my trousseau had instead been trickling into my apartment for years via birthdays and holidays and simple necessity. The KitchenAid mixer? Christmas 2003. The cutlery? IKEA, self-purchased. The Cuisinart? Birthday, age twenty-seven.

Maybe I'd originally promised myself that we would register only for things that we loved or needed, but what, really did we "need"? Not much. Our house was fully, if often cheaply, equipped. What was left, I realized when we arrived in Macy's home department, was upgrades. Instead of the hand-me-down Teflon pan, a $120 Anolon twelve-inch sauté pan. Instead of the stained khaki-colored quilt Greg had picked up at Bed Bath & Beyond eight years earlier, the four-hundred-thread-count Calvin Klein duvet. A complete set of matching luggage to replace the decrepit carry-on suitcase with a broken zipper that I'd toted around the world. Egyptian cotton towels. Soft, fluffy new pillows.

We were now fully cosseted in invisible abundance; no aspect of our life (hypothetically) unimproved. But did we really know anyone who would buy us a $225 duvet cover, let alone the entire $650 bed set? As it turned out, no. Nor did anyone want to buy us the high-end pots and pans, the luggage, or even the very reasonably priced pillows. No, people wanted to buy us those expensive but useless decorative objects, semifrivolous kitchen gadgets, and anything made from crystal or silver: Those gifts apparently felt more special, more fun to give. As the gifts continued coming—rice cookers! silver serving trays! cut-glass vases!—we realized that we might as well not have registered at Macy's at all.

We now had a slightly embarrassing four registries listed on the back page of our Web site—what had happened to our testaments to moderation?—but at least we were done registering, once and for all. Or so we thought.

ORREFORS CRYSTAL WINE GOBLETS, $25 EACH, FROM BLOOMINGDALE'S

I was the first of two daughters to get married and had learned right away that my mother had specific ideas about how it should be done. She had arrived for a celebratory cocktail on the day of my engagement with a bag full of ear-marked bridal magazines, some dated up to a year earlier. I was still enamored with the ring on my finger, but my mother had already picked out the table decorations for my wedding.

Overwhelmed by my mother's enthusiasm for the whole process, I had conferred with (and, occasionally, conceded to) her on almost every aspect of the wedding—location, attire, flowers, menu. The registry, I'd assumed, would be a sanctuary of decision making for Greg and me. After all, my mother wasn't going to be living with our presents.

How wrong I was.

Once our registries went online, the e-mails began pouring in from my mother, who was living four hundred miles north in a suburb of San Francisco. "Did you register for serving spoons? I didn't see a serving set on your list." "Do you realize there's hardly any silver on your list?" "I can't believe you want a knife block for $140!" When I didn't respond, the e-mails grew more pointed, such as, "If you want my advice on some items, let me know."

I didn't let her know, but she let me know instead. The biggest mistake we'd made—besides not registering for enough decorative picture frames and having so far failed to choose a silver pattern—was that we hadn't registered at Bloomingdale's. She called me, upset: "All my friends are going to want to shop for you at Bloomingdale's."

"We registered at Macy's and Crate & Barrel," I said. "Can't they go there?"

"The Macy's at our local mall is really tacky," she said.

"Then they can shop online."

The silence on the other end was deafening. "They want to be able to see what they're buying you. I don't know why you didn't ask me before you registered at Macy's; I would have told you that."

I'd already lost too many wedding-related arguments with my mother to get into another; I gave up almost immediately and told Greg that we would have to register at one more store.

"You're kidding," he said. "A fifth registry? There's nothing left to register for."

"We'll just replicate the registry at Macy's," I told him. "Both stores carry the same stuff."

"So we're going to knowingly ask people to buy us duplicate gifts? That makes no sense whatsoever," he said.

"It's for my mom," I muttered. "It's not about making sense. Just go with it."

But his ascetic's warning bells had finally decided to sound the alarm, and he refused to have anything to do with it. While he furiously gave his clothes away to charity to soothe his conscience, I spent a listless afternoon alone on the Bloomingdale's Web site, duplicating our registry from the four other stores without adding anything new. Once again, I requested the Swedish crystal from Orrefors, the Calvin Klein duvet, the Nambe bowls. But it wasn't fun anymore, it wasn't wish fulfillment or fantasy; it was a chore. I added Bloomingdale's to the list of registries on our wedding Web site, more than a little mortified by what it suggested about us. So much for not conveying "Gimme."

But my mother was thrilled. The next time I visited her in San Francisco, she insisted that we walk through Bloomingdale's together, to get a firsthand look at our registry. Watching her excitement, I realized that it wasn't her friends who wanted to see my gifts at Bloomingdale's—it was her. As much as I had fantasized about my future life with Greg—those roasts, those dinner parties, the endless display shelves—she had too. She was imagining herself at her daughter's well-appointed Thanksgiving table, excited by her daughter's happy marriage to a very nice young man. If the only way she could contribute to the bottom line of her own fantasies for Janelle & Greg was to help me pick out a timeless silver pattern and some steak knives, well, then, dammit, she was going to do it.

It was a small thing to concede to her, I decided.

VINTAGE JAPANESE LACQUERED SALAD BOWL, $59, FROM ZINC DETAILS

In our house, we now have an entire closet we refer to as the "schwag closet." It is overflowing with wedding gifts, most of which, a year later, are still in their original boxes. In the year since our wedding, the gifts have continued to trickle in; though, by this point, most of the stragglers have bypassed our outdated registries and are just sending cash or gift certificates. This is a good thing, since we no longer have room to store anything. (We had a mere one hundred guests at our wedding: I can only imagine the storage requirements of a couple who invited two or three hundred.)

A good half of our gifts have gone unused because our life is still too chaotic, too young and carefree, to merit their use. Last week, we once again had a barbecue for thirty people. As usual, we used paper plates. There wasn't enough German china for everyone, anyway. I put away the fancy new stainless and hauled out the old IKEA forks, just in case an inebriated friend threw one away by mistake. Greg did, however, inaugurate the coordinated barbecue set from Crate & Barrel, and I served salad in a vintage Japanese lacquer salad bowl, which, I must say, looked stunning even on our secondhand picnic table.

We have used the fanciest gifts—the crystal Orrefors glasses and the Nambe bowls—but only once, when my parents came to visit and we attempted to show off with a dinner feast worthy of the best Beverly Hills hostess. My mother was, of course, thrilled. Then everything disappeared back to the closet. I figure we'll break them out again in five or ten years; but it's nice to know they are there, just waiting for us to really grow up. Someday, we finally will, won't we?

If the life bequeathed to us by our registry hasn't yet fully materialized, there is an adult quality to our lives now, a sense of a now-and-future Us (right there, in that closet!) that wasn't there before. Whether this has more to do with the fact that we stood under an arch of flowers and committed our lives to each other or that we now own a full set of sterling silver flatware, I wouldn't begin to guess. But if we could survive the registry—exposing, in the process, our weakest and greediest selves, but loving each other anyway; forcing ourselves to accommodate each other's wildly different worldviews; but discovering, in the end, a common dream for a future together—our relationship can probably survive anything. Bleep.

weddings
& the
single girl

it all started
with princess di

daisy de villeneuve

29 July 1981, age 6, watch the wedding of
Prince Charles & Princess Diana on T.V.
with my sister.

Age 14, buy 1950s style wedding dress at
thrift store in Indianapolis, to dress up in.

At 16 my first boyfriend asks me to

sign a contract, which consisted of

a scrap of paper written in his

scrawly handwriting saying that on

this date in 1991 that I will

marry him in 5 years' time if we

are still together.

I sign the paper.

We break up a year later.

When I am 17 my best friend says to me,

"Do you think that I look like I'm
trying to find a husband in this outfit?"

18,   Get my Tarot cards read by Daphne's
mother. She foresees marriage soon.

Aged 19...
      "Do you want to get married?"
                  he said sarcastically.
"Yes" i said. "Don't look at me!" he said.

21, My ex-boyfriend becomes a professional
wedding photographer. I insinuate that
maybe he could take photos at my wedding
one day. "Yeah, right" he replies.

When I was 22, he said to me,

"We could get married, you know. I'm rich
you wouldn't have to work!"

23, Attend several weddings...

        knowing that in a couple years'
time, some of these brides & grooms will no
longer be married. My prediction comes true
& half of them aren't together anymore.
Whenever I see them now they always rant on
about their divorce & 2 kids.

When I met him I thought that he seemed like the
marrying kind. He was, he just didn't marry me.

Age 24

25 years of age...
        just as I was about to catch the
bouquet the maid of honour pushed in front of
me and grabbed it!

Insulted at 26 because one of my best friends
gets married & she doesn't ask me to be a
bridesmaid.   She asks 2 other girls instead.

I am 27, he is 3 years older.

We are in an Italian restaurant
when he pops the question. I am in shock &
I ask if he's joking. "Really is this a joke?"
I say. He says that he thinks we'd be good
for each other. I'm speechless & unable to
answer. I want to say YES but nothing comes
out. As I remain dumbfounded he starts to
backtrack.

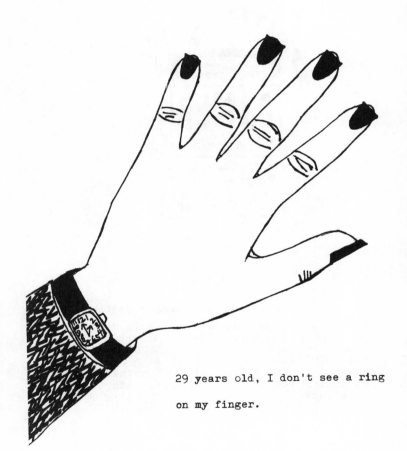

29 years old, I don't see a ring
on my finger.

Age 30, Go to engagement party,

Meet 2 guys that seem nice, interesting

& cute. Chat with them for a while. No
exchange of telephone digits. Consequently

this makes me feel sad; I cry on the subway
for the entire journey home.

31, Travel to Ireland to attend a
beautiful fairy-tale wedding in a castle.

This is what I dream of. Let's hope
that I too find my Prince Charming one
day....

THE END.

the honor
of
my presence

meghan daum

In all the weddings I've attended in my adult life, one of my more salient memories involves crouching over a toilet in the Helmsley Palace in New York City throwing up at least two of the three glasses of wine I drank in rapid succession on an empty stomach during the cocktail hour. I recall that my primary thought about this situation was not that I was a pitiful lush or even that I should repair to Park Avenue and hail a taxi but that if I was careful I could avoid messing up my dress and then return to the reception no worse for the wear. I remember hearing the primping noises of other guests outside the stall, the clicking of lipstick cases, and disingenuous compliments about hairstyles. I steadied myself between the walls, praising myself for the impressive soundlessness with which I deposited the last traces of Chardonnay into the exceedingly elegant bowl. This was me at age twenty-eight. I had no steady employer, lived in a sublet apartment filled with someone else's furniture, and had a boyfriend who lived a thousand miles away and whom I had no intention of marrying.

This was a period during which alcohol-induced vomiting, though not a regular occasion, wasn't exactly an anomaly. It was also a time when boyfriends and wedding invitations tended to drift into my life on the winds of a kind of anxiety and trepidation I can only describe as commitment apathy. This is not to be confused with commitment phobia, a condition from which I suffered as much as any culturally conscious urban twenty-something who believed in things like soul mates and the necessity of achieving professional and psychological nirvana before walking down an aisle in unsensible shoes. It was more like an identity crisis, a sensation of being unable (or unwilling) to slough off a layer of scaly skin. Every time I received a wedding invitation, be it the expected, long overdue kind or the kind that appears in the mail like a jack-in-the-box— "since when was she even *dating* someone?"—I could feel my life receding further and further to the margins of normal human society.

It wasn't a feeling I entirely disliked. If there was anything that could put what I believed was the moral, social, and psychological righteousness of my own life into high relief, it was a letterpressed piece of stationery requesting "the honor of your presence." If there was any better way to express the essence of that presence than to check the "will attend" box and show up six weeks later in a little pink dress, strappy sandals, and no date, I didn't know what it was. In my twenties—and well into my thirties—I saw going to weddings alone as a political act. I saw my dateless-ness as a proud and effortless statement of defiance, a piece of protest art displaying the ease and grace with which I carried my utter lack of need. The degree to which this posture did or did not align with the posture necessary to silently throw up in a toilet at the Helmsley Palace rarely occurred to me.

In the same vein, I rarely noticed in my twenties and early thirties that my boyfriends, such as they were (for the sake of argument, I'll include even those who resisted, on either semantic or neurotic grounds, the "boyfriend" label); often introduced to my life a certain queasiness. That's not to say I didn't want, at least on Saturdays and alternating Fridays, some sort of romantic attachment. But as attach-ment opportunities came my way and, as often as not, blew past me for reasons as far ranging as social ineptness to bad taste in books, it became increasingly clear that being single was, for me, a far easier hand to play than being in a rela-tionship. As much as I wasn't wild about being single, I was usually even less wild about the guessing games, tacit stand-offs, and manufactured coolness that seemed to come as standard features with every romantic entanglement I got into. If my dating history had a slogan it might be a cruel play on those "if you lived here you'd be home by now" condo advertisements that hover over the freeways of major urban centers. In my case, I could pass the sign a hundred times and still not register its meaning: "If this guy was your boyfriend you'd know it by now."

Those of us who miss billboards often need certain memos delivered to us in a handwritten envelope. Therein lies the job of the wedding invitation. To be a single person—male or female, I daresay—whose usual stack of bills, junk mail, and never-to-be-read issues of *Esquire* magazine suddenly includes a wedding invitation is to stare at your life as though the measure of your choices, failings, uncertainties, delusions, hopes, and, on some level, downright laziness is being spelled out in black ink. To be extremely single (as in the haven't-bothered-to-shave-legs-in-months variety) and receive a wedding invitation is to begin making mental preparations for the invariable purgatory of the "singles' table." To be moderately single (as in the dating-someone-who-calls-regularly-but-knows-neither-your-birthday-nor-your-mother's-first-name variety) is to enter into a form of self-doubt so intense and all-consuming that it's possible to feel nostalgic for the arid refuge of extreme singleness. If showing up to a wedding sans date is a small act of courage, showing up at a wedding in the form of a couple that's not sure it's a couple is a monumental act of . . . something. Only time—and maybe psychotherapy—will tell for sure. In any case it won't obviate the task of calling up the bride or groom and asking what feels a lot like permission to bring a guest.

The wedding hosts have, of course, every right to exercise jurisprudence over who will be consuming the food and drink that is costing them and/or their parents upward of $200 per head. And even when money isn't the issue (we all know a few of these people; they tend to own handbag boutiques in trendy urban neighborhoods), you can hardly blame someone for not wanting to share what is supposed to be the most sacred moment of their lives with strangers their friends met on Match.com. But this is the first crack in the inevitable fissure between single people and married people, a gulf that, despite the best efforts of both parties, will grow wider with each phone call not immediately returned, every Saturday-night plan rescheduled for a Monday, and every relationship crisis that neither friend, no matter how many romantic catastrophes they've seen each other through, will ever again fully understand.

In all cases, the single person will be the first to take notice of this phenomenon. That's because the married or about-to-be-married person will go through a long period of not noticing anything other than the color of her beloved's eyes and whether they match the place mats for which she registered at Pottery Barn. This is natural and at least temporarily excusable, the main problem being the ensuing confusion when a friend asks if it's okay to bring a semi-significant other to the wedding. For some brides, and even the occasional groom, the myopia of the relationship and its attendant party planning has made them unaware that the friend even has a new "other," be it significant, semi-significant, or just short of a houseplant. This, exacerbated by the tendency of unequivocally serious relationships to erase all memory of what it was like to be in the far more common "ambiguously defined relationships," makes the single person about as excited about the wedding as she is about an annual gynecological exam. Hence the inclination to put off calling for an appointment as long as possible.

SOON-TO-BE-MARRIED: Why haven't you RSVP'd yet?

PERSON IN AMBIGUOUSLY DEFINED RELATIONSHIP: I've been meaning to talk to you about that.

SOON-TO-BE: There are going to be lots of single people there, if that's what you're worried about.

AMBIGUOUS: Well, I've actually been seeing someone for a few months and I—

SOON-TO-BE: Who, that guy Joel?

AMBIGUOUS: No, this guy Will.

SOON-TO-BE: What happened to Joel?

AMBIGUOUS: Oh, you know . . .

SOON-TO-BE: Well, how serious is it?

AMBIGUOUS: I don't know. But it just seems weird to not, you know, bring him. . . .

SOON-TO-BE: There are going to be single men there. At least one, anyway. Probably.

AMBIGUOUS: We're not really seeing other people.

SOON-TO-BE: But you haven't even met this Bill!

Et cetera.

The confluence of the ambiguously defined relationship and the arrival of a wedding invitation is the defining drawback of being single. As cumbersome as holidays, parental visits, and company picnics can be for the not-quite couple ("this is my, uh, *friend* . . ."), weddings are a game of sudden death. By the time the band packs up, your relationship will have either turned the corner into a sweet, fierce intimacy or you will be breaking up in the car. Such is the tyranny of the power of suggestion. By so publicly raising their own stakes, the marrying couple inadvertently drags everyone else into their drama. Like a toddler whose pristine world is rocked to the nub when he hears a four-letter word on premium cable, the ambiguously defined couple can only squirm in their church pew as the protective bubble wrap of their oh-so-casual rapport is punctured with "I do"s and "till death do us part"s. Gone are the semiprivate jokes and references to *American Idol* that, in the past, glued the relationship together like a toy plane. Once a couple has attended a wedding, even the most affectionate form of banter won't cut it anymore. Try as you might to cast them aside, the echoes of those vows will reduce all other conversation to small talk. Like the turning of the seasons, the tint of every interaction will darken a shade or two, leaving you with a form of seasonal affective disorder that will feel like a venereal disease. Without warning, you become terribly alarmed about the other person's taste in sofas. Suddenly you must know where they really stand on Israel. At the very least, you need to learn their mother's first name. For all but the fortunate few, these questions will vacuum whatever fun in the relationship hasn't already been squelched by the wedding itself. It is at this point that you realize you are no longer in a relationship. You are in an expectationship. Plus you've shelled out a hundred dollars for a Pottery Barn gift.

Is it any surprise, then, that going stag to a wedding remains, if not necessarily an "attractive" option, a perfectly legitimate mode of self-preservation? Actually, yes. No matter how often people say, "Weddings are a great place to meet someone," the less repeated part of that sentence is "who will talk your ear off about annuities" (or, as I've experienced in the last three years alone, gastroenterology, horsemanship, and what a slut the bride was in college). No matter how many times the hard-partying folks at the singles' table declare, "This is the *fun* table!" when a visitor from Grown-up Land ventures over for a look-see, the implicit understanding is that the singles' table is essentially a kids' table with booze.

In the case of destination weddings, the kind that require airfare and taking days off from work, the singles' table extends into a kind of camping trip. These are the weddings where, unless you happen to be very old, close friends with a significant number of other single guests (think *The Big Chill*, minus the suicide), there is no surviving the situation unless you a) have a date and b) are having sex with that person on a regular basis.

Such were my circumstances almost a decade ago, when, having been summoned to Maine for an exquisite wedding for which the couple was paying everyone's accommodations (it was the dot-com nineties; they'd also hired a famous blues singer to perform under a tent), I sheepishly asked my ambiguously defined boyfriend to accompany me. Let me say right off that as far as ambiguously defined relationships go, this one was in an upper tier. We'd fallen for each other hard and fast, our mutual attraction (he looked just like the actor David Duchovny) and obsession with the films of Jim Jarmusch overriding our countless incompatibilities. After a less-than-cushy but not entirely awkward amount of time—we began dating in April; the wedding invitation arrived in June—I popped the question, an inquiry that in lesser hands might have emitted the sound of a vise grip closing in on a piece of lumber. But thanks to my already vast experience with ambiguously defined relationships, I inquired with such nonchalance as if I were asking nothing at all, which is in fact how the question was received.

ME: So, remember I mentioned my friends T———
and W———, who are getting married?

AMBIGUOUS BOYFRIEND: Uh, I guess.

ME: Their wedding is coming up. It's over Labor Day weekend. It should be fun.

AMBIGUOUS BF: Uh-huh.

ME: You're welcome to come with me if you want. You don't have to, though.

AMBIGUOUS BF: Oh.

ME: Do you want to?

AMBIGUOUS BF: Yeah, I guess.

ME: But only if you want to.

AMBIGUOUS BF: Yeah, I want to!

ME: Are you sure? Because you don't have to. We'd
    have to fly there. But I'd pay for your ticket.
AMBIGUOUS BF: It sounds fun.
ME: You really don't have to.
AMBIGUOUS BF: I want to!

He'd said yes! Twice, no less (and with *feeling*—I did
not add that exclamation point for emphasis; it was right
there in his voice). Gleeful with my ambiguously-defined-
boyfriend-isn't-so-ambiguous-that-he-can't-accompany-me-
to-a-wedding smugness, I RSVP'd for both of us, purchased
two tickets on US Air Express, and proceeded over the ensuing six weeks to lose exactly as much interest in him as he
lost in me, which is to say all of it. Suddenly, the flaws I'd
initially seen as youthful quirks—his perpetual cheapness,
his compulsive quoting of lines from *The Simpsons*, the fact
that he was still living in his ex-girlfriend's apartment (she
was no longer there, but all of her Williams-Sonoma cook-
ware was, which is why I'd tolerated it)—started to seem
like punishable crimes. As Labor Day weekend approached,
it was clear to both of us that our relationship was trailing
off like summer itself. The problem was the wedding. Ever
the pragmatist, I planned to take him to the wedding, enjoy
a final weekend of drunken celebration among strangers
who'd surely be impressed that I'd landed a David Duchovny
look-alike, and commence with an amicable breakup as
soon as the wheels touched the tarmac at home.

But two days before we were scheduled to leave for

Maine, the Ambiguous BF showed up at my apartment carrying the VCR I'd lent him some months earlier. Bad sign. We sat on opposite sides of the room and talked about the shocking news about Princess Diana, who'd died the day before. He told me that we'd had a wonderful ride together but were probably better off as friends. I wholeheartedly agreed, adding that friends sometimes accompany friends to weddings, so I hoped he was still game. He said he didn't think he could do it. Then he started weeping. I went over to comfort him, wrapping my arms around him and telling him it was for the best, that we'd still spend time together, that in a week we'd feel so much better. He began sputtering and gasping. "She was so young," he heaved. "Such an icon. And poor Prince William and Prince Harry, losing their mother like that."

Any chance that I was going to cry during this conversation vanished immediately. The conversation wherein I had to track down the bride at the hotel in Maine and tell her she had to redo the lodging and seating plans was another matter.

BRIDE: What happened?
ME: Well, you know. It just didn't work out.
BRIDE: How long were you guys going out anyway?
ME: I don't know, four months?
BRIDE: Oh, then you shouldn't be too upset. We had
    you guys staying in a suite with three other couples.
    You don't mind if we keep you in there, do you?

As it turned out, this ended up being one of the best weddings I've ever attended. The location was gorgeous, the rehearsal dinner was a lobster bake by the ocean cliffs, the blues singer was terrific, and the couples in my "couples suite" either got so drunk they couldn't walk or bickered for forty-eight hours straight about who forgot to pack the toothpaste. I didn't cry during the ceremony (it would be at least six years before I started crying at weddings), nor did I cry while lying alone in the double bed listening to the slurred whispers of my bed-sharing suitemates and thinking about the $200 I'd spent on the Ambiguous BF's unused plane ticket. Instead, I soldiered through the weekend, avoided throwing up, and returned home feeling empowered and even a little glad that the Ambiguous BF (emeritus) hadn't come. I then began sorting through my mail and discovered yet another wedding invitation. Gazing absently around my apartment, I caught sight of my newly returned VCR, not yet hooked back up, and burst into tears.

The funny thing about weddings is the way they capture the fantasies of the hosts and guests alike. For all the brides and potential brides who have dreamed about what kind of formal affair best expresses their personal and aesthetic values, there are even more of us who wonder when and where we'll find the person who will accompany us to our friends' and relatives' weddings, hold our hand during the ceremony, dance with us during the reception, and spend the car ride home not breaking up but gossiping about the other guests while Garrison Keillor drones softly on the radio. For some of us (okay, me, at least) this is a scenario that remains firmly in the fantasy category, because most of the men I've dated either couldn't dance or never really got the hang of post—social event analysis. If the worst part of going to a wedding with an ambiguously defined date is the pressure cooker into which it deposits the relationship, the worst part about going alone is that there's no one to talk to afterward about why the best man felt compelled to give his toast using a PowerPoint presentation. At the same time, if there's anything more exhausting than the hard labor of smiling and initiating conversations and figuring out where to position yourself on the dance floor without the ballast of a partner, it's hearing your friends take the most solemn vows of their lives, feeling the warm body of the person next to you, and knowing not only that you will never love that person enough to say those vows yourself, but that given the way the whole thing is going—so often a replay of the replay of the very first time love abandoned its post—you might never be able to say them to anyone.

I remember the first wedding I ever went to as a quasi grown-up. The friends weren't mine; they were old family friends of a boyfriend who had started out as ambiguously defined as they come but who, at some indiscernible point, had fallen in love with me to a degree of desperation that scared me to death. We were young; he was twenty and I was twenty-one, and we drove from New York City, where he lived and where I'd spent the last year, to New Hampshire in my rusty Honda like a pair of runaways. We were out of our depth. I should have been back in school upstate. He hadn't thought to pack proper shoes, which he didn't own anyway. We weren't familiar with the protocol of cere-mony seating, so we sat on the bride's side of the church even though he knew the groom better. This was a tiny, sparse, perfect chapel and the reception was on a large, sparse, perfect farm. We sat in the sun and drank cham-pagne. The guests were kind, quiet, Anglican types—the bride and groom had met in seminary school—and we managed to hold up our ends of the conversation, which was something this boyfriend had rarely managed to do in the year and a half that I'd known him.

That night we checked into a Motel 6. We were playing grown-up. Even with our cigarettes and tattered copies of Vonnegut novels, we thought we'd transcended the limita-tions of our youth. We thought we'd come into ourselves. We lay in bed and he gripped me as though I were falling off a cliff. "I love you,' he said. "There is no one I love more on earth. There is no one I will ever love more than this girl right here."

Tears erupted from me like sickness. Wrenching, miser-able, uncontrollable tears. I gagged on them. They cut off my air supply. They ruined the world. I did not love this man, this boy, whatever he was. I hated him for loving me and hated myself for having allowed him to. This relation-ship took place during a weird, hard period in both of our lives. We both had families in chaos, the city assaulted us daily, and of course there was the standard nonsense that comes from being twenty and twenty-one years old. We had a closeness that was both magical and suffocating. When we were together, which was most of the time, it was like we were sharing each other's organs. But I did not love him, at least not enough or in the right way. And that night at Motel 6, as the air conditioner buzzed and the air stank of carpet cleaner and smoke, I cried as hard as I'd cry over anything for years to come. I cried because I would soon hurt him more than he could ever hurt me. I cried because I feared then that I didn't have it in me to love someone enough to really be hurt, that I'd somehow damaged myself beyond all capacity to ever do something like stand up in a tiny, perfect church and do what people do to supposedly set their lives in motion.

Of course, twenty-one-year-old girls like to come up with dramatic, existential reasons for needing to unload their brooding, chain-smoking twenty-year-old boyfriends. Fifteen years hence, there have been several more brooders, a handful of unnervingly buoyant free spirits, and more wedding invitations than all of the boyfriends—ambiguous and not—put together. I'm a member of that demographic that marries late—last year alone, four friends over thirty-six got married for the first time—and that means that even though I was spared the onslaught in my mid-twenties that my mother warned me about, the invitations tend to arrive in the kind of steady trickle that keeps me up at night wondering if I'll ever find someone to fix the faucet.

But I still go to as many weddings as I can, and I'm proud to say that although much of the righteousness of my twenties has mellowed, I still harbor no jealousy of my friends who get married. I'd like to say that's because I know they'll owe me big-time when my turn comes, that I'll earn back all those gifts and expensive plane tickets when I decide to register at Bergdorf's and get married in Tuscany. But the truth is that, for me, the words "wedding" and "fantasy" have never quite fit together. To say I wouldn't have preferences regarding my own wedding if it were ever to occur would be overstating my (already significant) powers of indifference. But to elevate the wedding—even the distant notion of a wedding—to a landmark event that draws a line in the sand between *then* and *now* would be to forget that night in Motel 6. Real love, we all know, can hurt like hell. But love that's not quite real can choke the life out of you. That's why I still believe it's worth it to wait for the real thing, even if it means getting sick in a bathroom at the Helmsley Palace, even if it means—and I'll say it out loud—that it never comes at all. You may be alone, but you'll still be alive.

family
&
budget

parental control

amy sohn

My boyfriend freshman year of Brown was a six-foot five-inch black guy from Philly who played power forward on the basketball team. He was my first love and our relationship was deep and intense, but one of the main reasons I was drawn to him was because I knew my parents wouldn't approve. They are what you might call liberal conservatives: NPR-listening, cultured, Democratic-voting Jews, but my mom doesn't like women with visible bra straps and my dad doesn't feel comfortable around black men.

So when Kevin came to visit for a weekend the summer after freshman year, things were awkward. He towered over my five-seven bearded dad, who kept resorting to small talk about the championship chances of the 76ers. I insisted that Kevin sleep in my bedroom, even though my thirteen-year-old brother, Mark, was in the next room, and though we didn't have sex the slats on my platform bed kept falling and making loud clacking noises and in the morning my mother looked at us both very strangely.

After he went back to Philly, we would talk most nights, late at night after I got home from canvassing for an environmental group. Our relationship wasn't going well—I was always telling him about the new friends I was making at work and he was worried I was cheating on him, which I wasn't. I hung up in tears and when I walked into the living room my father said, "It doesn't sound like you're very happy."

"Of course I am!" I said, sniffling. "Happiness sometimes involves emotion."

"I know this might not be what you want to hear," he said, which was what he always said before he said something hurtful, "but Mom and I didn't get a good feeling about him when he came to visit. She doesn't think he's polite."

"Of course he's polite! What are you talking about?"

"Well, he called us by our first names before we said it was OK, and he takes very long showers."

"Oh, come on!" I said. "That is so hegemonic!"

"What's hegemonic?"

"It's racist and totally unfair! Why don't you just admit that you'd like him better if he were white?" I waited for him to tell me race had nothing to do with it; how could I accuse him of such bigotry when he was only looking out for my feelings?

"Of course I'd like him better if he were white," he said. "No question about it."

Kevin and I eventually broke up, for reasons that had less to do with my parents and more to do with all the fighting and crying. I didn't have any other serious boyfriends in college, so after I graduated I set about finding one. I moved into a share in Carroll Gardens, and at night I bar-hopped in the East Village with a girlfriend who had guys falling left and right for her because she smoked and knew how to appear disinterested. I, on the other hand, threw myself at every 120-pound drummer who gave me a second glance. I did magic tricks, the Cockney alphabet (A for 'orses, B for mutton, C for miles), and then I suggested openly that they come back to my place. None of this made for long-term relationships, so by the time I was a few years out of college I was still painfully single.

The only good thing in my life was that I had a job writing a weekly column about my dating life for a downtown alternative newspaper. My parents read it religiously and joked about it, although I knew it made them embarrassed and uncomfortable. One night I went over to their apartment for dinner, as I frequently did since I couldn't cook. My father was sitting on the couch reading *New York* magazine. "I've just read the most fascinating article," he said, "about a guy who should be your future husband."

The article turned out to be about a music-video director, Harvard grad, and former member of the Lemonheads named Jesse Peretz. He'd recently gotten into a terrible car accident, and the brush with death gave him a new lease on life. He had just directed an indie film and had decided to focus on projects he really cared about. "Not only is he bright, talented, and very handsome," my dad said, flashing me a large photo of him, "but his father is Marty Peretz, editor in chief of the *New Republic*, and I think his grand-father is I. L. Peretz!" I. L. Peretz was the most famous Yid-dish writer in history.

This guy had a pedigree to beat all pedigrees. He had an intellectual father, an Ivy diploma, a stint in a rock band, and a budding new career. Even his name was perfect: The Jesse connoted a freethinking, skateboarding hippie, and the Peretz conjured two generations of leftie Jewish cred.

Although my father had no idea what he was doing by showing me this article, I was in such a vulnerable state that I took it as an admonition. If I wanted his approval I had to find a smart, well-educated Jewish guy with an artis-tic but impressive occupation. A guy like this would be able to talk with me about art, literature, and love and still get married under a chuppah. We'd have a Jewish wedding offi-ciated by some hip downtown rabbi and invite a crowd of actor and artist friends. We'd buy an old loft in Williams-burg, drink microbrews, and have adorable punk-rock chil-dren with trendy names like Dashiell and Ruby.

I never met Jesse Peretz, but I spent the next eight years pursuing the Peretzian Ideal. I dated a string of actors, comedians, screenwriters, journalists, and novelists, all "names" to me if not the world. There was a guy who'd been on a sitcom, a downtown stand-up comedian, a young Broadway director, and a screenwriter who'd been nomi-nated for an Oscar. Some were depressed *and* Jewish, others just depressed, but they all had one overwhelming thing in common: None of them had any interest in marrying me.

What I didn't realize then was that guys with impressive careers are narcissistic and sought-after, so the last thing they want to do is commit. We'd go on one date, and then, when I called too often or told them I wanted to go out again, they blew me off with lines so repetitive I could have written them myself: "I need to take things very slowly" or "Career is the basement to my house" or "My last girl-friend and I got very serious very fast and I don't want to make that same mistake again." But I kept chasing them, imagining each guy shaking my father's hand after asking permission to marry me, and my father erupting in a sea of tears like Paul Sorvino at the Oscars when his daughter won for playing a whore.

By the time my twenty-ninth birthday arrived I was starting to lose it. I'd made a career of my singlehood (four columns, two novels, dozens of sex articles for third-rate women's magazines), but I was afraid that when I died my books would be all I left behind. So I decided to throw myself a birthday party to convince myself that friends were all that really mattered. I would invite a small, smart group, show off my new floor-through apartment in Cobble Hill, and show myself that I didn't need a boyfriend.

A few days before the party I decided I needed some art for my walls, and a mutual friend suggested I contact a painter he knew named Jack. So I called and left a message and a few hours later he called back. I was sitting home alone drinking a Corona and watching *Double Indemnity* on DVD, and when I answered the phone I heard a deep, sexy voice. Our mutual friend had said Jack lived in Brooklyn Heights and was eccentric, so I decided that despite the sexy voice, he was an over-the-hill weirdo with a rent-stabilized apartment and a bunch of cats.

I asked if he could lend me a few paintings, and when he came to my door with his portfolio I saw that he was most definitely not an over-the-hill weirdo. He looked to be in his late thirties (I later found out he was forty-two), and he was six feet tall, with red hair and tattoos of his own artwork up and down his arms. He was wearing a wide-brimmed tan felt hat with a string that attached it from his head to a button on his shirt, and there was something about the old-school nature of the hat that excited me.

It was obvious by Jack's last name, the tattoos up and down his arms, and his aquiline nose that he was not Jewish, but I didn't see him as husband material so much as a hot fling. I had been reading Anaïs Nin stories about perverted painters and their subjects, and I had a fantasy that Jack and I could live out one of the stories together. I led him upstairs, where I was cleaning the apartment in preparation for my party and into the bedroom so I could find a copy of my novel to give him as a thank-you. As soon as I walked in I saw my Hitachi magic wand sitting on the bed. "God, this is embarrassing," I said, yanking it away.

"It's nothing I haven't seen before," he said.

And that was how it started. He loaned me paintings, but declined my invitation to the party, and when he came to pick them up we went on a long walk. Because I wasn't thinking of him as a potential mate, I was myself when I was around him and not so nervous. Soon it became clear that in addition to being hot, he was also an avid reader, a gentleman, and a rough-edged romantic. He cooked for me, well, in his tiny galley kitchen. He read me Bernard Malamud at night. He bought me used books by Kleist and e-mailed me photos of vintage porn, saying the women's bodies reminded him of mine. We went to see Paul Thomas Anderson's *Punch-Drunk Love* and during the credits I told him I loved him.

I told my parents I was seeing someone new, and then one night a couple months after we met I invited them over for dinner. "I can't believe you're cooking," said my mother.

"I'm not. Jack is."

My parents and Mark came and we sat around my tiny table. Jack made a bouillabaisse with good salad and sourdough bread. My dad ate three portions. When my dad found out Jack had gone to Harvard for graduate school he seemed doubly impressed. Jack was not a Jesse Peretz or even a Jew, but he was a *mensch*, smart, and a good conversationalist, and clearly he loved me. The next day my dad wrote to say how happy I seemed and how beautiful I looked. I got choked up reading it because most of the time when he sent e-mails they were passive-aggressive and weird.

Over the next few months my parents got to know Jack better, and given the fact that he was from a different background and closer in age to them than to me, I thought they did a pretty good job of making him feel welcome. There was only one thing they didn't seem to like about him: They weren't exactly sure how he made a living. When they asked I explained that he sold his paintings, but I rarely gave details about how often or how many. Then I'd change the subject. Soon they stopped asking and we settled into a kind of uncomfortable silence on the issue.

That winter I invited him to spend Christmas and New Year's with my parents, Mark, and me at their country house in the Berkshires. On the night of Mark's birthday we invited our cousins for dinner. My mom usually makes lasagna but Jack offered to make it. "That's very generous of you," my mother said, but she didn't look happy.

In the morning Jack did his prep work, all except for the salad, and then he, Mark, and I went to see *Gangs of New York*. We got back at five and even though our guests weren't coming till seven, when we walked in I saw an entire salad in the bowl sitting out on the counter. "You didn't have to do that," Jack said, blinking.

"I was just trying to be helpful," my mother said.

Jack looked at the heap of vegetables on top of the lettuce—carrots, tomatoes, celery, and cucumbers. It was a Jewish salad, the kind I'd grown up eating, with everything thrown in. It wasn't an elegant salad like you'd have in a restaurant, with a couple leaves of romaine and a dash of vinaigrette.

Our cousins came over and Jack set out the lasagna, to oohs and aahs. I didn't see the salad, and when I looked up at him he was at the kitchen counter, with the garbage drawer pulled out, gathering the carrots, tomatoes, celery, and cucumbers and tossing them into the trash. I glanced over at my mom. She was squinting at Jack, her mouth in a tight, thin line.

Our last morning in the country, I woke up before Jack. When I walked into the kitchen my dad was sitting at the counter, already on his third cup of coffee. "So Jack's pretty amazing, isn't he?" I said, filling a mug.

"He's wonderful," my dad said. "Bright, funny, and what a storyteller!"

"I know," I said.

"I know this might not be what you want to hear," he started.

"Dad, please," I said. But he wouldn't stop.

"It's just something Mom noticed. Did you know that when he thought no one was looking he took her salad, removed all the vegetables, and tossed them into the garbage?"

"It was his dinner!" I said. "He didn't even ask her to make the salad but she did anyway!"

"That's not the point," my dad said. "The point is, *Do you think it's a good idea to be involved with someone so narrow-minded?* If you two get married, there will be a lot of decisions you'll have to make together, and it will be hard when he shows such a total lack of permeability!"

I stormed downstairs. A few minutes later I heard the Weedwacker. My dad always weeds when he's stressed. It helps him but it doesn't help the garden, since he has no idea what he's doing. A couple years ago he bought a chain saw, and even though the instructions said, "You must use motor oil or the belt will break," he decided he didn't have to obey. He started to chop down a tree, the belt broke, and the chain saw got lodged in the trunk. It's still there.

On the way home I told Jack what my father had said. I knew it might not be a wise idea to do this, but I was so hurt by my father's behavior that I felt I had to tell Jack, as someone who cared about me. "Can you believe he had the nerve to complain about you behind your back?" I whined.

"You shouldn't tell me these things," Jack said. "I don't need to know that your parents don't like me."

"They *do* like you," I said. "It's just that my mom has this competitive thing with you because you're a better cook, and my dad feels protective of her feelings. You can't undo thirty-five years of marital loyalty." He looked out onto the road. I said his name a few times but he was quiet all the way to Torrington.

One night in late June, about nine months after we met, we were lying in bed in Jack's apartment whispering in the dark. He was telling me he loved me, and then he said something about how we should get married. At first I thought he was kidding, but then I realized he was asking, for real. It was a moment I'd been waiting for my whole life, and I never expected it to happen late at night on blue sheets on a mattress on a floor in Brooklyn Heights. I said yes and then I asked him back and he said yes and the rest of the night I couldn't sleep.

A few days later I called my parents. "Jack and I want to stop over one night this week," I told my dad. "Just to say hi. How about Tuesday?"

"That's not going to work," he said. "Mom has folk dancing."

"What about Wednesday?"

"I have the co-op board meeting and on Thursday and Friday we have dinner plans." I couldn't believe it. My father was trying to cock-block my engagement.

"What about Sunday?" I said. "We're supposed to meet friends for dinner at eight but we can come over before, for a drink."

"Why do you want to come over if you're not staying for dinner?" my mom said. They do that all the time—both get on the line when I think I'm only talking to one of them.

"I just . . . wanted to see you guys."

"If you really want to," my mother said. Was she in on it too? It seemed they were doing everything in their power to prevent me from telling them I was getting married. It was the "if a tree falls in a forest" of engagements.

"We'll be there at six," I said, and hung up before they could protest.

Sunday night at five thirty I met Jack at a bar a few blocks from my parents' apartment. He said he was nervous and ordered a Maker's Mark on the rocks. "They're going to be so happy for us," I said. "You shouldn't worry."

"I'm not so sure," he said. "I'm not Jewish and I'm an artist. I think we should decide now if we're asking them or telling them."

"We're telling them," I said. "I'm twenty-nine years old. That's too old to ask permission."

"Good," he said.

When we got to the apartment my mother opened the door. "Dad's not here," she said.

"What?" I said.

"He's running errands on the Lower East Side but he should be home soon."

"Oh," I said. This was awful. If he didn't make it back in time we'd have to leave for our dinner and I'd have to postpone the whole conversation. Years would go by, in an endless cycle of New York–style postponements, and by the time we finally told my parents we were engaged we'd already have three kids.

We sat on the living room couch. Jack held my hand. My mother asked what was new. We both said "nothing" at the same time.

The front door opened and my dad came in. Then he disappeared into the bedroom and didn't come out. My mom bellowed his name.

"Sorry, sorry," he said, emerging in a T-shirt and khaki shorts. "It was very hot outside. I had to change."

He sat down next to my mom. "So anyway," I said, taking a deep breath and grabbing Jack's hand.

"Did Mom tell you I saw *Spellbound* last night? It was playing at the Heights Cinema. Excellent documentary. About these kids in a spelling bee. There was this one scene where this girl couldn't spell *viand*. I swear to you I was on the edge of my seat."

"We've decided to get engaged," I said.

"*Mazel tov!*" my mother said, rising to embrace us. My dad was smiling tightly. My mother turned to him and said, "Come over here and congratulate them."

He stood up and kissed me and shook Jack's hand and then he said, "Should I open some wine?"

"That's why he was late," my mother said, giggling. "He had a feeling this is what you were going to tell us so he went out to get wine, but he had to go to Chinatown since all the liquor stores were closed."

He brought out a bottle of rice wine with Chinese writing on the label and poured us a couple glasses. We clinked and I swallowed. It was awful. The price was on the bottle: $4.99.

"So have you thought about dates yet?" my mother said. Her cheeks were flushed and she was exuberant. I could see her imagining herself dancing at the wedding, and being a gracious hostess. I had always wanted a closer relationship with her, and I had a feeling my wedding was going to do it. We had always been so different, but now we would be the same in one way: We'd both be married women.

"We want to do it this fall," I said. "Grandmom and Grandpop are so old, and we want to be sure they can be there."

"Where do you want to do it?" she said.

"We'd like to get married in the Berkshires," I said. I knew that in Massachusetts you could be married by anyone, and Jack and I had an older, patrician friend we wanted to enlist so we could avoid the whole drama of trying to find a rabbi who performed interfaith weddings.

We started talking about possible locations and different weekends. My dad asked how many people we were thinking of having and I rattled off some names of friends. Jack mentioned a few of his, and since his friends were older and married with kids, his number was a little higher.

Before we left Jack took a picture of the four of us, using his long arm to hold the camera. My mom, Jack, and I were all grinning ear to ear, but my dad looked like he was constipated.

When we got home that night my mom had written to congratulate me. She said it was obvious Jack and I brought out the best in each other and would make each other very happy. There wasn't any note from my dad. I wrote back to my mom: "I'm so glad you're happy," I said. "I hope Dad is too."

"My mom sent me the sweetest note," I told Jack as we got into bed.

"Yeah?" he said. "Did your dad write?" I leaned over and turned out the light. "He didn't. I can't believe he didn't congratulate you."

"He probably read her e-mail before she sent it," I said. "To him everything that comes from her is from both of them."

The next morning I checked my e-mail as soon as I woke up. "Mom felt I should reply to the implied question. I really, truly, totally feel as she does. If I tell you that running through my mind was: 'But does she know how hard it is to live with someone for better or worse?' you have got to believe that that's how any eyes-open person would feel at a time like this."

That was his attempt to be nice? Each step he took to try to be gracious made him come off as more hostile and weird. I wished he had some ability to lie, to suck in his feelings when it was for the greater good. Didn't he know how important his support was to me, even if he wasn't totally comfortable with Jack? We hadn't known each other that long, but my parents had known each other only a year when they got married. Besides, they knew from reading my column that I'd dated around long enough to know what I wanted.

On Fourth of July weekend Jack and I drove to the Berkshires with my parents to go location scouting. Every place we saw was too stuffy or too WASPy, until my parents suggested a funky restaurant they'd eaten at, the Dreamaway Lodge. It was a former bordello in Becket that Bob Dylan had once visited. The furniture was falling apart and all the tables were mismatched, but as soon as I walked in I knew this was it.

"What do you think?" I whispered to Jack.

"It's definitely funk factor five," said Jack. "But I like it."

The owner, an affected former actor named Daniel, had hosted a few weddings before, and when I told him I wrote a column for *New York* magazine he seemed impressed. He gave us a tour, showed us some sample menus, and took us to a spot in the woods where we could do the ceremony.

"So assuming we have one hundred people," my dad said to Daniel, "do you think you could ballpark it for us?"

"Well, with three appetizers, it would be about fifty dollars a head." There was a stunned silence. My father broke into a smile. Even including the tent, the floral, and the band, he was going to get in and out for under ten thousand dollars. My lowbrow taste would wind up saving the day.

Over the next few weeks, as I made the other wedding preparations, my mother said she'd like a running tally. I took this to mean my parents were okay with paying for the bulk of the wedding as long as the costs didn't balloon out of control. And I liked this arrangement, partly because I didn't want to tap into my retirement savings to pay for my wedding, and partly because it seemed like they could afford it. Jack and I were paying for our own suits and dresses (at least $2,000 altogether), a photographer we liked ($2,000), and the liquor ($1,000). With all that money coming from us (which meant me) it didn't seem ludicrous to ask them to pay for the rest.

But when I found a klezmer band and the guy wanted $2,500, I decided to run it by my mother. My father answered. "Is Mom there?" I said.

"She's out folk dancing," he said.

"Oh," I said. "I just interviewed this band we want to hire."

"You can talk to me about it."

This was the point where I should have said no and hung up. She was out folk dancing, which meant he was watching crime shows and messing around on the computer. Nights like this he didn't eat dinner and got hypoglycemic. This was no time to talk money. Even though I knew all of this I got nervous, and because I was nervous I kept talking.

"Well, we listened to a few of their tapes and they're really incredible," I said. I told him how most of the band had been in the episode of *Sex and the City* where Charlotte has a Jewish wedding. "They cost two thousand five hundred dollars, and I was thinking we'd pay for half." He was quiet.

"I'm so glad you brought this up," he said. "I think you've gotten the impression Mom and I want to pay for the whole wedding when that's not the case. I don't believe in the tradition of the bride's family paying. I think it's outdated and unfair."

"Who paid for your wedding?" My mother's parents had paid for the entire thing, a swank affair for two hundred people back in 1969.

"That was a different era!" he shouted. "I've thought this over and we're willing to pay up to a certain amount or a certain percentage, whichever is lower."

"Whichever is *lower*?"

"I envision this as a shared expense, some combination of you, us, and Jack's family."

"But they're already doing the rehearsal dinner and it's going to be like five thousand dollars. It's not like they're not helping already. And Jack and I are paying for the photos and the liquor!"

"I undehstand that," my dad said. He didn't have a Brooklyn accent except when he said "undehstand" and "intehview." "But there's no reason the burden should fall on Mom and me when Jack's inviting so many more people than you."

"What are you talking about?" I said. We'd come up with a working list, and because I had a huge Jewish family I was inviting three times the number of people Jack was.

"When you were saying who you were going to invite, there were many more people on his side than yours." He had clung to this like a fact when it was just an initial conversation. He did this kind of thing all the time: believed an incorrect bit of information and then built up a month's-long resentment, without even knowing it was all predicated on a fallacy.

"Dad!" I screamed. "I was just going off the top of my head! I'd just gotten engaged. My head wasn't working right. We're inviting eighty-five people and sixty are on my side."

"Oh," he said. "Well, let me think this over and e-mail you some breakdowns."

I began to hyperventilate. I could do the whole thing if I really wanted to, but I would bust most of my retirement savings. And I didn't want to ask Jack's mother and stepfather to kick in any more because they'd already indicated they'd be giving us a substantial wedding gift.

What was my father's problem? Did he think Jack's father and stepmother were richer than they really were? They summered in Wellfleet, and my dad always raised his eyebrows when they talked about it, like they rented some huge cottage even though it was really a shack. Or was it all about Jack? I was convinced my dad wouldn't be fighting like this if I had married Jesse Peretz. (Then again, if I married Jesse Peretz, his video-directing money would have funded the entire wedding.)

Did my father know I made more money than Jack? Was he worried I was going to support Jack for the rest of my life

and afraid to be complicit in that, even symbolically, by paying for most of the wedding? If he knew I made most of the
money then he had to know that any contribution from us
was really a contribution from *me*. Why would he want to do
that to me? Maybe he felt that getting Jack's family to pay
was the only way to even things out, a kind of reverse dowry.

I went into my office and checked my in-box. There was
an e-mail that looked like an algebraic equation, outlining
three different ways of dividing the total budget between
them, us, and Jack's family. It contained phrases like
"where $Y = 60\%$ of total."

When Jack came home I was totally distraught. "It's
OK," he said. "Obviously your father has issues with me, so
let's do it all ourselves. I can't pay you anything now, but I
will pay you back, I promise. We'll cancel Dreamaway and
do it here, at City Hall, just a small dinner, immediate family. I'd prefer a small wedding anyway."

"I'm an exhibitionist!" I said. "I'm not going to do my
wedding vows for an audience of fifteen. That's fewer people than I had at my Barnes and Noble reading!"

The phone rang. It was my mother. "What is it?" I said,
my voice high and frenzied.

"You know that conversation you had with Dad?" she
said.

"Yeah?"

"Forget it. We'll do the whole thing."

"I don't understand. What happened?"

My father was on the line. "Mom came home and
brought me to my senses. I said to her, 'How did you

manage to defuse such a tense situation so easily?' She said, 'The same way I've been doing it for thirty-three years. It's called husband management.' " He got all choked up when he said, "husband management," like he'd realized how lucky he was to be married to someone who knew what to do with him.

The rest of the planning went by relatively smoothly, although there were arguments over how many people could be invited to the rehearsal dinner. (Jack and I wanted fewer, my parents wanted more.) The day of the wedding my father put on a suit and a carnation and, with his slicked-back hair and gray beard, looked like a real father of the bride. Even when the band went into overtime and the photographer turned out not to have the right equipment, my father didn't get upset. We danced together even though he doesn't like to dance and we made quiet small talk while everyone watched us.

At the toasts, Jack's friends stood up and said what a wonderful guy he was and my friends stood up and made jokes about how much I used to drink when I was single. My parents got up and my mother said, "We were going to read a poem but we decided it was too corny, so instead we'd like to give Amy and Jack a few words of advice about marriage." Then, in unison, they said, "When you're wrong, admit it. When you're right, shut up." It wasn't sentimental but it got a huge laugh. I wished they had said something nicer about me, or even about Jack, but I figured they decided less was more.

Two days after the wedding, after Jack and I were back in Brooklyn, I got an e-mail from my father. I was nervous to open it because the subject heading was "Misc."

It opened with a long and somewhat corny poem, the one they were going to read, about the joys of marriage with metaphors like "mountains and valleys." I wasn't sure who wrote it, but it looked like something he'd found on the Internet.

Underneath it, he wrote, "I'd have to say that one of the greatest 'values' of the wedding day (toasts plus conversations) was how much I learned about Jack . . . to his enormous credit! Maybe I wasn't observant enough, or other things got in the way of my realizing sooner and with greater certainty what a truly wonderful match you are for each other. Anyhow, you certainly 'have our blessing,' by which I mean that we think that your making a life together is a wonderful thing and we're glad we can learn from both of you over the coming years. Now, about this 'baby thing' . . ." After that, he put the sign for a wink. It's the only time an emoticon ever made me cry.

my
perfect
wedding

samina ali

♥

When I was twelve years old, I got my first period while my parents, two brothers, and I were spending Fourth of July weekend in the Wisconsin Dells, a gaudy tourist trap smack in the middle of the Midwest, which can best be described as a miniature and humble version of Disney World. There were bumper cars, twisting roller coasters, towering water slides, and, of course, the main attraction: the waterskiing show, where a troupe of expert water-skiers showed off their talents of impressive high jumps and twirls to a large, mostly white audience. All the hotels in the area were booked, and my immigrant Indian family had rented a room in one of the many crowded and nearly identical two-story hotels that featured a view of the main highway and a swimming pool adjacent to the asphalt parking lot. My dad liked to go to Wisconsin because, unlike where we lived in Minneapolis, fireworks were legal. In Wisconsin, he could load us up with firecrackers that my brothers and I would excitedly shoot into the wide gray skies at dusk.

My menses secretly crept up on me in the middle of the night. My mother woke me early in the morning, and when she saw the stains on the white hotel sheets, she led me to the bathroom and had me clean up before the others woke up. I still remember the confusion and horror I felt, this deeply private maturation process happening smack in the middle of a tourist trap in some cheap hotel room, where my father and brothers were steps away from my mother's commanding whispers and my quick and embarrassed movements. For the rest of the vacation, I felt strangely different but did everything I could to keep my sudden change hidden from the men, grateful it had been my mother who found me. Yet only a month later, my family flew back to Hyderabad and within days of our arrival, my father threw a party to publicly announce the onset of my menstruation. Rather than invite a handful of close relatives, as some families do to mark this occasion, my father, who is known for his dramatic gestures and his deep pleasure in entertaining, invited close to two hundred guests, most of whom I didn't know, hired three chefs from the best local restaurants, and lit off fireworks over the house.

For the occasion, I was dressed in the wedding outfit in which an older cousin had recently gotten married. The ensemble consisted of rich layers of red silk and a six-foot brocade veil that was wrapped around my developing breasts and over my head. My hands were intricately patterned with henna. My face was washed with turmeric, and kohl was deeply applied to my eyes. Gold bangles gently clinked on my wrists. Around my neck and ankles, dangling from my ears, down the center part of my hair, and cinched around each finger, were fifteen pounds of gold. I was seated on a center stage in the huge living area of the old house, and my mother and aunts, the women of the house, fed me sweetmeats and draped me in fragrant ropes of jasmine and marigold. After the ceremony was completed, my mother took the crook of my arm and led me across the wide, open room to greet the guests. As a traditional Indian bride would, I kept my head bowed low, not out of obligation, but because I was deeply ashamed over the public production. My two brothers, whom my parents had firmly admonished not to tease me, kept to the background, providing my only relief. That night, when all the guests were gone and the house was quiet again, my parents sat drinking chai on the verandah underneath the clear dark sky. I overheard my father telling my mother he had received fourteen marriage proposals. This, of course, was the real reason the celebration had taken place, to announce that I was of marriageable age.

When my mother asked what he was planning to do, he said, "Nothing, she's far too young. Tonight we were just having fun."

. . .

The traditional Hyderabadi Muslim wedding ceremony lasts five days, each ceremony bearing its own ritual along with its own color. The first three days are gold, promising fortune and fertility; the wedding is the bloodred of union; and the groom's dinner that is thrown the day following the wedding is the green of Islam, the color of submission. The bride and groom are both expected to be virgins. Though the wedding has been arranged and the two meet for the first time on the wedding night, a successful consummation is expected, which is what, traditionally, the groom's dinner publicly announces.

I was nineteen when my marriage was arranged to a Muslim Indian man in Hyderabad. I was born in India, and though my parents immigrated to Minneapolis when I was six months old, I was raised to know that it was to India that I would return to get an arranged marriage. When I attended school in the United States, I wasn't allowed to date or even have male friends. I couldn't even accept their phone calls at the house. Each summer, to remind me of who I really was, my father sent me back to India, where I was also enrolled in school. I grew up in both places, fluent both in Urdu and English as well as in American and Hyderabadi Muslim culture. It never occurred to me that I might not participate in an arranged marriage when everything in my life was preparing me to be a proper Indian bride. The man my parents chose was exactly the type of man they had prepared me for: Indian, Muslim, educated, and from a similar social and economic background. Marriages are arranged around such commonalities to ensure that the daughter, who has grown accustomed to certain types of comforts in her father's house, continues to enjoy those privileges in her husband's. There was no surprise. I was relieved, however, to find that my future husband was handsome, even by my standards, and young, just four years older than me. In this roulette wheel of fate, anything is possible: My parents could have agreed to a match with the man who recently had one lung removed or with the widower who was fifteen years older and had three school-age children about my age. Of course, there were also the handful of suitors whose attributes were indistinguishable from the one they ended up choosing, and it was only after my parents completed thorough background checks and careful character assessments that they made their final decision. Which is to say that by any standards, my parents chose wisely.

The wedding was a grand affair that lasted two weeks. Musicians were hired and installed in the inner courtyard, where they played throughout the day and evening, stopping only for lunch and afternoon tea. Colorful strings of light blazed down the four floors of the exterior of the house and over the enormous front gates. Lights were wrapped around the trunks and branches of the guava and coconut trees. Beauticians were hired and brought to the privacy of the house in order to wax my full arms and legs, thread my brows, and apply henna to my feet and hands. Each day, silver trays laden with sweetmeats and silk saris arrived from well-wishers and neighbors. My wedding dress, a stunning burgundy silk full-length skirt threaded with gold sequins and brocade, came with a matching cropped top that tied with gold thread just below the breasts, and a six-foot veil that was designed specifically for me and fitted by the best tailors. Around my slim bare midriff, my mother wrapped a stunning silver chain. I was lost in the revelry, almost taken by surprise, at once excited and frightened, as any bride, of getting married, but also deeply afraid of what I was actually getting into. Doubts I never had before suddenly overcame me, and the years of preparation my parents had provided began to seem like nothing more than a gentle and loving indoctrination. I was as American, I realized, as Indian, as free to invent any new custom as I was tethered to continuing these age-old traditions. Yet it wasn't really true. These were just the final rebellious thoughts of a nineteen-year-old. I knew the truth. I wasn't free. I was my father's daughter. Having brought me up in a restrictive and closed environment, he had deemed I was now the right age to get married.

A wedding hall the size of a small mansion was rented for the wedding, along with elephants, horses, and camels to carry the five hundred guests to ride in honor through the palatial gardens. A long line of seven cars led me to the site, which I could spot from a mile away because of the fireworks exploding in the tropical sky. At the front of the cars, a brass band played to announce my slow journey through the streets, then rose to a cacophony when I at last arrived at the wedding hall. As I was exiting the car, two fire-breathers crouched on either side of me and threw their heads back to scorch the night air. A richly sequined veil covered my modestly bowed head down to my knees. When I moved I heard the swishing of silk and the gentle clink of gold. A group of women quickly led me into a separate room where a mullah quietly asked me if I agreed to the marriage. By Islamic law, no woman can be married against her will, and the Muslim priest was here to make sure I wasn't being coerced. I didn't answer him right away. Again, I was plagued by doubts. I didn't know what it meant to be married, outside of my parents' visions, and I had no ideas independent of them. Through the years, without fully being aware, I had adopted their dreams as my own, not from force or manipulation but because what they had described over and over seemed like it was written, something inherited with my brown skin, my thick brows, and my full lips. The mullah repeated his question, and a cry went up around me among the women: The bride hasn't agreed! There are no vows in the ceremony that a groom and bride make to one another before a congregation. A marriage isn't even a covenant according to religious doctrines. Under Islamic law, a marriage is nothing more than a business contract between two people who are meant to provide solace and sustenance to one another. Comfort in partnership, protection, and sexual fulfillment. When a woman marries, she automatically signs what resembles a prenuptial contract in which she can bind her husband to anything she fears might be withdrawn after the wedding: the right to continue her education, the right to work, the right to mobility, even the right to how often she wants sex. None of these went into my prenuptial agreement. It was assumed I had these rights. Nothing was being taken away from me. Unlike most Indian Muslim brides, I wasn't even moving into my in-laws' home; instead, I was bringing my future husband with me back to the United States. The only stipulation in my contract was that if either of us exercised our religious right to divorce, I would receive a specific amount of alimony in one lump sum. Because I wasn't even sure how much to put down, my father set my price.

On the wedding night, I could tell my husband was as nervous as I was. We were locked in a large bedroom in his parents' home with a queen-sized bed draped on all four sides with ropes of marigold, and rose petals were scattered across the velvet blankets. We each took turns using the bathroom, where we each, by turn, locked the door behind us to brush our teeth and then change into our pajamas. When I came out, my arms were full of silks and gold and, not knowing where to place them, I stood before my new husband in some strange stance of spiritual offering. He understood and quickly cleared one of his shelves, then thought better and emptied a drawer. Then we lay side by side under the thick layers of the mosquito net, the breeze from the overhead fan not quite reaching us through the heavy ropes of flowers. The closed room was sweltering. At one point, he got up and opened a window just above the bed. The band was still playing outside, probably just under the bedroom window, judging from its deafening noise. It was four in the morning. He closed the window again and lay back down. He asked if I was hungry, and I said no. He asked if I'd been able to eat anything at the wedding ceremony, and I told him no again. He said he hadn't been able to eat anything either. Then we went to sleep.

Two years later, we still hadn't consummated the marriage. By then, we were living in America. Within months of our moving to Minneapolis, however, he had quickly left for Chicago in order to pursue a master's degree while I stayed on in my parents' home and went to the local university, as was my husband's wish. During my occasional visits to his apartment, we sat on the couch and watched a Hindi movie. He made no advances toward me, and if I attempted a gesture, he quickly distanced himself. What had seemed to me at first to be an undiscussed mutual agreement to slowly get to know one another, possibly even to fall in love before we became intimate, eventually became apparent as his exclusive determination to keep away from me. It wasn't just that we weren't having sex; he was also emotionally distant. He refused to answer innocent questions about how he passed his days, to share anything of his history in India, to even include me in his phone conversations with his parents, which he conducted in Gujarati, a language I didn't understand. When I went to my parents for help, they advised me to be patient. They continued to believe, as I once had, that my husband and I were getting to know one another. They had never known any couple to not end up falling in love, as they did themselves, and held firmly to their dream for me. After all, love comes after marriage in this culture, not before. The commonalities of language, faith, customs, education, and economic status are all in place to help cajole these tender feelings. In the same way I had felt gently trapped into getting married, now I felt trapped to remain in it. Divorcing would mean losing my family and everything I had grown to know. Still, at twenty-two, when I peered honestly into my future, I saw year after year of devastating isolation. The truth was, despite all the superficial connections I shared with my husband, we didn't share a basic human bond. We remained the strangers we had been on the wedding night. By then, I was finishing my college degree and possessed more confidence than when I got married, more self-assurance and independence. This time, I did what I didn't have the strength to do before and went against my parents' wishes. I filed for divorce. Ironically, my actions freed my husband to tell me what he had been hiding all this time: He was gay. Because he came from a good Muslim family, he knew there was no way for him to express it. He had married me believing he could repress or even change his homosexuality.

.   .   .

The next time I married for love. I met my husband in graduate school in Oregon, where he was studying poetry and I was studying fiction. Though he claims we met on the first day of orientation, I didn't notice him until the end of the first year, when a group of us rented a beach house for the weekend and spent the days hiking along the jagged cliffs and sunbathing on the pebbly beach. We bought fresh oysters for dinner and barbecued them on the wide balcony overlooking the ocean. It had been three years since my divorce, but I remained stunned by my first husband's revelation. Somehow I was deeply embarrassed, as though it had been my fault that he couldn't overcome his sexual preference. In looking back, it's easy to see why I took responsibility. Our divorce scandalized the provincial Indian Muslim community in which I had been raised in Minneapolis, and though I was exercising the rights Islam granted me to fully and safely divorce, the followers of this very faith attempted to snatch away those rights in order to keep me in my place as a woman. I underwent a psychic stoning. While the families dismissed my husband's confession as a moment of confusion, they criticized me for ruining a perfectly good Muslim man's reputation. Although my parents had always encouraged me to have patience, the community claimed that no woman possessed the kind of patience needed to endure two years of a sexless marriage. I was accused of lying, of covering up the supposedly real reason I was leaving my first husband: I had an American lover secretly stashed someplace. One of my father's close friends even suggested I was a "whore." This is what I left behind when I went to Oregon and, not yet knowing how to understand this betrayal and suffering, I kept from telling my classmates what I had been through. Like those days in the Wisconsin Dells, I once more hid my body's secret experience.

That night in the beach house, however, when all our friends turned in for the night, leaving the balcony one by one, only Tim and I remained on the balcony under the bright night sky. He told me about his travels through India, his botched affair with a woman he had met there, his revelations so honest and intimate and vulnerable that I was inspired to confess my own failed marriage. We spoke through the night, naturally sharing in the way I had tried to force with my first husband, then crawled into our separate beds when the sun appeared red along the horizon. Two days later, he drove me back to my apartment in Eugene and we continued the conversation in the car. It was a relief to have a companion to share with, someone to hold my secrets, to help carry my burdens, to laugh. In this way, I guess we had the traditional American courtship. We went on dates to restaurants and concerts and slowly got to know one another. He grew up in Palo Alto, California, with a poet father and an artist mother, had already gotten his master's degree from Berkeley in English literature, and was expanding with a second one in poetry writing. He had traveled to most every corner of the world, to places I had never even heard of, and spoke three languages fluently. Like me, he possessed both an insider's and outsider's view of America. We were already falling in love when the school year ended, and I returned to Minneapolis for the summer and he to San Francisco. For three months, he wrote me long letters filled with his poetry, his visions of our future together, and I, afraid of my father, checked the mail early each morning and smuggled in these treasures under my shirt. When it was time to return to Oregon, he flew out to get me and we drove my car back west. For two weeks, we traveled through barren canyons and deserts and lush forests where I heard owls hooting in the middle of the night and the scurrying sound of jackrabbits. He read me his poetry while I drove, and I talked to him about my novel. By the time we arrived in Oregon, we knew we were going to remain on the journey together, and a year later, when we made our feelings official, all our friends said it was fated.

The wedding he and I planned was very private. We decided to hold the ceremony in the back garden of his parents' house and invited thirty-five of our closest friends and relatives, though my father, who was against my decision to marry outside my faith and culture, didn't attend. We held the humble affair in the afternoon, and that morning, I rose early to get to the local spa, where I had my hair pinned, my makeup professionally applied, and my hands and feet manicured and pedicured. On the second floor of his parents' house, I wrapped myself in a gold sari my mother had brought for me to wear, not especially designed for me, just something she thought was pretty. The only flowers were those I carried in a bouquet. I didn't wear a veil, and no women surrounded me; no brass band announced my arrival. There weren't any fireworks. At the scheduled hour, the sitar player we had hired played a traditional raga and I walked down the aisle, so to speak, out the back garden doors, down the patio, and through the garden to where Tim stood. My older brother gave me away. My best friend from Oregon was my maid of honor. Tim's parents were part of the local literary circles, and the man who married us was a prominent writer who didn't possess a license, which meant Tim and I later went to court to register. Another prominent writer videotaped the ceremony. Yet another photographed it. In front of our loved ones, he and I shared vows to love and cherish one another, through sickness and in health, after which Tim read a love poem by Rumi and I cried. A local Indian restaurant catered the celebration and, because I wanted to hang on to it, I didn't throw my bouquet. We rented a grand hotel room for the wedding night, with a hot tub on its private terrace, where we whispered and kissed into the warm silent night.

I wish I could say that our bond of love has grown stronger through the years and that we are still together, each day finding creative ways to bridge our cultural and religious divides as we so beautifully did on our wedding day. But our marriage ended after seven years. By any standards, they were the severest and most trying years anyone could face: In that period, we buried both his parents, one who died slowly of advanced lung cancer, another suddenly of a heart attack; I suffered significant health setbacks after a very complicated delivery of our son; and Tim was diagnosed with a rare, inoperable, and incurable brain lesion. It was our deep love for one another that kept us striving through the earlier misfortune, an optimism that inspired hope that we could make it through. But the catastrophes piled one on top of the other, and soon our different approaches slowly divided us. Other than our love, we didn't have anything in common, and this is what became apparent. I turned to my faith to imbue me with courage, while he grew uncomfortable with what he thought was my naive belief in some greater force, like a child still clinging to visions of Santa Claus. During the worst period, when I considered taking a quick trip to Hyderabad to visit relatives in order to regain my strength, it only reminded him that both his parents had passed away, and he was unmoored. He left his poetry while I dived into my fiction. Soon, we began differing on how we would raise our son. The journey we had undertaken together split into two separate paths, and we found ourselves strangers not only to one another but also to our own former selves who had fallen in love.

When I think about my perfect wedding now, I don't think about the day itself, the glamour and hoopla, the fireworks exploding overhead or the gentle sitar music in the background. My mind automatically wanders to those many days and months and years that come after the ceremony, when two people are traveling side by side, agreeing from moment to moment on how mutually to confront disappointment and disaster or celebrate the milestones of their children. Whereas my first marriage may have been conducted solely with intelligence and thought and the second entirely with the heart, I have come to see that if and when I get married again, the two—mind and emotions— must join. That is the perfect marriage for me, because a union within one will bring about the union with the other. There is a practicality that weighs down my floating feeling of love that, at an earlier age, I would have condemned as unromantic but which I have come to see as realistic. Now that I am in my mid-thirties, when I honestly peer into my future, I see myself reaching my peak, then hitting middle age, and eventually slowing down. The man by my side will witness the gentle unraveling of my glory, as I witness his, both of us an audience to the other's impressive twirling and high jumps as well as the private vulnerabilities and embarrassments. The bond that will take us to the end can only be that of love, but a steady and mature love toughened by defeat, compromises, and worthy celebrations.

going bridal

farah l. miller

♥

It was three a.m. on a twenty-nine-degree January night in New York City, and I was climbing out the window of my fifth-floor apartment in an oversized T-shirt and cotton pajama pants to cry my heart out on the fire escape. I'd been crying for three hours inside, and when my fiancé, Scott, told me to calm down and try to sleep, I decided it was time to get some air.

"What are you so upset about?" he asked. He knew I'd found out earlier that day that my best friend Jamie's step-sister wanted to buy the wedding dress I had my eye on. I told him about my phone call with Jamie, how I called her sister names. He knew that Jamie wasn't returning my phone messages now. Still, as I look back, I'm the first one to admit that none of it added up to middle-of-the-night theatrics.

I wouldn't come back in. I folded my knees into my chest

and rocked back and forth, mimicking Demi Moore's depressed Jules pose from the end of *St. Elmo's Fire*.

"Farah, please . . . what the hell are you doing?" Scott asked.

"I don't"—gulp, sniffle—"want to have a"—sniffle—"WEDDING!" I said.

Why was I acting like a toddler? How did I get to this point? It couldn't have been about the dress. I never even thought I'd wear a wedding dress. Four years earlier, I'd gone with my friend Julie to a Vera Wang bridal collection sample sale, held in a huge ballroom at a hotel in midtown Manhattan. It was insane. First, we waited on a queue of five hundred nervous brides. Then, we watched them rip $6,000 gowns from the racks and strip down to their sports bras to try them on. When Julie found the one she wanted, she ordered me to "Hold on tight and don't let anyone else touch it!" I hugged the bodice like a new puppy and used the skirt to whip unsuspecting shoppers if they so much as asked if they could try on Julie's dress.

Later, this made for hilarious storytelling because Julie, the woman who had spent her girlhood role-playing weddings and imagining what flowers she'd carry down the aisle, got me, the woman who always made fun of her for it, to "go bridal," when I was never the bridal type.

Seeing my classy friends don their veils and gowns on their own wedding days always looked absurd to me, like a uniform, and not at all romantic. This might have had something to do with the fact that I had to wear a uniform to each of their weddings. In a few short months, my closet had become decorated with a rainbow of bridesmaid dresses and accoutrements. I complained to my mother about how much this was all costing me.

"Honey, nobody I knew in the sixties had a traditional wedding," she said. "I can't believe how many of your friends want you to wear bridesmaid dresses." I thought about the bits and pieces I'd heard about how she married my dad in Las Vegas after a two-month trip across the country with a jaunt down to Mexico. But I didn't dare ask her for details.

Then I met Scott. I was producing content for the relationships channel of a major women's Web site. We dispensed tips on every topic from how to "Find a Man in 30 Days" to how to "Unleash Your Inner Sex Goddess." The punch line was that I had never had a real boyfriend. I was faking my way through "Love Lessons on Breakup Recovery" and "Reviving Your Sex Drive." The only content I felt fully confident in writing was my "Is Divorce Holding You Back from Happiness?" quiz.

Then Scott and I fell in love. I was twenty-six years old; he was twenty-nine years old. He met my mother. I met his father and stepmother. We flew to California and he met my father and stepmother. We flew to Florida and I met his mother. It was the twenty-first-century American meet-the-parents tour. I found a new job with a book publisher that made me happy. Being a chef, Scott also found a new job at a restaurant that made him happy. He moved into my apartment and we were happy together. It was unbelievable.

I went from being the most single person I knew to being someone who used the word "we" whenever people asked what I did over the weekend.

Two years went by and my attitude about weddings started to change. I went to a bridal shower, where I expected to initiate my normal routine of finding a seat, ordering a coffee, and drowning myself in it just to stay awake through the gift portion of the afternoon. Instead, at this shower, as the bridesmaids asked the bride-to-be to answer questions about her fiancé, I thought about how I'd answer them at My Bridal Shower. Maybe this is something women do, but I'd never done it before. It led to other strange behaviors. I'd be hanging out with Scott. He'd say something sweet. I'd think, "I want to marry this person," and suddenly I'd wonder who would be invited to our wedding. What wedding? As I made this fictional guest list, I couldn't help but wonder if I'd be able to have both my mother and father in attendance.

The most common question I've been asked in the twenty years since my parents divorced is, "Do you want them to get back together?" My answer has always been a definitive, "No." The notion of wanting to marry Scott with both of my parents as witnesses seemed completely ridiculous to me. But once I started thinking about my real wedding and what it would be like, I knew I'd want both of them there.

When Dr. Judith Wallerstein's *The Unexpected Legacy of Divorce: A Twenty-Five Year Study* first came out in 2000, I was so relieved that someone had published a tome on how much your parents' divorce can leave its mark, even years after the divorce took place. I called her to find out if it was possible that I had a delayed "child-of-divorce" reaction.

"A lot of the youngsters say that the parents' divorce ended the childhood," she told me. "You may have grown up feeling you haven't had as much time to play."

Later that year, my dad, who lives with his wife in northern California, came to New York on a business trip. Scott had just started a new job at a downtown restaurant that critics were raving about. It's an impressive, funky space, and there is a good-looking clientele and open-air seating. I took my dad there to make him proud. He's an ex-hippie who's always a little stoned, so wowing him isn't a tricky endeavor. (He once bragged to his wife on the phone about how cool it was that I took him on the subway.)

We've lived three thousand miles away from each other since my parents' messy divorce got under way when I was nine years old. My dad moved out. My mom picked me up from a friend's house one day with an apple and a note that read: "We're moving to New York!" And we did. Any hope of a father-daughter bond was demolished.

The court system dictated when my dad could phone me, and my mom chaperoned the calls. The joint custody arrangement dictated when I was to fly to California to see him, but it was always during school vacations. I never wanted to go. It wasn't until I turned eighteen, when the court order no longer applied, that we started to have a relationship. I called my dad from college and found a person who not only loved me, but who understood me. He told me stories about growing up in a Long Island suburb, which was an experience similar to my own. He showered me with praise. This is what dads do, I realized. I didn't want to punish him anymore. Instead, I let him in.

That night at the restaurant Scott wanted to impress my dad, and he sent us eight courses. We had *baccala* (or cod cakes) on toasted Italian bread, calamari salad, and a rich mushroom risotto, all before our main courses even came out. We drank a bottle of wine. I found myself in a gastronomic coma.

It was a beautiful late-summer night in New York, and my dad and I decided to walk off our dinner with the twenty-five-block walk back to my apartment. He told me how much he liked Scott and how happy he was that I had found someone to love and be loved by. I told him that I thought we'd get married soon. When we got to my door, I told him that more than anything I wanted him to be there when we did.

Two months later, Scott and I were officially engaged. We talked about the options. My mother told me how much she had to spend on a wedding, and it was more than I ever expected. After doing a little research, I found out that the average wedding in New York costs $30,000. My mother's offer wasn't enough on its own. My father offered to help pay as well. But if they both contributed, one thing was certain: My mother and father would need to be at our wedding together—in one room for the first time in twenty years. I didn't know if any of us could handle that. I tried to consider our options:

1. Plan two small weddings—one with Mom in New York, and one with Dad in California.
2. Have one very small wedding, but choose only one parent to attend.
3. Get married at City Hall—and save the money to buy an apartment.
4. Throw a destination wedding with friends. No parents.
5. Plan two weddings—the one with Mom would be the destination wedding, and the one with Dad would be in California because that's like another destination wedding. Still equal.

   This is where it got tricky. It felt like we were going around in circles. No matter what, options 1–5 meant I would have to choose which parent would be there for the "real" wedding. So option 6.

6. Have one wedding with a $30,000 budget from my mom, my father, and some help from Scott's family as well. Invite one hundred friends and family members to serve dual purposes as company and divorced-parent buffers.

For some reason, it seemed easier to make a decision to spend all of this money on a one-night affair if it were the only logical choice. When I told my hip colleagues at work that I was going traditional and having a real wedding, I could explain that this was The Only Way.

But once you decide to have a real wedding, a big wedding, you become a Bride-to-Be. You buy magazines to learn how to plan what is essentially a big party. You watch any television show that mentions the word "wedding." You ask every married person you know ridiculous questions like "Did you send save-the-date cards, and if so, do you think it's okay if they're rectangular?" You stay up too late searching Web sites about venues, menus, and hairstyles. Without ever meaning to, you become the type of woman who cries over a wedding dress on a fire escape.

Except I don't think that's why I was crying.

In the four months leading up to my glorious midwinter's-night breakdown I had bargained, begged, fought, and ended up in a therapist's office with my mom to get my dad involved in the wedding. And not even that involved. I told her that he wouldn't walk me down the aisle, and we wouldn't dance together, and he wouldn't talk to any of her friends. In return for these sacrifices he would be allowed to give Scott and me a large chunk of change for the festivities and have the chance to show up. The final condition she gave me was that he had to put all the money in a bank account before we booked a venue. She wouldn't agree to come to my wedding until I promised her this was done. I was twenty-eight years old and I was in the middle. Again.

"People think divorce begins and ends at the time of the breakup," says Dr. Wallerstein. "Divorce goes on throughout the child's whole life. The issues go on. Every decision has to be made long distance, and a wedding brings up every one of those decisions. The child is in high sea. In an intact family, you would sit down at the kitchen table and hash it out. In a divorced family, the wedding becomes a matter of state policy."

Every time the planning got rough, I fell apart. All I could think was, "I-don't-even-want-a-wedding-this-is-going-to-be-a-disaster-anyway-*whatamIdoing*?"

I Googled "divorced parents at wedding" to try to find a solution to my problem, but instead found a Q&A from an etiquette expert about where divorced parents should sit in the church during the wedding ceremony.

I tried "child of divorce getting married" and found a book published by my company about getting remarried after you've been divorced and have kids.

I lurked on the Dealing with Difficult Family Members message board on a Web site for independent-minded brides. Someone posted about her alcoholic stepfather, and others advised her to let him walk her down the aisle if it "felt right."

Ah, the aisle. The traditional role of the father of the bride is to walk his daughter down the aisle and "give her away." I had bartered with my dad's role to get him invited. That was out of the question. Then, I saw another message board post from a woman who had decided she would walk down the aisle with her fiancé. I loved this idea. Scott and I would walk in together. We'd start our lives together. I'd be a feminist and a diplomat! And my dad's feelings wouldn't be so hurt.

"But *my* feelings are hurt," my mother said to me with tears rolling down her face. We were in her therapist's office again. Discussions about the wedding could no longer take place without a mediator.

"Can you explain to Farah why it's so important for you to walk her down the aisle?" the therapist asked my mom, wiggling her toes in her Birkenstocks.

I don't remember what she said, but I walked out of that appointment having agreed to let my mother escort me into the arms of my new husband. We'd been a team for so long. She'd raised me. She wanted the wedding to reflect that, and suddenly it seemed as though I did too. She'd taught me to do my homework when I got home from school. She fought with me through my crankiest teenage years and laughed hysterically with me about everything from made-up Scrabble words to old-time family videotapes. I may have started to have a relationship with my dad, but my mom has always been my best friend. I was choosing her all over again because I knew she realized she'd been replaced in a way, and not by an ex-husband she thought was evil but by Scott—a partner she said she was happy for me to have found.

"Children in divorced families learn quickly that they have to adjust to different ways of being," says Dr. Wallerstein. "They have to be chameleons. They learn to be foreign ambassadors who aim to please everyone. They don't have the sense of 'I can be who I am.'"

By the time July rolled around, my dad was back for another business trip, and Scott was working at another new restaurant getting rave reviews. It was one of those uncomfortable sticky Manhattan summer days. This restaurant was a thirty-seat noodle bar, so the three of us sat on stools together watching Scott's boss and fellow chefs plate beautiful bowls of ramen. We were no more than three feet from the action in the kitchen.

My father was on a mission. He'd told me before he arrived in New York that he wanted to Talk About the Wedding.

"Farah, I want to give you away at your wedding." Scott looked up from his noodles. My father was sweating something fierce.

"But you agreed. . . ." I didn't know what else I could say. If I played ambassador now, my mom wouldn't come to my wedding. Why did everything come down to this minute-long walk down an aisle? I stood up and walked calmly out into the sweltering city streets. I turned the corner and tried to breathe. I couldn't. I decided it was time to call off this charade.

Yes, I called off the wedding. Try telling people that and explaining that you're not calling off your *marriage*, just your *wedding*. They think you're hiding something. They ask questions like, "Will you give the ring back?" And you wonder if you should stop wearing it, because when people see a shiny diamond on your finger they inevitably ask you when you're getting married.

I called in for reinforcements. My girlfriends came over the weekend after my dad left New York, and we went through the original list of options again. We decided I was making the right decision. Inviting my mother and father to the same wedding was out of the question.

There was only one problem. Scott and I had planned a totally kick-ass party. Our wedding was scheduled for December 10 at an inn in the Hudson Valley. We'd booked a jazz band from Brooklyn led by a woman who dyed her hair bright red and sang Miles Davis as well as my favorite song from *Willy Wonka and the Chocolate Factory*. And they included a vibraphonist. My mom and I had finally found a dress that didn't swallow me up in chiffon or satin or tulle, and it was a one-of-a-kind sample made by two men in Chelsea who gave it to me for 50 percent off the price. Not only did I love it, I looked thin in it. We were having an ice-cream-sundae bar.

And we wouldn't get any of our deposits back.

"So call your mom's bluff," my friend Andrea told me. "She's not going to really not show up at your wedding."

"Tell your dad he's not walking you down the aisle and he's gotta get over it," Jamie said.

"You can't cancel your wedding because of your parents!" many people said.

"My mom thinks you're right to call it off," my friend Jen countered. "You're spending too much money to throw a wedding that might turn into a disaster."

I probably asked too many people what they thought, and the one person I wasn't asking was Scott. Somewhere in the middle of my mom and my dad, I'd forgotten about him. When we finally talked about the situation, he was practical. He thought the twenty grand still left in the wedding bank account would be best spent on a down payment on our first home. He also didn't want to see me hurt.

"I just . . . I really want to have our wedding, though," he said.

"Me too," I said. "And I don't think I care if either of them is there."

I may have been lying to myself, and Scott may have known it. But that didn't matter. For the first time in twenty years, I realized my mother and father would never speak to each other. They would never understand why this upsets me so much, but it doesn't matter. I was done with the tears. I was mad at them for making this wedding so difficult.

"Scott, I want to have a WEDDING!" The anger felt so much better than trying to make anyone happy.

My parents didn't speak to each other at the wedding. My mom ignored my dad's side of the family. My father was nervous and awkward around her side. And none of it mattered.

Something magical happened. First, it snowed twelve inches on December 9. Big white fluffy flakes that stuck. We were in a winter wonderland, and all of our friends were there. My mom "gave me away" in the best possible fashion—when we got to the chuppah she beckoned for Scott to come take my hand and gave him a warm, welcoming smile. Scott delivered vows that made me fall in love with him all over again. At the reception, everyone twirled me around during our jazz band's version of the horah, even my dad. Later, the DJ played the Beastie Boys, the White Stripes, Bowie, Def Leppard . . . there was a sing-along to

"Eternal Flame" by the Bangles. My hair looked really healthy. I lost those last five pounds. I let go of my illusions about my parents. I realized that they don't have to reconcile in order for me to be happy. I found happiness in a more likely way; I married a man I love.

my
mother's wedding,
myself

From City Hall to Having It All

gina zucker

I crashed my mother's wedding. Before I go further I want to state up front that I love my mother. She buys me goofy socks and has nursed me through a thousand heartaches, and I am forever grateful to her. But she didn't tell me about her wedding. The only reason I did find out about it—just in time to crash it—was that my stepsister-to-be called me.

Ann's call came at work on a winter morning. At first I thought someone had died. My future stepsister and I liked each other but we rarely spoke on the phone. Although her father, Mannie, had lived with my mother for twenty-four years, Ann and her brother had grown up mostly with their mother. We were at different stages of our lives. Ann was thirteen years older, married, with kids, and spoke to her parents voluntarily and often, whereas I, in my twenties, avoided communicating with relatives as a rule. I had important things to do, such as drinking, meeting boys, hearing bands play in bars, and cultivating a writer's persona while doing as little writing as possible. So, Ann knew about the wedding; I didn't.

The gist of our conversation went like this:

ANN: Did you buy your plane ticket?

ME: Plane ticket?

ANN: To Burlington. They're getting married at City Hall. Tomorrow.

ME: Who?

ANN: Daddy and your mom.

ME: (*Dumbfounded silence.*)

My mother could at times be circumspect about her private life, and I wasn't the easiest person to reach, but the fact that she appeared to be sneaking in a marriage without notifying me came as a shock. I had been raised by her and Mannie, after all, and in their decades together I'd heard nary a peep about nuptials. Plus I was her only child. How could she have kept this from me?

Having worked myself up into a lather, I said good-bye to Ann and dialed my mother at her studio in Vermont, where she was making abstract sculpture inspired by before and after images of women who'd had plastic surgery.

"Why didn't you tell me?" I shrieked, momentarily forgetting where I was (in the busy office of an entertainment magazine where I'd just been hired).

"I don't know," my mother replied vaguely. "I wasn't thinking—I was trying to get everything done."

"Uh-huh," I said.

"Gina, it's just a civil ceremony; we didn't tell anyone. Are you upset?" Then my mother giggled, sounding uncharacteristically giddy.

"Yes, I'm upset," I said, trying to keep my voice down so my new cubicle mates wouldn't hear. My mother apologized, but I got the sense her mind was elsewhere. I felt like an indignant parent berating her child for eloping. Except the person eloping was my fifty-seven-year-old-divorced-feminist-artist-tenured-college-professor mother.

Well, I thought, *at least now I can call Mannie my step-father and not be lying*. A little background at this point might help. My father (who had a son from a previous marriage) moved out when I was four; my half brother went with him. A year later Mannie moved in, and never left. This turned out to be a good thing. When Mannie's first marriage ended he'd been so certain he wanted no more kids that he'd undergone a vasectomy. But from the beginning he treated me as a daughter. An architect and bon vivant, he cooked gourmet dinners and helped me with my math homework. He took us to Italy, his native country, for glorious vacations. He taught me to ski, drive a stick shift, and use a computer; most important, he survived both my and my mother's volatile temperaments with his love for us intact.

As for marriage, this institution was viewed in our household with a kind of amused irony, as if it were a quaint fad, a convention for people caught up in the petty trappings of bourgeois life. Born to artist-political radicals who fled Europe for America during World War II, Mannie had an instinctive aversion to governmental meddling. He saw no reason to bring the law into his love life. My mother, a 1970s feminist who battled for the ERA and began the first all-women's art gallery in the United States, came to see marriage with my father (an unrepentant old-school chauvinist) as a sexist construct that was more of a burden than a privilege. With Mannie, she had independence paired with the security of being loved by someone who shared her values. For the most part they kept their assets and finances separate. They traveled frequently—together and alone; they had their own careers and many friends, some mutual, some not. They were involved in local politics. They liked to throw dinner parties and eat and talk late into the night. As my mother once told me, when she and Mannie got together they'd started a conversation that had never really stopped. That was what made their relationship tick—not "some piece of paper."

As nicely as their unmarried status worked for them, it did cause some trickiness for me growing up. People often assumed Mannie was my father, or at the very least my stepfather. At some point I began to refer to him jokingly as my "Adult." To call him "my mother's boyfriend" seemed reductive, but I didn't want to call him "stepfather" either, since it implied a marriage that didn't exist. And he wasn't my dad—I already had one of those, every third weekend and for two weeks in the summer. Some people might have judged them, but to me, my mother and Mannie's decision not to marry seemed natural. That was who they were. And while I wished sometimes that my family were more "normal," I respected their choice.

So what was with the sudden hush-hush wedding? My mother assured me that no one was sick, no one was dying, but I felt unsatisfied. Telling only Ann, I got the next day off, bought a one-day round-trip ticket, and flew home.

.   .   .

As far as wedding crashing goes, my appearance went over well. When I showed up at my mother and Mannie's door a few minutes before they were to leave for City Hall—my flight had been delayed by a snowstorm—my mom screamed at the sight of me. "You came!" she yelled, jumping up and down a little. "You came!" In contrast to her blue wool dress, her face was bright red, a probable combination of excitement, anxiety, and high blood pressure. After a round of hugging, the five of us—Ann, my mother's best friend, the happy couple, and me—squeezed into the family Saab and drove into town.

The no-nonsense civil ceremony was officiated in a gray-carpeted room on the third floor of the courthouse on Main Street, by a female judge friend of theirs with blond highlights. It would have been dull, were it not for my mother's hysterical weeping throughout the entire event. From the moment the judge began to recite the vows, my mother started gushing—not discreet tears that one dabs at with a hankie, but full-on waterworks and wailing. I can still hear her repeating, "For richer and for poorer, sniff-sniff, in sickness and in health—WAAAAAAAH-HAAAA."

No one else cried. I think we were slightly stunned by my mother's show of emotion. Secretly, however, I related. The truth was, at twenty-eight I'd been fantasizing about my own wedding for years. No matter how stressful things became with the boyfriend of the moment, I could always lose myself in a warm and fuzzy matrimonial daydream. The ceremony would take place on the beach where I'd spent my childhood summers; I'd wear a flowing gown and flowers in my hair. My father and Mannie would both walk me down the seashell-strewn aisle, and my mother and grandmother would weep copiously (how my wheelchair-bound grandmother would maneuver herself onto the sand was something I'd figure out later). My bridesmaids would wear pretty sundresses. Every friend I'd ever had, plus a few famous writers and musicians who magically became my pals for the occasion, would assemble in an adulatory crowd. Afterward, as the sun set over the dunes and the sea turned purple, witty toasts and bacchanalian dancing would ensue.

The only thing missing from my flight of fancy: a groom.

But at my mother's wedding I felt strangely removed from the proceedings, as if I were the one who was missing. My mother's best friend videotaped the ceremony as Ann and I stood off to the side, Ann smiling, me zoning out. Mannie kept patting my mother on the arm. When it was over, my mother stepped back, stared at her new husband, and said in a voice full of wonder, "I did it! I married you!" At that moment I felt the significance of what they'd done. It was a fleeting but powerful rush. Maybe, if you found the right groom, you could do without the grand setting and all the rest.

. . .

Now, seven years later, Mannie and my mother are still happily hitched, and I, at thirty-five, have finally become engaged. It took two long dead-end relationships, a few hundred dates, and several hundred more sobbing heart-to-hearts with friends, my mother, and my shrink, but it seems I've finally found a groom with not only a face (handsome) and a body (hot), but a beautiful soul as well. Although Russ and I come from very different backgrounds (let's just say his family would never give Fidel Castro a letter saying *Mi casa es tu casa*, as Mannie once did), we share the experience of having divorced parents and strong, career-minded mothers.

The morning after Russ proposed, the first thing I did was call my mother. "Are you sitting down?" I asked. "I'm engaged!" It felt surreal—I'd been waiting to say those words to her for as long as I'd been waiting to hear, "Will you marry me?" from a man I love. I was expecting a scream, but instead my mother asked me to repeat myself.

"Engaged," she said, almost whispering. "Wow. En-gaged." I felt a pang of uncertainty. Did I sound bour-geois?

"Yes, Mom!" I spoke loudly to make up for her under-whelming response. "Russ and I are getting married!"

"I guess you really love him," my mother said. I re-pressed the urge to hang up. Russ and I had been together for a year and three months. He'd met my various parents a few times, and while my father jokingly called Russ "the best thing that ever happened to me" (meaning to him), it was hard to say what my mother thought of my fiancé.

On a rational level, I couldn't blame her reticence. Until now, all my romantic relationships had ended in tears. What mother wants to see her daughter heartsick? But this love was different. Wasn't it? When we announced our news to Russ's family over lunch in Brooklyn, their reaction struck a different tone. "OH, MY GOD!" his mother boomed as she rushed around the table to embrace us both. "OH, THAT'S WONDERFUL!" echoed his grandmother and his aunt. In turn, his brother, his uncle, and his mother's boyfriend rose to kiss me and slap Russ on the back. Russ's mother wanted us to "TELL HER EVERY-THING" about our plans for when and where we'd marry and what my dress would look like—stuff we hadn't even begun to consider. It was overwhelming, and I liked it.

So began the planning of my long-dreamed-of wedding day. By now I had attended most of my friends' weddings, not to mention their kids' first and second birthday parties. I thought I had a pretty good idea of what to expect and what to avoid. No grotesquely swollen wedding budgets for me! I would do things my way—laid-back yet elegant, fun, and unpretentious. I discovered that a wedding on the beach in the Hamptons, or anywhere in the Hamptons for that matter, would be prohibitively expensive and complicated. We began to look in our own neighborhood—Brooklyn—for a venue. But even when I spotted a "reasonably priced" caterer listed on the Web or tracked down a reception hall that charged less than ten thousand bucks a night, the ease with which I could see our life savings dwindle boggled the mind.

As Russ and I struggled to figure out what sort of wedding we wanted and what we could actually afford, I couldn't help but think about the way my mother and Mannie did it. When I told my mom how things were going, she tried to reassure me. "It's not a competition. You don't have to spend a lot of money if you keep it small. Mannie and I didn't spend anything on the ceremony except for the marriage license." I reminded her that they'd had a big bash several months later to celebrate with their friends. But I knew the party didn't cost much—they had it at a friend's house, the hostess cooked all the food, Ann brought cupcakes, and Mannie and my mother bought the wine.

"You don't have to make yourself crazy," my mother continued. "Keep it simple. It sounds corny, but the wedding is just one day. The real celebration is the rest of your lives—focus on that." How right she was, and yet I found myself resisting this wisdom. Who cares if it's just one day—it's the day I've been waiting for my whole life! I called my grandmother, who put in her two cents. "Have a little luncheon; lots of people are doing it now, and it's much less pricey." I got a few e-mails from Mannie. He wrote: "I think weddings should be done at City Hall, by a justice of the peace. That's how everyone in my family got married. Have a party later, when you have the time and money. All that other stuff is advertising." My father was concerned about money in his own way—he said he couldn't pay for a wedding, and I knew he was hoping my grandmother, mother, and Mannie would pick up the slack.

I was grossed out by Bridezilla culture, but each time I talked to one of my "keep-it-cheap" relatives my reaction was increasingly, "Bring on the pouf and circumstance!" In a fit of mixed emotions, I bought the spring issue of *Bride* magazine. As I perused its glossily exotic pages, I was only partly amused, partly turned off by its siren call to wedding frippery; the other part of me was absorbed by the signs and symbols harking fairy-tale bliss. I asked Russ what he thought—should we just go to City Hall with the dog walker as our witness? Though this option appealed to both of our practical sides, Russ wanted more, too. "If nothing else," he said, "I want our ceremony to be special; I don't want to stand in line in some grimy room downtown."

Right on! I thought. Maybe the bells and whistles were important because they represented something missing from our childhoods: tradition. Now tradition could be ours! In my case, my parents chose unconventional relationships (my father has had many girlfriends over the years and married none of them), but I didn't want one foot out the door of my marriage. A wedding ritual with trimmings underscored my hope for permanence. It was a way to trumpet the beginning of something strong and stable.

I explained this to my mother. "I get it," she said. And did she. A check for several thousand dollars came in the mail. Apparently she talked to Mannie, because he pledged the same amount. My grandmother said she would help cover what was left.

Then my mother called and announced she'd bought me a dress. She braved a one-day wedding-gown sale in Vermont and scored, for $98, a white, puffy department-store sample with silk flowers and buttons sewn down the back. It sounded utterly unlike the more modern look I'd imagined for myself, but the dress from Mom was like a green light. In a flurry, Russ and I chose a park on the water for our ceremony, with views of the Brooklyn Bridge and the Manhattan skyline. We booked a light-filled loft for the reception, signed on an Asian-themed caterer, a funky florist, and two talented friends to sing songs for the processional and recessional. We found Jesse, a self-anointed "Rabbinister" who practiced "humanitarian pagan spiritualism," to marry us. In honor of my Jewish heritage, which I mostly ignored until becoming a bride, Jesse would help us incorporate some Jewish-wedding elements into the ritual, such as the chuppah canopy and breaking the glass. I even went shopping with one of my bridesmaids and ended up with three bow-adorned Diane Von Furstenberg sundresses that complemented the dress my mom gave me.

. . .

It is now just under three months until the wedding. Every once in a while I second-guess myself. Despite my conviction not to become the full-time control-freak bride featured in reality TV, sometimes she possesses me. I do nothing with my days, it seems, but research, plan, and think obsessively about the details of my wedding. There are epic struggles over the guest list with our mothers; my poufy gown turns out to be sun-damaged and has to be replaced; I have paroxysms of anxiety about rain. In these moments I shove aside the bursting folder marked "wedding" and drop my head between my knees, wondering if the expense and effort are really worth it. The invitations are not yet in the mail; we haven't found a photographer; the caterer and florist and loft people have not been paid. We could still call it off.

I do what I always do when tormented by confusion: I talk to my fiancé. Only today, when I ask him for the umpteenth time if we should elope, Russ—my rock, my font of calm and reason—doesn't give me an easy answer. He doesn't reassure me that everything will be fine and that I should just relax. Instead, he says, "The guest list is three-quarters your family and friends." I cringe inwardly. "So if we call it off, it's not such a big deal for me. I'm perfectly happy to have a small ceremony in the park and then go out for dinner with a few people. But is that really what you want?"

I think about it. I consider our friends and relatives, ready to show up and rejoice. I see them getting jiggy on the dance floor to the music Russ and I have compiled and sung to, out of tune, in our car. I picture my three oldest friends—now wives and mothers—wearing their bridesmaid sundresses, standing by me as they always have. I envision the dramatic views of the city that will be the backdrop to our wedding vows. I think about walking down the aisle with Mannie on one arm and my dad on the other, and me probably bawling like my mother, who will be bawling in her chair as she watches me finally do this thing. I look at Russ, who is looking back. The answer seems clear after all.

father of the bride

kathleen hughes

♥

A little before three o'clock in the afternoon, I climbed into the driver's seat of my sister's Volvo, still wearing the well-loved cotton housedress that reminded me of my great-grandmother. My wedding dress and veil, both of which had been worn by my mother, were laid out in the way back of the wagon, and my sister, seven months pregnant and counting, smoothed her bridesmaid dress down before sitting in the passenger seat. Mom, my four-year-old niece—the flower girl—and my sister-in-law, also seven months pregnant, sat in the backseat. We were quiet. It was hot, suddenly, after a spate of cool weather the previous week, and there was a haze over the lake that meant you could not distinguish the horizon from the sky. I felt calm, almost vague.

I drove along the big lake—Lake Michigan—to the point where an unruly inlet lake interrupted our progress. I was aware that Tim and I were about to do something rather intimate in front of one hundred or so people. I wondered what he was doing at that moment, how he was feeling. I wondered how my brother was feeling as he prepared to escort me to the altar. I wondered one last time about the details, as if watching a roller coaster tick up the crest of a hill—the music at the church and at the reception, the four-course dinner coming from eighty-year-old kitchen equipment and an insufficient amount of fridge and freezer space. The wine and booze and buttercream-frosted cake and the band I still worried might not show up. The Porta Potties, which had been delivered in error to some poor stranger's front yard. The previous night's cookout and beach bonfire felt so immediate, I could have believed it was still going on behind me, and I wished it were. Guests had trickled in from the same time zone and from several zones removed; some I hadn't seen in several years, some I had seen ten months ago, at my father's funeral. Time felt like it was accelerating; I would have preferred it to slow down.

It was the last turn around the back of the little lake, approaching the bridge where swans and fishermen gathered, when Meghan took a framed picture of Dad from her bag and said, "I brought this along for you."

"Thanks, that's nice," I said, reminding myself that I wasn't interested in crying. Crying in public has always been deeply embarrassing to me. When I was a young competitive swimmer, I was proud that I did not cry after bad races, or at least, I did it underwater on my warm-down laps, where no one could see or hear. As an adult, I simply don't cry in public. Though crying in a car with my family would not constitute crying in public, I was afraid that if I started, I might not stop. There was also the fact that I'd long since decided the day was meant to be about Tim and me, not about my father's death. I pushed my eyebrows close together and clenched my throat tight.

A mile farther on, nearly to the church, I brushed the bumper of a farmer in front of me who was turning with irresponsible slowness. I laid into the horn. "GO, you fucker!" I hollered. He gave me the finger and crept through the intersection with all the haste of a slug.

"She's the bride, you a-hole," my sister said inside the car. We laughed. Meghan looked at her watch. "Kath, you've got plenty of time. Really."

I nodded but accelerated quickly anyway. Adrenaline still floored me. I wanted this to go well. My wedding. *Our* wedding.

In the balcony at the church, flowers were waiting and the brass quintet was warming up. This was good. My brother arrived with a cold can of beer for me (at my sister's wintertime wedding, he'd brought a flask of bourbon). I left the cotton dress in a pile at my feet as I stepped into Mom's wedding dress, and as Meghan and my sisters-in-law worked on the many buttons, I took a gentle, careful swig of Coors Light, thinking I probably hadn't had one since high school. I peeked over the balcony to see Tim striding up to the front of the church, talking to the grooms-men, looking a little anxious. I wanted to be down there with him already, but I was eased just to look at him.

. . .

The previous summer, we had gathered around my dad's hospital bed in Indianapolis, where I grew up, playing his favorite music and saying whatever we could think to say— "last words," in theory, though I found the concept ludicrous. (He couldn't hear us, not with all those drugs, and what would I say anyway, with everyone gathered?) He had lost a medical lotto of sorts, improbably spawning a septic infection after relatively minor brain surgery, related to a small, benign tumor. The jackpot was four weeks on a respirator in intensive care, with a second infection and sepsis as the final bonus prize. That morning, fatally low blood pressure meant his veins resembled a deflated pool raft, and synthetic adrenaline was keeping him alive until his sister arrived on a plane from Washington, D.C., and my brother on a plane from New York.

At some point, Mom said to him, "I guess you won't be able to walk Kathleen down the aisle." She resumed crying, and I moved my face in an expression of disgust that got us off the topic of my wedding, which didn't even exist at that point. I was exhausted, nauseous, and the events around me were ungraspable. Everything was distorted, a bad cliché. The only way I knew that my father's impending death was real was that I couldn't say it out loud. I'd made several phone calls that morning. "Please come," I'd said to my mother's brother, trying to pull out the ugly warbles in my voice. "As soon as possible."

"Come today," I said to Tim, when I called his office in Rhode Island. "Pack your suit. Call me when you have your flight. OK?" Then I hung up.

I hated what my mother said about Dad not walking me down the aisle because it contributed to the melodrama, the TV version, the, in fact, *silliness* of it all. What about his missing the publication of my first novel, which he carefully edited? What about the fact that my children would have no idea what he was like? I also hated the wedding reference because it was so exclusively about *me*, and although I'd done a fair amount of feeling sorry for myself that month, most self-absorption evaporated the moment I realized he was, in fact, going to die. *I* would assimilate to his death. Most everything I wanted from life I could still have. But *he* would be gone and he would leave a thready, unmendable hole in the world for many people. He had so many talents, so many pleasures, so many ways of living. It would be easier, I thought, never to speak to him again than it would be to get used to the idea of his not being in the world. And this, above all, is why I scoffed at my mother's comment. Who gives a shit, I wanted to say, about one currently nonexistent big expensive party where I wear a white dress. Dad won't be *anywhere*.

. . .

Perhaps I would've been more concerned about my father missing my wedding if he hadn't known Tim, if it hadn't already seemed likely that we'd marry. Tim had known my father for two years before his death. On their introductory dinner, my dad described a shaggy dog of a dream that had us all scratching our heads, but then the punch line involved white mules, the mascot of Tim's alma mater, and the compliment inherent in Dad's scheme—he paid attention to how I sounded about Tim on the phone; he was going out of his way to flatter Tim—flushed me with pleasure.

There were a few Christmases and Easters and one Indy 500 spent together. Then, during the first week of Dad's hospitalization, Tim joined me in Indiana and took a couple two to six a.m. bedside shifts, doing crosswords and holding Dad's hand and making gentle jokes about it, since Dad was still somewhat lucid, and he wasn't someone who usually wanted his hand held by his youngest daughter's boyfriend. We had one hotel room across the street, since the nine-mile drive to my parents' house was too far the first week, and Tim and I rotated through naps in one of the beds, while my mother, my sister, my brother, and/or my brother- or sister-in-law slept in the other bed. Tim's truest induction into my family came that weekend, and although my father was in and out of sedation, I know he knew Tim was there.

I picked Tim up myself at the airport an hour after Dad died. Memories of that time exist in still frames, and I remember Tim rising off the escalator, and I see myself not wanting to meet his eyes. I'm surprised I can see at all, I feel so swollen, so disoriented, plus the usual, excruciating embarrassment of crying in public, and then he's dropped his bags and his arms are around me.

.   .   .

When we were all together for a September 11 funeral about eight weeks after Dad's death, Tim asked my mother about proposing marriage to me. He asked my sister and brother next, and he finally asked me to marry him in late October at the bottom of a bluff on Block Island. Though I was a little surprised at the timing, or afraid that others would be troubled by it, I also felt stronger for it, and brave and honest—we wanted to get married and we didn't expect anyone, including me, to put aside sadness. What, I asked myself, did I consider "better" timing—when exactly would my family and I be less sad? I thought back to sitting around in the living room the night Dad died. There was an extra car at my parents' house, and there had been a several-months'-long discussion of who should have it. Tim's car had recently been stolen and so I'd asked for the extra car for us a few times. The extra car was Dad's Mazda Rx-7, retired but beloved. That night, we talked about many logistical things: the calling, the funeral, who would do what the next day. I have no memory of the prompt for what came next, and very possibly there was none, but with Tim sitting at her feet, Mom blurted out, "Tim can have the Mazda when Kathleen gets a ring." She wasn't thinking and never meant to say such a thing in front of Tim. But we all laughed long and hard, even on that night—even then. The memory of it made me think that our wedding could similarly be a single, happy spot in a long, tight spell of sadness.

We planned a small Midwest wedding away from Indianapolis—away from where we'd have to avoid the funeral church and reception country club, and where the list could easily grow past one hundred, which I felt I couldn't handle. Pentwater is the rural Michigan beach town where I'd spent many summers, always romantic in my life, and romantic in a way that Tim and I shared: good food and long beach days and books and sports and family and music. Pentwater was also Tim's kind of place more than any city or country club would be, in part because he had grown up in a small Rhode Island beach town. To boot, he wouldn't wear a tux in Pentwater, and the dance floor would invariably be dusted with white sand. Though Pentwater was rife with memories of my father, I believed a wedding there could be both more intimate and more appropriate to Tim and me.

I asked my brother over the phone to walk me down the aisle. He wanted to know if he could wear seersucker and I said yes, absolutely. I wondered after hanging up if I hadn't squandered a nice moment by asking this over the phone, but my instinct was to ask casually, so I did. As for the rest of the planning, I had visions of it being a true, portentous Tim-Kathleen partnership. Yet the reality of tiny Pentwater being eight hundred miles away and unfamiliar to Tim meant I planned much of the three-day event myself with a notebook full of scribbles and phone numbers, while he took on the "mystery" Canadian honeymoon. In my file cabinet, the wedding file rotated ahead and behind, in between "Dad Memorial Contribution thank-you" and "Dad medical bills," which were my other consuming activities at the time.

Perhaps I missed my father the most during the planning stages. He would have given the process grace, confidence, and a simplicity that I could never feel. Instead of my disintegrating notebook, he would have had a three-ring binder, divided by days and by food, lodging, guests, maps, music, and he would have had definitive opinions and gut takes on people, like the band agent and the caterers, who baffled me. My dad was also a map guy, so when that task fell to me one miserable half-rainy-half-snowy day in March, it was excruciating. I couldn't get a map of the area right—and given that the wedding was literally in the middle of nowhere for the many guests flying in or driving numerous hours, we needed a good map. Tim will point to that day and say I kind of lost it then, holing myself up with the computer and then at Kinko's for too many hours, speaking few words until it was complete, then crashing into bed and not being able to sleep.

I thus discovered that I'm a doer of a griever. I become slightly manic to distract myself from grief, then wonder why I don't feel much (besides exhaustion). Finally, something like map day happens, and I simply drop, out, down, away. It was funny, therefore, to be occasionally pigeonholed as a manic bride, because I rarely felt, during the engagement, that (manic) bride and (grieving) daughter were distinct from each other. And this feeling, perhaps, above all, meant I was determined not to be either one on the actual day of my wedding.

I arrived in Michigan with only my mother and our dogs two full weeks before the wedding. I communed with my father and exercised my body and spirit in the best way I knew how. I used a putty knife to clean accumulated dirt, crud, and maple wings from between the deck boards, all one thousand square feet of them. I located the origin of a potent stench—a rotting raccoon in the woods—and asked my year-rounder neighbor to bury it. I washed all the outdoor furniture and realphabetized the spice drawer while listening to show tunes. I walked the dogs on the beach in the morning and at night. During long runs, I wrote a hundred eloquent, subtle toasts to my "husband." And though I continued to hope that I'd be awakened one morning by Dad firing up a power tool downstairs, I knew how much he, too, would love the coming weekend, and that made me happy, not sad.

Tim arrived on Tuesday before the wedding, and we ditched family to go out to dinner alone. After eating, we walked out onto the long cement channel that provided boat access from Lake Michigan to the Pentwater Harbor. I remember only the revelation of being together again, after a few weeks' separation, of being together in that place, with a notion of what we were about to do, of having stolen time away from our families and the numerous "to dos" to enjoy each other. I think my calmness that weekend, the sense of sailing across an almost unnaturally calm surface, began with our date that night, standing on the channel at sunset.

As most wedding days do, mine flew by. After nearly rear-ending that car and flipping the bird right back at the driver, the afternoon and evening were a blur. My young nieces and nephew were shy and serious and perfect in their roles. I breezed down the aisle. My brother Jimmy kissed Tim at the altar, awkward if it hadn't been on purpose, and then I immediately set to calming Tim down. I mixed up right from left during the ring exchange. We had tin cans tied to the back of our car, and we laughed through our whole fox-trot. Dinner was delicious, the wine was perfect, and my toast was bumbling. And I felt like I exhaled one breath for a solid five minutes as Tim and I drove out of town the next morning with our dogs barking in the back of the Volks-wagen. It seemed about four hours since the whole weekend started.

· · ·

A half year later, at Christmastime, I had a late-morning dream that we were having another wedding, except this one was in Indianapolis, at the church where I grew up, and Dad was organizing it all. Wedding guests were every-where. Dad met me in the parking lot. His suit was perfect and his shirt seemed starched, though starch irritated his skin, and he wore a yellow pocket square and a yellow striped tie. I was pleased because he looked so good, like himself, not like he had in the hospital. We had the pre-dictable father-daughter moment, and I said it was time to go into the church and he nodded: "Yes, and it will all be fine. But I have to go now. I can't stay." Even in my dream, I was thinking, *This is such a stupid dream, this is so "ABC After School Special,"* but I was gasping hard, sucking in, wheezing with shock, and I couldn't speak; Tim, awake and spooning me on the real-world side of things, asked me if I was okay, what was wrong, why was I breathing like that, while in my dream, I crumpled to the asphalt: Dad had left.

Every so often I'll wake up knowing I've dreamed of Dad, knowing I'll spend the day once again getting used to the idea of his not being at his desk in Indianapolis, his voice not greeting me on the phone. Surely I missed having my father at my wedding; surely it was "easy" not having him there because I wanted it to be "easy." But I also know Dad would have wanted it that way. Though he loved good traditions, such as walking his daughter down the aisle, he was also one of the most considerate, self-deferential people I'll ever know. He would not have considered the walk down the aisle or the father-daughter dance at the reception the primary aspects of my wedding. He would have emphasized that he was essentially a bystander to Tim's and my joining, and this must be why, in my dream, he sent me in alone.

getting
hitched

first, reader,
i made him up, and
then i married him

jacquelyn mitchard

I used to buy wedding dresses. Ivory lace jackets. Delicate beige suits. Costumes for second weddings. It was a kind of hobby because I never really expected, after more than four years as a widow, to marry again. I would sometimes, though, take out my picture hats and fingerless lace mitts and try them on, to imagine how I might look on the day I confounded the odds.

But every day, the odds seemed stacked more firmly against me. And I was so bored and discouraged by dating that I'd given it up.

How is it possible, you may ask, that a widow aged forty years old with four children under the age of twelve (including a toddler and a rebellious boy) *could* get sick of dating? Isn't the better question to ask, how does such a woman, who does not resemble Demi Moore or Susan Sarandon or even their fatter sisters, even have the *option* to give up dating at all? I was a woman living in a populated area, at the end of the twentieth century—not the kind of nineteenth-century widder woman a cowboy might marry for love of her barn—in other words, for security and three square meals a day. I had assets, but not necessarily the kind that modern men considered value-added.

And yet, I am not lying.

People did come a'courting and I, alas, did tire of them.

They were all nice enough fellows.

There were sweethearts from the past with busted marriages, orthodontists I approached with fervent hopes for free braces in the future, a hotelier and former English soccer pro young enough to be my, uh . . . younger cousin. But all of them failed the critical test. They weren't father material. If I were to marry, the man would be the only father my children would ever know, the only father whom the young ones would truly remember. Either these men blanched when they heard about the size and variability of my brood or visibly glazed over when I regaled them with tales of my posse. For me it was a case of this: Love me; love my crew. And that wasn't happening.

And so, as I have done so often, trudging grimly across an arid expanse, I cried into my pillow and turned to my pages.

In my second novel, I created the man I wouldst marry, no Tim, Dick, or Harry, but Charley Wilder, a sexy younger guy with a ripped T-shirt and ripped biceps beneath it, who had a degree and a tie, liked classical music, and considered the idea of having a big family deeply erotic. "Too bad Charley Wilder doesn't exist in nature," my friends wrote as I sent them chapters to read. A free spirit, Charley slept in a woven hammock from the Yucatán he'd strung across his living room. He had a tool belt with three pockets instead of the usual two. He knew all about botany; he could dance, and (most urgently, as I am shallow) he looked like David Duchovny. (And yes, that last part really made my friends snort.) But I could dream—the law against it had not yet been passed in 1998—and Charley on paper was more fun than Joe or Mike or Eric or Ted in real life. In my book, he courted the stiff and edgy lawyer Annie Singer until, against all reason, she gave in. He came to do carpentry on her house and ended by covering her bridal bed with orchids. They had a baby, although she was too old, because he just couldn't wait to have a family.

No wonder reviewers found the story line unrealistic.

My author's copies of *The Most Wanted* were sitting unopened in the hall on the morning the doorbell rang, and my daughter Francie, wearing her floor-length summer nightgown, her long dark hair in a tangle, opened it. I heard a voice ask her, "Are you a Mayan princess?"

Francie answered insouciantly, "Yes, I am." She was two at the time and didn't know not to talk to strangers. So I unrolled myself from the couch where I'd been catching a postworkout nap, resplendent in my ripped biking shorts and Texas Rangers ball cap, and looked into the clear-water-blue eyes of one of the cutest guys I'd ever seen. My assistant would later tell me I had that look people get after a near-death experience.

"Hi, sport," said the guy, who looked to be about twenty-one. (He was, in fact, thirty-two.) I felt myself assume the demeanor of a puddle of warm pudding; and the fact that I could neither speak nor look at him did not augur a relationship. I pointed the way upstairs to where he would be doing . . . carpentry, and though I was too young for a hot flash, I flushed when he strapped on his tool belt (three pockets, not two). He was obsessed with measuring, he later told me in passing, because he liked a tight fit. I remained conscious.

The next morning, I prepared to greet him—having employed mascara and a curling iron. He didn't show up. By ten, I was furious. By eleven, I had decided not to put my faith in tool belts. I had changed back into a sweatshirt from a sweater by the time he showed up in his absurd yellow van. He apologized. He had remained up far too late, reading my novel, a copy of which my assistant had thoughtfully given him, and he wondered if we might later take a few minutes to discuss it.

Discuss my novel? A guy who looked like this wanted to *discuss my novel?* In my experiences, deltoids like his did not usually coincide with bookishness. But my first novel, he mentioned, had been one of his mother's top ten all-time favorites. He had himself not read it, but hoped to.

And so, we began to spend half our workdays gabbing in my garage, sitting on overturned plaster buckets. I was fixing up my house to sell and working on my third novel.

Chris had a degree in studio arts but was proud of being a carpenter. He had made beautiful environments, gazebos, multitiered and unusually shaped, and loved the botanical aspect of his work. He hoped within the year to move to New Mexico. I caught myself hoping against his hopes.

It didn't take a psychic to recognize that I had conjured up Charley Wilder . . . from longing and imagination, and somehow, the universe had listened and sent my vision to me. He had the look, the demeanor, and the, ah, equipment of the man I'd created in the novel, the one who convinced Annie Singer (who, like me, had been around the block before the block had sidewalks) to give up her misgivings about men in general and be swept away—into his hammock and his love.

Still, I wasn't sure for some weeks.

What I had, I realized in days to come, was a giggly teenage crush. So did Chris. We rode around in his van and sat on the hood looking at the stars. We lost a combined total of about twenty pounds. And we never did a single thing but hold hands. Chris didn't want to kiss me, he told me, because he didn't like things that ended, and if this was to be a thing that ended, he wanted it to end with a friendship instead of a premature and truncated love affair. Still, late at night, he called me, and while my children banged furiously on the bathroom door, we talked absurdity and gush for hours. We sang to Tom Petty on the radio. We talked obliquely about how some men *liked* marrying women with children, and how some older women needed a younger man to keep up.

The first time I visited his sparse apartment, I noticed the eighteen-foot hammock from the Yucatán strung across the living room.

The second time I visited, he proposed. The way he put it was this: "I've been wondering. I think you're remarkable. And you seem to think I am. And so, I thought I'd ask if you would do me the honor of marrying me?"

I reminded him about my children, with whom he'd been playing basketball in our yard after work, the closest I'd ever allowed any man I had dated to come to them.

"I'd like ten children," he announced.

I asked when he hoped this nuptial event might take place. He said, "Well, let's see, what's today? Saturday? Do they do weddings on Monday?"

I gulped. But the universe had indeed handed me my fantasy on a plate. I gulped again and nodded. Mad with excitement, unable to sleep, we went for breakfast at one of those horrible pancake places where everyone is up too early or too late. In what I would learn was a statement characteristic of him, Chris said, "Tonight, I'm only grateful that I'm not anyone else on earth." He paused, glancing at the behemoth farmers and scrawny Goth children around us. "Especially anyone in this restaurant."

At six a.m., we went to the house of my best friend, who'd been a rabbi, and asked her if she would marry us on Wednesday. She had been invited that coming Wednesday night to a dinner in Ohio to sit with President Clinton. She declined in order to perform our marriage instead. Finally, we headed to my house.

When I told my sons I was going to be married, after nearly five years of widowhood, my eldest wondered, "May I ask, to whom?"

And my youngest son pulled me aside and asked, "Does this mean he'll *live* here?"

I'd phoned the people whose country house I was in the process of buying to ask whether I might bring by a few friends to see the place on a night just a few days hence. How we pulled this together is still a mystery. Of course, I had the dress—I had a closet of selections. But I needed a bouquet with violet orchids (an obliging neighbor and bridesmaid went to work on that). We made phone calls to extra-close friends and relatives, many of whom had the same reaction as my ever-tolerant brother: "Married. To the Zen carpenter. Wednesday. Right. Well, game on!" My father was so confused he thought I was asking him to *someone else's* wedding. One friend surreptitiously surprised me with a gift of two white limos that showed up later in the afternoon, drawing the attention of the neighborhood. My assistant hired out a room at my favorite Italian restaurant, and a baker buddy whipped up a multitiered carrot cake for the chocolate-allergic bride. A photographer who'd often taken book publicity shots for me agreed to shoot the wedding all in black and white, and on two days' notice. When Chris's dad asked what the rush was, we were able to reply that it wasn't us; it was everything around us. We weren't afraid we'd back out; we were afraid that so many people would give us so much adverse advice that we wanted to put their words back into their mouths before they came out.

Though all the bustle, I was curiously calm, and "calm" is not a word often used in connection with me. In fact, a friend once told me of the Zen philosophy "Be like snow," in other words, fall softly on the earth but still nurture it, as does the rain. She said, "In your case, I'd suggest, be like hail." I had chosen the loveliest and laciest of my wedding dresses: an ivory ballet-length skirt and a fitted bodice with a high neck in front that dropped away in the rear view to nothing at my waist. It was May thirteenth; I got twenty-one mosquito bites on my beautiful back in the twenty-minute ceremony, in which we promised to honor each other with all that we were and all that we had, in a variation of the words from the Book of Common Prayer.

The previous owners of the house I was buying, who were still in residence, promised to vanish but later heard about the limousines in the neighborhood, and we heard they got a giggle out of it. Chris's mother, who looked to be the same age as her son, pulled him aside and said, "All I asked you to do was get her to sign my book!" My brother hugged Chris and asked, "Have you ever seen my sister . . . get mad? Think the Red Queen in *Alice in Wonderland.* I admire you."

Each of my three boys had chosen a passage to read. The eldest read from Robert Frost's famous poem, "Two roads diverged in a wood, and I, I took the one less traveled by, and that has made all the difference."

My middle son read from *A River Runs Through It,* "Eventually, all things merge into one, and a river runs through it . . . on some of the rocks are timeless raindrops. Under the rocks are the words."

And my youngest son, just seven, read from *Charlotte's Web*, "It is not often someone comes along who is a true friend and a good writer. Charlotte was both."

At the reception, friends made side bets on how long this marriage, a culmination of a five-week courtship, would endure. The long shot was a year.

But it has been eight years, three more children, whales of laughter and oceans of tears since that day. We married in haste and wondered at leisure just what we had done. But I am stubborn and so is he. And we were both committed, in part, to prove the doubters wrong. The children quickly let it be known that even if we occasionally yell at each other like people in an opera—and, at first, we did—no one was going anywhere. And no one has.

Writing has its own way of making things manifest. I don't have a spiritual bone in my body, but putting things down somehow seems to nudge at least some of them into being, perhaps because, as we write them, we bring them forth so utterly from the core of ourselves. Silly as it sounds, I'm convinced, this one time, that I fictionalized not my own past, but my own future.

And by the way, we got four hammocks as wedding gifts.

the second trimester

ruth davis konigsberg

♥

Our engagement came as a surprise to no one, especially me. Eric and I were both thirty-five. We had met at a dog run where we took our canine companions, Camby and Rennie, a scenario so marvelously clichéd it recently found its way into a mediocre John Cusack movie. Two weeks into our relationship, we were already talking about spending the rest of our lives together. Eric was everything I wanted: caring, highly literate, in therapy. When you're in your mid-thirties and finally fall in love, things can happen awfully fast.

Five short months later, Eric proposed. Once engaged, we had no problem with the wedding planning being as whirlwind as the courtship, and it seemed as if no hurdles could get in our way.

We began the premarital merging of two lives; we each sold our apartments, with no regrets plus great nontaxable capital gain, and moved into a cozy two-bedroom apartment in Greenwich Village. Even before Eric popped the question, we'd scouted out our ideal wedding location—an old hot springs resort in southwestern Montana—and immediately reserved a date. Eric's parents, who were throwing the rehearsal dinner at their house near the resort, announced that they'd be giving us an exotic honeymoon on safari in South Africa as a wedding present, the trip of a lifetime.

Even buying a dress was swift and painless—I chose one off the rack at RK Bridal, an unglamorous warehouse in midtown Manhattan, for $800. It was off-white with blue embroidered floral trim, perfect for a ceremony taking place in a field of alfalfa with the northern Rockies as a backdrop. The A-line cut accentuated my best feature, my waist, but the sleeveless bodice accentuated my worst, my upper arms. (When did all wedding dresses start looking like *ball gowns* anyway?) Undeterred, I ordered a bolero jacket to throw over my shoulders during the ceremony and take off as the evening progressed indoors.

Since I'd recently left my editing job to become a freelance writer, I decided that I finally had time to hire a personal trainer and get in shape. But not just any personal trainer. I called the author of an exercise book entitled *Buff Brides* and arranged to begin sessions with her right away. That gave me at least five months before our wedding date in late June.

At some point during this flurry of activity, I started having the following thought: *I'll be thirty-five this year. If we want to have kids, it can take anywhere from six months to a year to conceive.* And then this thought: *Why not "start trying"?* I did some quick math: If I got pregnant now, I'd be in my second trimester for the wedding, late enough so that I wouldn't be puking and early enough so that I wouldn't be enormous. I broached it with Eric. He was on deadline with his first book; it had been five years in the making. "Okay, cool," he said. "Maybe they'll come out at the same time." Unfortunately, I didn't pose this question to anyone else, or I might have been told what I would say to anyone who asked me today, which is, "Be careful what you wish for."

I was afraid of waiting too long and discovering I was infertile, but I gave little thought to what it would be like to be pregnant so early in our relationship, and even less to what it would be like to actually have a baby. Now that I had every other aspect of my life perfectly lined up, or so it seemed, I couldn't handle the procreative uncertainty of a woman who had finally found a partner but was no longer in her prime childbearing years.

The obvious flaw to my thinking, of course, was that the only way that I could know for sure if I could conceive and bear children would be to actually conceive and bear a child.

In this regard, I have to admit that I wasn't simply going to "start trying"—that left too much to chance. Getting pregnant became a full-scale project that I embraced on every level, from taking folic acid to painstakingly reading the book *Taking Charge of Your Fertility*, by Toni Wechsler. Per Toni's instructions, I began to chart my basal temperatures every morning. Not content with this time-honored but low-tech method, I also threw into my arsenal an ovulation monitor with a computer chip that could read my hormone levels and "memorize" my cycle. Wake up, take my temperature, pee on a stick, and repeat. When, two weeks later, I realized that I had, in fact, gotten pregnant right out of the gate, I was stunned by my own success. I shouldn't have been—I had engineered the whole thing, down to having sex on the day all the signs were saying that one of my eggs was already making its way down my fallopian tube.

All of a sudden, things were going so fast that two of my life's biggest milestones were getting compressed into one, and it was my own damn fault. I wasn't worried about any kind of social stigma attached to my "*condition*" at the wedding, especially since we were already having a civil and not a religious ceremony. In fact, both my family and Eric's were quite happy about the events being packed together, as my eldest brother and his wife had done the exact same thing two years earlier. But there was no denying that both our wedding and the birth of our child would be irrevocably changed by their proximity to one another. I had been trying to make up for lost time, but now there was no turning back. The train had left the station.

First, I focused on the logistical adjustments, such as the dress, which had already been ordered and paid for. I called RK Bridal and explained the situation. "Well, all we can do is wait for the dress to come in and see what we can do," said the clerk.

"But this must happen all the time, right?" I asked nervously.

"If we can let the dress out, we'll let the dress out," she said, sounding as if my situation hardly qualified as a bridal emergency. "If not, we can try sewing in some kind of panel over the stomach."

So much for my nice waistline. At least my personal trainer had a retailoring plan ready to go. It turned out that she was at work on a follow-up to *Buff Brides* called *Buff Moms-to-Be.* But I only made it through a couple of sessions with her until nausea and fatigue hit. I had so little energy, I couldn't see the point of expending it in the gym, and so I stopped going altogether. I would have to put vanity aside and make do with having a swollen, ungainly figure at my own wedding. By this point it was almost March, and already my pants were getting very tight around the waist and my bras felt like torture instruments. By the time late June rolled around, I would be almost six months pregnant. My best hope was that my jacket and some creative pashmina placement could diminish the bulge.

The next disappointment: our honeymoon plans. As I was now in the habit of sleeping ten hours at night, my dream of waking at five a.m. to search for rhinos in the savanna no longer seemed wise, or even feasible.

"I still want to go," I told Eric and anyone else who asked, and I did, desperately. I've always loved animals, and I'm a sucker for nature shows on public television. Since I would never feel comfortable splurging on a safari for myself, getting one as a wedding present seemed like my only chance. But was it safe for me to travel to South Africa? I checked the Centers for Disease Control Web site:

Travel to a Malaria Risk-Area During Pregnancy is NOT Recommended. During your pregnancy, you should not travel to an area with malaria unless travel cannot be postponed. If you get malaria, you may become more ill than a woman who is not pregnant would become.

The CDC's warning didn't leave much to interpretation. But I was still torn, and I made an appointment with an infectious disease specialist, who informed me that if I really wanted to, I could take the antimalarial drug mefloquine, also known as Lariam.

"Excellent," I said. "That's a relief."

But the doctor wasn't finished. "The thing is, there haven't been any studies of what effects the drug might have on unborn fetuses," he said. "Why don't you find a nice beach in the Bahamas?"

Back at home and on the Web, I discovered that studies *had* shown that Lariam can cause depression and psychotic episodes and was even suggested to be the cause behind the high number of soldier suicides in Iraq. That decided it for me: I called Eric's father and apologetically told him to cancel the safari. Then I went into our bedroom and cried. Eric couldn't understand why I was so upset. "Are all the hormones from pregnancy making you emotional?" he asked. I just shook my head and kept crying.

My reaction seemed out of proportion because it wasn't just the loss of the honeymoon that I was mourning; it was the loss of control. When you're planning a wedding, every step along the way is an opportunity to broadcast your preferences, to make a personal statement by picking a country-and-western band over a string quartet, or blue hydrangeas in buckets over white lilies in glass vases. For that matter, our relationship also seemed to be a clear articulation of choice: making the decision to be together, and feeling, in that decision, that we were finally getting what we wanted. I had been riding high on this notion for months and was only now crashing back to earth. Now that I was pregnant, many of my choices were being made for me, down to which wines we would be serving, since I wasn't allowed to taste any of them. What was more, all the time I was supposed to spend writing that spring—one of the other "perfect" changes I had managed to make in the year of having everything go my way—was getting sucked up by morning sickness and doctor's appointments. Even my body was no longer mine; it had been taken over by that baby growing inside of me, and it didn't seem fair. Planning a wedding may be an exercise in exerting control, but getting married, and certainly starting a family, seemed to be all about losing it.

. . .

A month before our wedding date, when the manufacturer delivered my dress to RK Bridal, I went in for a fitting. Luckily, I had ordered one size up before I got pregnant; the plan had been to take it in around the chest and waist. And even though, of course, the dress was now tight and unflattering, there seemed to be an inch or so of inseam that could be let out. The jacket, however, was a different story, and there was nothing to be done about it: When I put it on, it hit at exactly the wrong place, my widening and protruding belly. At four months, I was definitely showing, but I tried to find comfort in the knowledge that at least I wouldn't have to buy an entirely new outfit.

The dress was altered and shipped to Montana, and soon Eric and I were packing for our own journey in a rental car with our dogs in tow. We would be flying back east right after the wedding and continuing on to a honeymoon in the doctor-sanctioned Caribbean, leaving the dogs behind with Eric's parents. I was excited to see all our friends and family gathered together in a place that we loved, but I no longer wanted to be the center of the show, the woman of the hour. After watching my best-laid plans orbit into chaos, I wanted to take a backseat and let our guests enjoy themselves. And they did, with gusto. They went horseback riding up mountain trails and fly-fishing on the Yellowstone River; they frolicked in the natural hot springs pool at the resort and drank beers from the adjacent honky-tonk bar. I couldn't help but notice the guests who'd left their young children at home: They seemed especially liberated by their freedom, while I felt as though mine was becoming increasingly curtailed. What had I gotten myself into?

The morning of the ceremony, I nursed a headache with Diet Coke and Aleve. I had planned to do my hair and makeup myself, but Eric's mother was wise enough to hire a nice woman from a local salon to come help me on my Big Day. My mom came by to keep me company, and so did my close friend and maid of honor, Anya. When it was time to squeeze into my dress, it was tight and uncomfortable, and I trudged up a hill to the meadow where everyone was waiting. The jacket was boxy and big, which would have worked fine, except that I had lost the "line" that made the outfit work in the first place——my stomach stuck out and my chest rose to meet my neck too quickly. I felt like a plus-sized woman trying to get away with wearing a slender woman's dress. I had always thought that walking down the aisle would be a moment I would try my hardest to remember in the future but would never quite be able to summon; instead, I recall it easily, because the contents of my mind were so mundane: I was not at my best on the day when every woman is supposed to be at her best. It was late in the afternoon, my usual pregnancy nap time, but I had to smile and put on a show. I had at least six more hours of hosting ahead of me. I already felt exhausted.

During the cocktail hour, while everyone was sipping prosecco, I slugged a giant bottle of Pellegrino. At the reception, I watched from the sidelines as my mother and aunt led a group of women, young and old, into a spontaneous cabalistic circle on the dance floor. They flaunted their bodies freely, all of them taking turns in the center of the circle for solos that grew more and more flamboyant, while I clutched my pashmina close and laughed in delight at their lack of inhibition. Six months earlier, I would have joined them. There were moments that moved me out of my spectator's role, such as when Eric and I danced slowly together, or during some especially charming and heartfelt toasts. But for the most part, I felt I had missed my chance to be the kick-up-her-heels bride and had already taken on the somber role of the expectant mother, with all its obligations and responsibilities.

Not that I wish I'd acted otherwise. It would have seemed forced, dumb even, to carry on as if things hadn't changed. In many ways, giving up stewardship of my own wedding was good preparation for the greater surrender I'd have to make once our child actually arrived. Perhaps it was enough to observe the revelry from this weirdly ambivalent vantage point instead of as a true participant. I may have lost the freedom of the carefree bride, but I was getting a jump start on celebrating the beginning of our family.

As the reception wound down, while waiters cleared tables and my father-in-law tipped the band, one of our friends announced a midnight migration toward the hot springs pool. We told everyone to go on ahead, we'd come by to say hi in a few minutes, although I intended to take Eric's hand and turn in for the night instead. I was tired, my feet hurt, and I couldn't wait to get out of that dress. But then I felt a twinge of guilt; all these people, who had come all this way for us, were trying to keep the evening alive; we owed it to them to bear witness to their good time.

When we arrived at the pool, about twenty of our friends were already in their bathing suits waist deep in water, cavorting and passing each other cans of Budweiser. I asked Eric if he wanted to jump in. He grinned and said, "I will if you will."

Eric stripped to his boxer shorts, and I neatly folded his custom-made suit so it wouldn't get wet. "Come on," Eric said, so I slipped off my shoes and put down the jacket and pashmina. And then, in my extremely tight wedding dress, I took my husband's hand and the two of us descended the steps of the steaming hot pool.

A loud cheer went up from the crowd, and I felt myself reinhabiting my body from wherever I had been all night, floating above and watching. Eric pirouetted and then splashed down backward into the water. I wasn't about to do a swan dive, but I carefully plunged in headfirst and then came up for air. I tried to stand, but my waterlogged dress suddenly weighed about fifty pounds. I dog-paddled in deeper. Someone threw me a beer and made a joke about how our baby ought never to see any photos from this moment, with me clearly pregnant and drinking—and in a hot tub, no less. I laughed, cracked open the can, and sank into the water, forgetting for a moment my responsibilities to the child on the way and enjoying my own party at last.

Postscript: A year after my wedding, *The New York Times* reported that due to increased demand, wedding dress manufacturers were now creating maternity lines.

my so-called
indie wedding

lori leibovich

♥

A few months before I got married, I wrote a manifesto. In it, I railed against the multibillion-dollar wedding industry, whose sole purpose, as I saw it, was to perpetuate outdated traditions, stunt individuality, and scam vulnerable couples. I called on my fellow brides-to-be to hold tight, stay firm, and make sure that every part of their wedding accurately reflected them, or their partner. I said it was up to us, the first generation of what I called "Indiebrides," to break free from the tulle handcuffs that had been binding women for centuries and make sure that our weddings reflected our fiery, feminist selves.

My manifesto was the first article published on Indie-bride.com, a Web site I founded soon after I became engaged. I started the site for women like me who didn't see themselves represented in the shiny pages of mainstream wedding magazines. I wanted to create a place where women could grapple with the thorny and emotional subjects—family, faith, money, tradition, commitment—that inevitably get dredged up when one plans a wedding. "Indiebride is a place for would-be brides who have more on their minds than planning a reception, women who never for a second believed in Prince Charming and who have not, despite all of the cultural cues, been breathlessly awaiting their wedding day for their whole life," I wrote in the manifesto.

An initial e-mail announcing Indiebride, designed like a formal wedding invitation with curlicue script and delicate flowers, was sent to one hundred friends. Within days, the site had hundreds, then thousands of visitors. These women (and a few men) gathered in the chat area, Kvetch, debating gender politics and offering each other advice on everything from meddling mothers-in-law to how to get grass stains out of a secondhand gown bought on e-Bay. I published an essay about a bachelor party that got so out of hand the marriage ended before it began, and a six-hundred-dollar Vegas-themed wedding where the groom dressed up as Elvis and the bride like a showgirl, and the guests ate deli sandwiches and danced to the King late into the night. I posted an interview with a therapist who counseled brides having second thoughts. Soon I was being invited onto radio shows and interviewed in newspapers about "Indie-weddings," what National Public Radio dubbed "independent productions that make up in integrity and creativity what they lack in budget."

In these interviews, I admonished women not to let their weddings control their lives and happily dispensed money-saving tips—buy your dress at a sample sale, serve homemade cookies and cupcakes instead of wedding cake, ditch the band or DJ and use an iPod and a pair of speakers instead. I reassured engaged women across the country that if after all the planning and obsessing, their wedding day wasn't the happiest day of their lives, like the magazines insist it must be, that's okay—the pressure to have the ultimate wedding was just another way for society to make women feel like failures. "Don't do anything you don't feel comfortable with," I said again and again. "Be true to yourself."

And I meant it. There was only one problem. No matter how many times I told other women to let go, be themselves, buck tradition, save money—I couldn't shake the exacting standards I had set for my own wedding. In the early morning hours after my husband and I were engaged on a Martha's Vineyard beach in August 2000, I scratched my first of many, many wedding lists. This one, titled "Musts," included a country setting, a weekend-long celebration, wildflower arrangements, sumptuous food, dancing all night. . . . When we finally settled on a date (the following August) and chose the place (a restored barn in western Massachusetts attached to an inn) I realized I wanted a bacchanal more than a wedding, and my vision, it soon became clear, would require a lot of cash and massive amounts of planning. With that, of course, came a lot of stress.

Within months my desk was littered with color-coded folders stuffed with clippings, and the walls of my office were plastered with Post-its. I spoke daily with my mother (who tackled the details with the same sense of urgency as myself) and to a coterie of far-flung vendors. I had to figure out how to air-condition the barn, find dozens of rooms in a tiny Massachusetts town for our guests to stay in, and convince my beloved hairdresser to give up a Saturday at her salon and drive three hours north because I couldn't entrust my tresses to anyone in the Berkshires. . . . Deep down I think I knew, during these chaotic months, that there was some disconnect between my public and private personae. But it was the day I found myself at Barneys shimmying into a couture wedding gown that cost more than three months' rent that I had to come to terms with the incontrovertible truth: There was nothing very "indie" about me or my wedding.

It was a stale gray February afternoon when I emerged from the Barneys dressing room in a body-skimming dress made of such supple silk I still have fantasies about tasting it. I mounted the platform in front of a three-way mirror and studied my reflection. Instead of feeling like a princess, as the bridal magazines say, I felt like (a shorter, darker) Uma Thurman. The dress, had it not been white, would not have been out of place on the red carpet at the Oscars, and I knew I had to have it. My friend Heather, the most fashionable person I know, was with me, and she practically cried as she studied the lace detailing on the train and the spray of sequins on the bodice. The saleswoman fluttered over to me and began to arrange a veil on top of my head. "No, no," I said. "No veil for me." The woman, reed-thin, wearing a perfectly cut beige suit, looked at me skeptically. "Oh, you don't mean that," she said. "You *have* to wear a veil! That's what brides do! Plus, you need something to *tie everything together*." After a few more rounds of polite arguing, I finally relented, saying I would try it on "for fun," certain that when I saw myself in it I would dissolve into chuckles. I thought most brides who wore veils looked like they were playing dress-up or wearing a costume, not to mention that veils historically represented purity and virginity. But when the sleek saleswoman planted a cathedral-length piece of tulle on top of my head, and I saw myself in the mirror, I gasped audibly—from horror or delight I'm not quite sure. And somehow I walked out of the store with a three-hundred-dollar piece of gauze I didn't want or need.

Now, I'm not a total hypocrite—remember, part of what I preached was that a couple should have the wedding they want, not the one their parents want, or the one they feel they *should* have, and in that way I stayed pretty true to myself. The wedding was elegant, but not fussy. Every guest was known to and loved by me and my husband. The word people used again and again to describe the weekend was "warm." Besides the veil, there really wasn't anything that didn't feel right. There were no bridesmaids or groomsmen, we nixed a videographer, knowing we'd never watch the video, and we ditched the idea of wedding cake (and the inevitable smashing-cake-in-each-other's-face photo, too) in favor of a tower of cupcakes topped with marzipan replicas of our dog and cats. It goes without saying that I did not don a garter, toss a bouquet, or use the word "obey" in my vows. The fact that I drove myself—not to mention my husband—mad by my neurotic fixation on details such as whether or not we should serve sea bass at the reception (it was just becoming endangered) is really part and parcel of my obsessive personality—I've never been mellow in my life. So when I advised other brides not to get too wrapped up in planning their own weddings, undoubtedly I was projecting onto them what I wished I could do myself: lighten up. But weddings are obviously exactly the wrong time to try to change your personality. By encouraging others to fly in the face of tradition, I think I wanted to live vicariously through them. As much as I sometimes wish I were a renegade, that's just not me. I'm essentially a good girl, and when it came to my wedding I just wasn't going to wear a red dress or elope to Vegas. Did this threaten my street cred? I wasn't sure.

Which is why I always become a little nervous when people I know through Indiebride ask me about my wedding. I imagine they're expecting to hear about a backyard BBQ where I wore overalls and served burgers, or a barefoot-on-the-beach ceremony with me in a sarong and one of our friends officiating. When I tell them the truth, that we got married on a Saturday night, with a rabbi presiding and a traditional Jewish chuppah sheltering us, that I wore a white dress and a veil, and that we had a sit-down dinner for 180 people, I worry I'm going to disappoint them. But the important thing is that I didn't disappoint myself. Much to my surprise, my wedding was—as the bridal magazines suggested—the happiest day of my life. Not because I followed the prescriptions dispensed by the magazines or bought into the fantasies they tried to peddle. But because when our wedding day finally arrived, I allowed myself to truly inhabit it—and celebrate the fact that my husband and I had found each other. I allowed myself, in other words, to experience joy—and then to savor it.

Last year, while I was taking an introduction-to-meditation class, my teacher instructed us to close our eyes and tap into a feeling of peace and contentment. Sitting cross-legged on a pillow, I immediately conjured images from our wedding day and played them like a slide show in my mind as I deepened my breathing. I imagined the dappled sunlight filtering through the maple tree outside the window of my hotel room, and the cloudless, cobalt sky. I felt the tickle of the makeup brushes as my hairdresser applied some combination of cosmetics that made me look not like a bride, but like me, only way better, and the crisp mountain breeze that kissed the back of my neck as I walked down the aisle at sunset flanked by my parents. I recalled the taut, somewhat painful feeling in my face from the might of my smile. My thoughts drifted to the reception and the earthy scent of wildflowers and late-summer fruit wafting from the centerpieces on the table, the foot-thumping bluegrass music, and how for hours I flailed my arms, shook my ass, and twirled around the dance floor with my friends.

Finally, before I fell into a state of meditative calm, I summoned the image of myself and my husband at three a.m. on our wedding night at a house down the road from the barn. We gathered with my hard-partying Argentine cousins and some of our closest friends. Someone had taken all of the leftover food and arranged it on a table, and we picked at cold steak and crusty rolls. My husband and I had gotten up to dance, grabbed hands, and leaned backward, spinning each other wildly in circles like children on a playground. My hair, perfectly styled a few hours earlier, was a tumbled mess, and the back of my gown lay in shreds. My feet were bleeding from dancing for so hard and for so long. My husband's suit jacket had been tossed on the floor, his white dress shirt rumpled and spotted with sweat stains. "Beautiful Day" by U2 screamed from the boom box on the floor, and I didn't want the music or the night to end. I wanted to spend the rest of my life in that swirl of motion, our hands clasped, our eyes locked, free, but also joined.

weddings aren't just for straight people anymore

anne carle

We walked out of the back of the house onto the deck and there they were. Our oldest friends, our favorite coworkers, our grad school allies, our families. Our entire support system right there in our backyard. We'd sent 110 invitations, and 108 people said yes and then actually showed up exactly when we told them to. They brought food, abundant, delicious food, like we asked. They bought gifts. Some stood and spoke about our meaning, individually and together, in their lives. On our right was a string duet someone had donated; on our left was a band waiting to give what some of our friends called the best local live show they'd ever seen. And way in the back was the caterer friend who donated her unmatched organizational skills. A wedding photographer friend and a wedding videographer friend each donated their services, too. And there we were. Standing right up front under the arch, which was under our Bradford pear tree, in our backyard, in Richmond, Virginia. Beside us was our "officiator," Barb. Our spiritual guide, our mentor, one of the best therapists in town, our friend and outdoor adventure buddy. We smiled back at our people, blindly, as the five p.m. sun lit us up. Slowly that sun descended below our cedar fence, as Barb got things rolling.

. . .

We got married on October 15, 2005. We didn't have a priest, a judge, or a marriage license. We didn't have wedding gowns or tuxedoes. We didn't have a church or a high-rise cake with two plastic people on top. Some of this we chose not to have. But because we're gay, some of it wasn't our choice. What did we have? A community event, a unifying celebration, a commitment ceremony. We designed it to be us presenting ourselves to our community and committing ourselves to each other before them. And more than that, it was designed to get a commitment from our community to stand by us, to rally around us, to think about us and our commitment.

Lots of people hesitate to call our event a wedding or our "arrangement" a marriage. Here's a common awkward moment: "Hey! Anne! I heard about your . . . thing! Your . . . I don't want to call it a wedding . . . what do you call it?" They stumble for a second because they don't want to offend us. But it was a wedding and this is a marriage. In a million ways, it looks just like any other marriage. Most of the time we enjoy spending every passing minute with each other tremendously. Sometimes we don't. And we make both difficult and fun decisions together. We help each other through hard situations, we hold each other accountable, we fight, we hurt each other's feelings, we make up, we agree, we disagree. We want to be doing this together for the rest of our lives.

MARRIAGE ISN'T JUST FOR STRAIGHT PEOPLE ANYMORE

I remember the minute I realized I really wanted to get married. It only came after a long path through lots of experiences I didn't really want or enjoy. I'd had several vaguely close approximations of wedding lust before my actual moment of clarity occurred. I inherited, like lots of girls seem to, this idea that marriage was kind of important. That's an understatement, of course. But there were ways I expected myself to be immune to it. The obvious way was my gayness. But being gay wasn't that simple for me and isn't for any gay person, really. I didn't "come out" as gay (tell people, send press releases) until I was thirty-four. By that time I'd been gay for about twenty years, in my estimation. I knew from forever that I was gay. I had so many crushes on girls—classmates, teachers, rock stars—that I lost count. I can safely say that I never had a real crush on a boy, ever in my life. I faked crushes on boys, though. In fact, I faked crushes on boys up until my thirty-fourth year. A couple of these boys I loved enough to feel lots of pain when it didn't work out. One boy I moved across the country with against all common sense, and then he left me, for a much less gay woman, and I was alone on the other side of the world. But this fake relationship had gotten so far that I'd imagined, if only briefly, that we might get married and have kids, and it might be an OK thing to do. His parents had mentioned it, after all. It turned out to be a good thing that we never got that far. When I moved back home, I figured out that enough was enough.

Home again, I gave up on men. I had a couple more crushes on women. One was fleeting and utterly not serious, the other changed my life forever. I tell Chris now that I knew I loved her when I heard her voice on the phone for the first time. She was organizing a ski trip that I'd signed up to take. Talking to Chris was like chocolate. Or color television. Or something strong and comfortable at the same time. And because the ski trip was a total, utter blast, we became friends. We watched the Winter Olympics together. One night when I was cooking dinner for Chris (sweet potato and black bean soup), I realized that I wanted to be with her. I wanted to be in the position to make dinner for her as often as possible. I had a crush on Chris like I'd had on dozens of other women. And for a few weeks I entertained just handling it the way I always had, by doing nothing, saying nothing, and keeping it to myself. But somehow I realized that what I was really doing was never, ever asking for what I really wanted. And this was suddenly a lot lonelier, and more wrong, than it had ever been.

To say I was raised Catholic is the hugest understatement ever. I was raised by the most conservative, orthodox, throwback Catholic father in an abundant community of conservative, orthodox, throwback Catholics. I got the message early from the community I was born into that there were lots of ways I could end up in hell, but there was one particular way that came with an all-expenses-paid, express ticket: being gay. When I was fourteen I prayed and prayed to be different than I was. And in high school when I couldn't care less for boys, I went on dates anyway, humored their horrible, sloppy French kisses, and said and did as little as possible. Then I went on like this for years. And finally, when I was thirty-four, I called Chris one night and told her I loved her. "I know you think I'm straight," I said, "but I'm really not." In some ways it was easier to say how I felt because Chris was gay and out already. She came out when she was right out of high school (no small feat for someone raised in Lynchburg, Virginia). But it didn't mean she loved me back. I said, "The most important thing is that I told you." I said I wasn't expecting anything just because I told her. But of course I was. I had crossed over into the land of "I know what I want" and there was no going back. For better or worse, I'd reached out.

And then there was this period of about two weeks where I'd said what I said, Chris had responded with kindness but not in kind, and we were just hanging out like we always did. We went bowling on my birthday, where (she likes to remind me) I totally crushed her. And I went to a wedding by myself. A gay wedding. There, as two of my dearest friends committed their lives to each other in front of the many people who loved and supported them, I discovered what else I wanted. I wanted to get married. I wanted to marry a woman. I knew this so certainly, and this was so different from the almost ambivalent interior interrogations I held about every last man I dated or even thought about: Could I date him? Would I consider spending more than two days in a row with this guy? Would it be so bad to have sex with him? What about for the rest of my life? This moment was so different. I felt clear. I wanted to love and marry Chris. It may not happen, I said to myself, but this is what I want. And I finally knew.

As it turned out, all I needed to do was plant that seed in Chris's head. Chris and I had our first date less than a week after my friends' gay wedding. We became inseparable and moved in together six months later. By now, we've faced lots of challenges together—we've left bad jobs, taken new less-bad jobs, bought and renovated a house, started graduate school, raised kittens, put down one of our well-loved dogs, raised a new puppy, and negotiated the perils of a shared bank account. That's just for starters. The challenges we face together go much deeper, too. Chris and I have always been clear about what we're doing together—leading purposeful lives. Starting very early, Chris and I had long, fruitful conversations about our dreams, our spirituality, and our individual paths to emotional health. And as our dating became more than dating, I stated my most heartfelt intention: "I want to grow with you." Chris agreed, and this is the ball we've always had our eye on. We ask ourselves, are we growing? Together and individually? As our relationship has evolved, growth always comes to mean different, more challenging things. Eventually, it meant marrying each other in front of a community of friends and family.

At this writing, we've been officially married for six months and joined at the hip for four years. We're both thirty-eight years old, acting like some weird combination of boy and girl tweeners. This is who we are, and this is what our life together is like. We can't get enough of each other. But what about the world outside our front door?

GAY MARRIAGE IS EVIL!

Behind every together moment of our lives is a background of contentious politics. We live in the giant shadow of "family values," which, despite all we know and feel, does not include our family in its approval zone. We're married lesbians in Virginia . . . which is actually an oxymoron. Virginia's informally known as the state that's least friendly to gays and lesbians, particularly because of legislation aimed at barring the recognition of same-sex couples. But Virginia also definitely reflects an unfortunate national mood. The recent tension has been building, nationwide, since November 2003. That's when things looked like they were going our way, toward an atmosphere of declining hatred and discrimination against gay people and same-sex couples. In November 2003, a judge overturned Texas legislation that outlawed consensual homosexual acts: an antisodomy law.

It was a huge victory. A victory for our morale for sure. But it didn't last very long. After a very brief gay marriage movement in California, New York, and other places, America's conservatives pulled together in a massive movement that was eventually called family values. They set loose a campaign of fear that seemed to climax with George W. Bush's reelection. It started in reaction to the gay marriages, and a number of states started enacting fear-inspired legislation.

This legislation, born of the fear of difference, is also doing a pretty good job of scaring the crap out of us. Here's how some specific Virginia legislation could hit us where it hurts. We've bought a house together and we own three vehicles together. We're sharing our lives. If someone was interested enough, say, one of my throwback Catholic aunts (you know who you are), they could dissolve everything we've built together. For example, if I were to be hit by a bus, someone could step in and challenge Chris's right to keep the house, keep the minivan, inherit my life insurance, and on and on. In fact, if I didn't die right away, someone could prevent Chris from making the decisions that only she could make about my medical care . . . they could even prevent her from seeing me or being present when I woke up or died. George W. Bush's reelection, riding as it did on the coattails of the family values issue, seemed to bring these possibilities closer than they'd ever been before, right into our living room.

Chris admits now that she was in such a funk after the reelection that she wondered why we were even trying . . .

why were gay people even trying to establish safe and sound lives for themselves, together as more or less traditional families? Why not just play to the stereotype and just screw around and drink and drug ourselves to death? Or simply give up altogether, wander off alone, and wait to die?

OUR GAY WEDDING

That's when we decided to turn outward instead of inward. In fact, our whole relationship so far had already represented a turning outward. I came out. I reached out of my homophobic distress for Chris, and she reached back. Now, in what seemed like the perfect time for a gay couple like us to lock the doors and hide our relationship behind the sofa, we reached out together to the rest of the world we knew.

Chris used to say, earlier in our relationship, that she didn't care about gay marriage, because she didn't want to get married. She had no use for trying to fit as a lesbian into "straight" establishments like marriage. I was in a different place because I'd had my moment of clarity about wanting to marry Chris, but I was still conflicted over what this would look like. We watched some couples around us plan weddings that seemed to be imitating, as closely as possible, a straight marriage, some right down to a gown and tux. It seemed laughable and it seemed degrading. We aren't proud now of the feelings we had then. But there was something that rubbed us the wrong way . . . actually, there was something terrifying about what these couples were doing. Gay people, like any group that experiences oppression, have a lot to be scared of. What would possess a couple to expose themselves to what feels like the whole mean, angry world like that? What we fear, we make fun of. So we laughed and laughed at the formal invitations complete with onionskin and embossing. And we didn't go. Then when all the bad family values legislation started to flood in, I started to point out to Chris, to both of us, that it didn't matter whether we wanted to get married or not. The country was moving toward moving backward, in a civil rights perspective; legislating against a certain group of people in a way we hadn't done since a distant, less enlightened time.

It was on New Year's Day 2005, right in the upswing of the George W. victory lap, that we both simultaneously warmed to the idea of marriage. We spent New Year's Eve with a friend who had rented an old, drafty farmhouse in Bath County, Virginia, right on the edge of Douthat State Park. On New Year's Day, we went hiking. We were by ourselves, Chris and I, on top of a small mountain, and I had a vision. I asked Chris, why don't we take a backpacking trip and have a ceremony for ourselves out in the woods? The way I saw it, it could just be three of us. Me, Chris, and our dear friend Barb, who would perform the ceremony. It seemed like a good idea. We committed ourselves to thinking about it. Personally, I had no idea where thinking would take us. But all ideas, if they're allowed to see daylight and breathe, will evolve. First there was a new idea I had of having another friend come along—a videographer. Wouldn't it be fantastic to document this somehow? Maybe even make a documentary? It was that idea of documenting that added a dimension to our ceremony. Why document? Over the next three months, we answered that question: Because this is important and we want people to see it. It was brewing somewhere in both of us that we didn't want to do this alone, unseen, unheard. So in March, Chris essentially announced that our wedding was too important to hide in the woods on a mountaintop. Chris was right, and we made a new plan. Our wedding had to take place in the center of our universe, in front of our community. We agreed to have a huge-ass rocking ceremony. In our backyard. In Virginia, the most un-gay-friendly state in the entire country.

GROOMZILLA, BRIDEZILLA, AND THE SAVING ANALOGY

We started talking about a ceremony. And then I almost don't remember anything between that moment and the moment we walked down the aisle and turned around into the blinding light . . . almost. What I remember is panic, worry, cold feet, and sometimes total and utter numbness. A coworker asked whether I felt like Bridezilla . . . but I actually felt more like Groomzilla. Chris pretty much planned everything, while I would nod and say, "Sounds fine." And it did sound fine . . . Chris has always had a great instinct and imagination for planning things. I always had a great yawning terror of it. So I went comatose for a little while.

I had some opinions about some things, and shared them. But I felt for a few months like I was underwater. When I finally came to the surface, I freaked out. Sixty days out I could think of a million ways things could turn out terrible. I fixated on very specific details, like parking. One hundred and eight people? Where would their cars go? There was a church parking lot about three blocks away that we could borrow, but what if people didn't park there and just piled their cars up on our street, making our neighbors hate us and creating some kind of incident? What if the police came? I also freaked about having a registry. I'd never in my life sent out little cards to people essentially telling them to go shop for me. And now I was telling them to do it because, yay, I'm gay! And at the very root of these panic attacks was the serious doubt that I really had a community. I was watching all these people say they were coming, and all these other people say they'd do this or that for us for free (catering, music, photography, videography), and I couldn't fathom it. Something must be wrong here. Something's going to screw up. I knew it. A mushroom cloud billowed in my head. Groomzilla was becoming Bridezilla.

Then came the Saving Analogy. Chris might say we both came up with it, but I think she's the one who pulled it out. Essentially, the Saving Analogy illustrated how we were two different kinds of person, and we could take two different roles in making this event happen. Here's the analogy. When we go to Kings Dominion, a local amusement park, Chris is the one to actually get us there. She's the planner; she gets us to pick a date, pile in the car, and drive there. But once we're there and we get to our absolute favorite ride, this bungee jump–swingy thing, I get us all harnessed up and hauled up about 150 feet, and I pull the rip cord. With no hesitation whatsoever, I pull the trigger, and we free-fall, screaming like freaks. So, Chris suggested, she would "drive" us to our ceremony. I would pull the trigger. I'd get us in front of our people, and I'd get us through the nuptials. And I did. Once the moment came, Chris turned from rock to jelly, and I emerged from my gelatinous form and held us up in front of that brilliant sun.

WE'RE GAY, WE'RE MARRIED, AND WE'RE NOT ALONE

Now that we're married, our community totally lumps us in that "married" category. And there are added communal responsibilities. Three separate families, including my two sisters, have asked us to be on the list to take their children into our homes as our own if anything should happen to the parents. We're so honored to be nominated by our community as good candidates. And we're more than willing to come through for them. In fact, this willingness of ours to be there for other parents and children has become the bedrock of our conscious decision not to have our own kids. When I say it's a "conscious" decision, it might bring to mind this question: "Isn't parenthood for gay people always a conscious decision?" It might seem that way, because obviously, Chris isn't going to get me pregnant accidentally.

But there are ways that gay families and parenthood have become a less conscious decision in our eyes. As soon as we got married, we were asked no less than five times by family and friends whether we were going to have children. The question alone is kind of a compliment. But it also reflects a growing expectation (in the gay-friendly world) that any "good" gay couple will build their own family, however they can manage it.

We've been invited to two gay family baby showers in the last three months. In case anybody's curious, I think that baby fever is now just as prevalent in gay people as it is in straight people. And I'd be lying if I said I didn't feel tempted. Sometimes I have a very secret, unexplored desire to be pregnant (I can hear my sisters choking, a whole state away from here). And Chris is like a genius with kids. She's been working with them for decades. So we've talked about it. Before the wedding, since the wedding. But we, both separately and together, have resisted a full-on commitment to the idea. And it took lots of talking to figure out why. We know right now that the best way for us to grow our community is not to have our own kids but to continue putting ourselves out there as allies to both our parent friends and our children friends. For us (not for everyone, we know), having our own children would mean building a separate family unit . . . and along with this comes a kind of insularity and isolation from the larger community. We've seen it happen to lots of straight people, to my sisters and our best friends especially. If we stay childless but reach out relentlessly to our sisters, friends, and their children, our family unit will swell and swell. And it's also a way we can complete the circle. These are the people who, when we reached out and held a ceremony, reached right back and held us in their hearts and minds.

SCENES FROM A GAY WEDDING: PRESSING REWIND THREE HUNDRED TIMES

Whenever we need to remember we're not alone, we pull out the wedding video and watch our favorite parts. Over and over. Just like any normal bride (and maybe groom) would, right? Here's a moment from our wedding video. My friend Sally stands up to give the last of about ten blessings. "I have faith in the union you are forming today, Anne and Chris, and I believe in the paradoxical beauty of two separate individuals forming one complete love. May you continually meet each other anew each day, and never cease to discover the distinctions that define your individual selves, for they will surely compound and enrich the building of your unity." In her own words, there was some happy crying and sputtering, too.

Sally was supposed to be the last to stand and give a blessing. We'd planned it out, at Barb's suggestion, to prevent our ceremony from becoming as long as Charles and Diana's. But an unplanned blesser stood up. It was Chris's mother. It was a surprising twist. She hadn't been asked to give a blessing because we considered it enough of a beautiful victory to have her there and completely engaged. That had taken some work. Watching Chris open her mother's heart was one of the most amazing things I'd ever seen. Here's how it began. In March, Chris called her mother and told her about the ceremony, saying that she'd really love for her to be there. Her mother's first response? "In October? I might be at the beach that week." It's not the response a bride expects from her mother. As a lesbian, Chris had lots of reasons to expect much less from her mother. And her father offered plenty less. He ignored the invitation, wouldn't talk about it, and didn't show up. But as weeks and months passed and October 15 crawled closer, Chris's mom warmed up. This was partly a result of the persuasions of Chris's older brother, Bill, who's also gay. Between Chris and Bill, Becky began to dip her toe into the pool of mother-of-the-brideness.

Then complete and utter chance stepped in. Chris was featured in an article in the Richmond newspaper a few months before the ceremony, an article about her mentoring a local gay youth who was now struggling with thoughts of being transgender. It didn't occur to Chris to share this article with her mother. She imagined her mother would simply never see it. But she did see it. A cousin happened to be in Richmond the day it came out and brought it home to Lynchburg for the entire family to read. When Chris's mother called her, it went something like this: "Chris. Why didn't you tell me you were in the newspaper? The whole family saw it before me. And now they all want to go to your ceremony. You have to send them invitations." We thought getting Richmonders excited about a gay wedding would be hard enough. We didn't expect to get an excited, engaged crowd from Lynchburg, the home base of none other than Jerry Falwell. But we did.

Then Chris's mother contributed money toward getting our invitations printed. She called often and asked about the arrangements. Becky had always been nice to me, but she became more than that; she was now warm to me. She was embracing me. Which felt even more special because my own parents were deceased. And not only was she going to come to the wedding, but she was going to bring her boyfriend, and they'd stay in town for the night. We thought, victory. But she wasn't finished yet. She stood up and blessed us. "I'm Becky, Chris's mother, and this is my boyfriend, Bob. And I just want to welcome Anne into the family." It was short, but it was sweet and very, very important. Our ceremony was the first step in our pursuit of a community larger and wider than our immediate families. But in the process of finding this community we rediscovered the people who had loved us the most from the very beginning of our lives.

CLOSING WORDS ON OUR GAY WEDDING

We did actually say vows. But we didn't gaze into each other's eyes and spill our guts about our undying love for only each other. We could save that for the decades to come.

Chances are, we'll need it. Instead we turned outward to our 108 people and said some words from a Native American blessing called The Beauty Walk. Here's a sampling:

> Let us be embraced with the love by which the whole creation is moved, the very essence with which all things are held together. Dependent, yet independent, whole yet individuated, in which all are our relatives.

A love by which the whole creation is moved. That's what we shared with our people that day. And they shared it with us. By showing up; by bringing food, gifts, chairs, tiki torches, and lots of other extremely useful things; by standing before everyone and offering blessings; and by saying yes when Barb asked them, at the end of the ceremony, to commit their love and support to our relationship. This love shone a bright light on the dark moments of our lives: my tortured Catholic life in the closet, Chris's homophobic family and hometown, our despair as we witnessed homophobia becoming more and more politically fashionable. When light hits these dark moments, it becomes a lot clearer that our lives are actually big enough to survive and surpass them. We stood under our Bradford pear tree, smiling like crazy, and we knew this. And as the ceremony ended, right at dusk, Barb presented us to our community and they clapped wildly as we walked to the back porch and into the house. But we were going to be right back. After all, the band had started to play, the tiki torches were lit, and the party was just beginning.

rubber chicken

julie powell

♥

It's not as if I was a scary child bride or anything. But I was nearly a full decade younger than what most of my big-city friends considered marriageable age. Don't get me wrong—I'm glad I got married. And our wedding was beautiful; I've got the pictures to prove it. (Looking at them I am reminded that, at the very least, marrying early means those photos to be treasured for eternity capture a comparatively lithesome version of things.) But maybe it was because I was so young that things turned out the way they did. Anyway, in retrospect, I would have done it differently.

When I imagine now the wedding I might plan if I had the chance to do it all again as a savvy thirty-three-year-old New Yorker, I picture some fabulous vintage cocktail dress or maybe a Catherine Malandrino gotten on sale off bluefly .com. I imagine a ceremony downtown at City Hall, with a small bouquet of wildflowers and perhaps a chic hat, then a boozy party at some classic old-school joint—Peter Luger, maybe. Porterhouse for forty, and the vegetarians can stick to martinis and creamed spinach.

But I wasn't a savvy thirty-three-year-old New Yorker when I started planning my wedding. I was a twenty-four-year-old girl with a possibly regrettable expertise in romantic fiction. As such, being proposed to in my parents' kitchen by my boyfriend of seven years, the answer a foregone conclusion, didn't quite live up to my exacting fantasy standards. The situation was saved, just, by the utter sweetness of the man who would, in six months' time, be my husband, and by the nicely poignant touch that he did his proposing the night before getting on a plane to Kazakhstan, not to return until five of those six months had passed.

So, armed with long-distance yearning and a good jolt of self-pity, I commenced planning the event that would, I was convinced, secure me everlasting love, bring all of my family and friends together in perfect accord and giddy celebration, represent with crystalline truth the essence of my vivid personality, and finally introduce me to adulthood. So thinking, I went for the whole princess package. My dress was white and poofy, and the service and reception were held on the gardenlike grounds of my hometown's art museum. There were flowers in abundance—green hydrangeas for my four bridesmaids in their custom-made white shift dresses, white tulips for me. Paper lanterns hung like moons in the live oaks, candlelit tables scattered beneath them.

And the food? Despite all my obsessive efforts—rubber chicken.

Though I was young, I was already something of a foodie, by which I mean that I had developed a cluster of firmly held culinary prejudices, a mishmash of New York snobbery and reactionary regionalism that, considered together, added up to a telling, not altogether flattering self-portrait. I despised on principal vegetarians, dieters, and the allergic. I held in utter contempt any Yankee-fied personage who saw extreme spiciness as a flaw in the dish rather than evidence of their own weakness. And I abhorred every meal I'd ever eaten at a wedding or benefit. I was better than that. This was to be the first night of the rest of my life, my first night as hostess and wife, and the food served on that rented china atop those be-tableclothed tables under the live oaks was going to be the proving ground for a lifetime of hospitality, grace, and good taste.

What I didn't realize was that I was messing with a law as immutable as entropy or gravity. Hundreds of guests + unreasonable expectations + catering − billions of dollars = rubber chicken. Hubris, that was my problem.

.   .   .

Some people might think it cowardly of my fiancé to cook up a five-month trip to Asia just to avoid participating in the planning of his own wedding. But I, on the contrary, credit our continuing union to just that wise decision. Five months of being double-teamed by future wife and future mother-in-law, pelted with incomprehensible questions about chafing dishes, plagued with endless menu permutations, subjected to unpredictable hors d'oeuvres–related tantrums, would make the saintliest of feet cold. Colder, even, than five months in Kazakhstan. So he got on a plane, and instead of dragging my fiancé along to tastings and meetings, I dragged my much more willing and comprehending mother.

This is exactly the kind of thing my mom likes best. An interior designer with a particular obsession for obscure brands of lighting equipment, she is a woman who never tires of jigsaw puzzles and insoluble problems. She and I went immediately to the best-regarded, most expensive catering services in my hometown, our eyes narrowed into canny smirks before we even walked through the door. My mother and I sat down with Mona, the catering coordinator assigned to us, with pencils in hand. Mona asked me—well, us—all kinds of questions: Buffet or sit-down dinner? Formal or semiformal or semicasual or casual? Is there a particular ethnic food I like? What's the overriding theme of the event? (I didn't know weddings had to have themes, but I did the best I could to answer on the fly. "French Quarter," I said, because I'd recently been to New Orleans for the first time, and because there was Spanish moss in the live oak trees on the grounds of the museum where I had just decided I was going to get married, and Spanish moss seemed New Orleans–y to me.)

We were keeping a firm hold on the purse strings, our eyes on the bottom line. We opted for the buffet, convincing ourselves that those sit-down dinners just tie people down when they want to be joyfully mingling. We only needed three passed appetizers, rather than the obscene suggested number of five. We brutally cut out the Hoffbrau chopped salad, because who really cares about the salad anyway? We even, regretfully, nixed the mint julep martinis I had found on the Food Network Web site, and that my parents and I got completely plastered drinking one night around their kitchen table, in favor of the simpler and therefore cheaper margarita route.

So we thought we were prepared. But we weren't.

. . .

$11,871.73.

For a moment I thought the stress was getting to me at last, that my eyes had doubled up on some digit somewhere. "That can't be right. Is that right?"

But the digits remained just as they were. The figure was right. The catering for my wedding was going to cost more than the dresses, venue, and band combined.

That my mother was not so shocked I attribute to the facts that a) she is an interior designer, and thus accustomed to obscene amounts of money spent on throw pillows and side tables and recessed lighting, and b) I was twenty-four, and had never paid for a child's orthodonture or college education. For my mother, this was merely one more in a long line of expenses necessary to her only daughter's happiness, and thus to be borne without undue complaint.

Still, we trimmed where we could. Cut out another appetizer, downgraded from roast beef to ham. I called my fiancé, nine time zones ahead, to discuss crudités and different cheap champagnes, and he was patient, the poor dear, even though the connection was bad, the toilets were Turk-ish, and he'd probably been propositioned on the freezing walk back to his horrid apartment by some prostitute with very few teeth who thought he was a rich-oil-baron-type American, rather than the poor-anthropologist-type Ameri-can he actually was. And by the time I'd talked at him for half an hour about all these terribly urgent choices I had to make, and he'd cooed through his chilly lips that it all sounded delicious, and I'd told him I loved him and hung up, I'd decided on the glorious food that would be served at my wedding.

This was the menu:

Passed Hors D'oeuvres

Cheese Beignets on a Bed of
Freshly Grated Parmesan Cheese

Spicy Chicken Creole Turnovers

Dinner Buffet

Shrimp Emeril
(A Refined Take on Cajun Barbecue Shrimp)

Southern Baked Ham
with Buttermilk Biscuits and Creole Mayonnaise

Citrus-Scented Wild Rice Salad
with Toasted Louisiana Pecans and Fresh Mint

Roasted Diced Vegetables with Fiery Vinaigrette

Spiced Boursin with Homemade Croustades

WEDDING CAKES

Sour Cream Bride's Cake
with Fresh Fruit filling and Cream Cheese Frosting

"Tower" of Chocolate Cupcakes

It looks good, doesn't it? Interesting, regional—"French Quarter," even. And not a chicken breast in sight! But of course, what I didn't realize then was that rubber chicken needn't be made of chicken at all. I was also too young to recognize the rubber chicken warning signs.

Very long names for things, that should have set off the first alarm bells. The long-name thing is something that works for fancy restaurants. But when caterers employ the trick it's to try to convince you that they are fancy restaurants rather than what they are, which is caterers. Unlike the chefs at Jean-Georges—or Peter Luger for that matter—caterers do not cook to order. Caterers cook great huge batches of things, then pack them into large tin containers and carry them in vans to convention centers or church basements or the grounds of local art museums, where they reheat the food on chafing dishes. Many foods can be eaten very satisfactorily this way, but these foods usually have simple names—macaroni and cheese, barbecued brisket. Certainly not "Citrus-Scented Wild Rice Salad with Toasted Louisiana Pecans and Fresh Mint."

Plus, "citrus-scented"? Since when does rice need to be scented? I'm supposed to be eating this stuff, not scrubbing my toilet with it.

I also should have worried about the shrimp. Nothing remotely Cajun should ever be referred to as "refined." You might as well just say "an utter travesty of the dish that made Uglesich's famous."

The tower-of-chocolate-cupcakes groom's cake I stole off Martha. (I was at the time in the thrall of a fairly hard-core Martha Stewart obsession, referring to her by her first name and tearing pages out of the magazines and becoming briefly, uncharacteristically organized. I am happy to report that I have since recovered.) Everything else was straight off the catering company's "sample menus." Which is fine, of course—you don't go into Daniel Boulud's restaurant and demand he change up the menu. But such is the bride's self-absorption that she thinks it perfectly reasonable to demand a sparkling new culinary evocation of her unique little self for her special day.

Luckily for caterers everywhere, such is the bride's self-deception that she can be easily fooled into believing that is just what she's receiving, given a decent vocabulary and a

word processor. Name the same old chicken turnovers "creole" and throw a celebrity New Orleans chef's moniker
onto that faithful sautéed shrimp dish, and I'm happy.

.   .   .

The six months flew by as the six months before weddings
tend to do, between the planning and the obsessive exercise
and the long-distance calls to Kazakhstan and the bridesmaids' dress crises, and suddenly my fiancé is home and I'm
rushing him to the tuxedo rental place, and my brother is
home and he's shaved his head and my mother bursts into
wild tears and has to take a Valium, and I am filling hundreds of tiny plastic boxes with chartreuse and white jelly
beans, and also with little slips of paper on which are written, instead of fortunes, scraps of love poetry and songs,
while my fiancé wastes the whole damned day on the
damned lake, canoeing. And there's a rehearsal dinner and
a breakfast and I'm scanning the sky for rain clouds and I'm
packing my dress into my parents' car and now it's hanging
from a paper towel dispenser in the bathroom where I and
my bridesmaids are bumping into each other trying to get
dressed, and I'm just so glad that the food, at least, I don't
have to think about. The food is perfect.

The service goes off practically without a hitch, except
that I start down the aisle too early so nobody knows to stand
up. Everyone cries, including my fiancé and my brother,
who never cries—everyone except my mom and me, that is.
We're just relieved that nothing terrible happened, and
secure in the knowledge that on the verandah the food is

being laid out even now, and that the food is perfect. And my husband—my husband!—and I have our picture-taking session with our goofy photographer who wanted Eric to ride on an antique bicycle in a newsboy cap for our engagement photos, and then we're walking back up to all the lovely tables set beneath all the lovely live oak trees. The evening is beautiful—we'd been afraid it would be too hot—and my husband (my husband!) is beautiful, and I am beautiful. We're so beautiful, in fact, that everyone has to talk to us *immediately*. My husband is swept off in one direction, I in another, with no time for anything but a sip of champagne together and a peck on the cheek.

This, from what I hear, is where wedding planners come in very handy: for handing the bride a plate of food. But I had no wedding planner, so I didn't get around to eating anything until the reception was nearly over. I didn't even drink anything—trust me, this was unusual. Occasionally I passed someone with a plate piled high, and I asked them how they were enjoying it.

"Oh, it's very good! Congratulations!"

They smiled when they said this and nodded their heads. But I was obscurely disappointed. Where were the ecstatic protestations of joy? Where was the oohing and aahing? This was the unique culinary evocation of me, remember?

I met my husband, at last, under the verandah. Our eyes met over the trays of Emeril Shrimp and Roasted Diced Vegetables with Fiery Vinaigrette. Cajun polka music drifted among the Spanish moss. "I'm famished," I confessed.

"Me, too!" sighed my husband.

So we piled our plates high and sat on a stone wall beside the dance floor. I spread a napkin across my lap to avoid the heartbreak of Creole Mayonnaise on silk organza. I speared a shrimp on my fork and bit into it.

Crap.

Rubber chicken.

.   .   .

The trouble with rubber chicken isn't that it's bad; it's that it's not much good. It is also, alas, inevitable, I see now. The memory of my rubber chicken is a continuing heartbreak for me, but I have finally stopped trying to assign blame, either to the catering company, which really is quite an excellent one, or to some personal failure of nerve or imagination.

Rubber chicken is just what happens when you want the impossible. When you want to make a meal for hundreds into an expression of who you are.

The only way to deal with rubber chicken is to embrace it for what it is: an excuse to bring these people you love together, a way to mark time while everyone you know does the thing they really came here to do; to celebrate this wonderful day, the day that you married the sweetest, kindest man in the world. Honestly? Nobody gives a crap about the food.

So in retrospect, I think if I were to marry again at the age of twenty-four, I'd keep the poofy white dress and the tulips and the paper lanterns in the live oak trees. I'd even keep the rubber chicken. But for real this time.

My theory on the ideal perfect chicken is this: It should be cheap, it should be at least a little tasty, and it should be inoffensive. Roasted chicken breasts with fennel fits the bill nicely.

ROASTED CHICKEN BREASTS WITH FENNEL

Smear some olive oil on a cookie sheet, toss the chicken breasts on there, and broil until the juices, when pricked, barely run clear. Set aside and throw some sliced fennel on the same sheet. Brush them on both sides with more olive oil, season them with salt and pepper, and squeeze some lime juice over them. Broil about five minutes, until the edges are slightly blackened. Turn them over, sprinkle with a generous dusting of Parmesan, and broil again, until the cheese begins to brown. You can serve this warm or at room temperature, and the fennel adds just a bit of interest. Spoon the fennel over the chicken breasts before serving, sprinkle with a bit more lime juice, and serve to as many hundreds of people as you like. Or let the catering company do it, rather. And relax, remembering that your rubber chicken is fine, but your rubber chicken is *not the point.*

The point is you. And your husband. And your family and friends.

Oh, and booze, of course.

MINT MARTINI

This is the drink I wish I'd served at my wedding: Put a few mint leaves in the bottom of a highball glass. Add a tablespoon of simple syrup and some crushed ice, and mash it up with the handle of a wooden spoon, to bruise the mint leaves. Pour in the vodka—Belvedere is good—and shake until thoroughly chilled. Strain into a martini glass and garnish with a sprig of mint. This is delightfully refreshing, slightly sweet, and packs a serious wallop. One or two of these and all impatience with rubber chicken will melt away.

But in case you're now thirty-three? The number for Peter Luger is (718) 387-7400. The steak is to die for, and the bartender makes an excellent martini, though not girly mint ones. It's probably the way to go.

Really.

to have
or have not

Sex on the Wedding Night

jill eisenstadt

Four a.m., one hour till dawn, and our four-star suite was still full of revelers. One hour in which to get out of our wedding clothes, tally the gift checks, *have* sex. It was our wedding night. Of course we'd do it. This I truly believed despite the hour. Blame it on bridal magazines, Hollywood, or my own naïveté, but when I agreed to take part in the marriage rites I assumed that meant all of them. Why else would I have worn the (new) white gown, the (old) tiara, and the (borrowed) garter that gave me prickly heat? Why would I have held up the ceremony to shove something blue (a Canada Dry label) into my cleavage? And allowed my parents to give me away? Maybe it was unrealistic to expect all-night bubble-bath erotica. But surely our vows would be consummated. For all I knew, our license wasn't even valid otherwise: Unravished come sunrise, I'd turn into a pump-kin, or worse—a single girl again.

That I hadn't technically been a girl in a while only heightened my anticipation. What could be more intense than a second chance to lose your innocence? This time without pain or hair-trigger conclusion. What more fitting way to mark the commitment to exclusive lovemaking till death (or divorce) did us part than with *la petite mort*, as the French like to call orgasm, preferably followed by rebirth and fireworks. After years of "sin," what could be more thrilling than the inaugural bedding of a legally married woman?

Unfortunately, I had to wait for the answers to these questions. It appears that a great many of us have had to wait. "Did you or didn't you?" I began asking friends and acquaintances over the months, then years that followed my wedding. Not the most scientific method, yet the responses were revealing. Many laughed nervously, evaded the question, changed the subject. But the overwhelming majority finally gave an excuse:

"Bladder infection. I cried."

"I spent the whole night on a plane."

". . . in a car."

". . . sitting in traffic."

". . . mile after mile of no vacancy signs."

"We fought about what he said to my high school friends."

". . . fought about my ex-husband."

"Pillow fight."

"Morning sickness . . . Yes, at night."

Of the few who did claim victory, only one ever described the act as being anything out of the ordinary. And, I quote: ". . . a little like date rape." The others just thought they "had to" or "should." They just "did it" to "do it." Laugh we might, but somehow, we still feel we're just *supposed* to have sex on our wedding nights. When we don't we think of it as a bad omen. Or as one friend, Tara, put it: "I felt like we'd flunked some kind of test."

After years of living together, she and her fiancé, Bill, had spent a chaste prenuptial week in separate (but equal) apartments. He wasn't allowed a preview of her "virginal" gown. She wasn't allowed a review of his "worldly" bachelor party. From the proposal on bended knee to the send-off under a shower of politically incorrect white rice, they'd performed their traditional bride and groom roles flawlessly.

"We had the honeymoon suite with a king-size water bed, the complimentary champagne, the works. . . ." But then something—or rather, nothing—happened. "We conked out."

"Blacked out."

"Crashed. The whole wedding party in a big pile."

Barring the religious, most people nowadays wouldn't dream of marrying somebody with whom they hadn't slept. Common sense says that ignorance is dangerous. Better to know the body to which you're pledging monogamy. Rule out incompatible fetishes and irreparable conditions. Decide you like the bed you're getting into. A lot. Marrying later, we're hardly naive. So what's all this hullabaloo over a one-shot screw? Why is everyone still playing the old game, pretending that the bride is still a virgin?

In earlier times, that kind of false advertising would have gotten a girl stoned to death. Those bloody sheets had to be hung out as proof. If the marriage was deemed void, she might be sent into a life of prostitution or—perhaps worse—back to her father's house, shamed.

If nothing else, the number of sexually experienced brides today makes punishing all of them impractical. It was with the invention of latex and dependable condoms that women in the Western world began taking the risk. The Kinsey reports from 1920 show only 50 percent of brides in this country at that time were virgins. The difference was they didn't sleep with the men they were marrying. Makes you wonder over their wedding-night scenarios. Maybe they fooled their new husbands too. But more likely they were just like us.

"Too exhausted . . ." for intercourse. Planning a wedding is said to rate in the top five for stress, along with air-traffic controlling and death of a spouse.

"Too hungry . . ." Only those who elope get to eat at their weddings. And brides typically don't eat for weeks before either.

"Too preoccupied . . ." partying.

"Too drunk . . ." if too preoccupied.

"Too hungover . . ." if the wedding was over before nightfall.

"Too many buttons. Forty or more buttons. I swear, I gave up."

"He couldn't get it up. All of a sudden."

I heard all these reasons and most of them thrice. But all I really heard was that no one is having sex on their wedding nights anymore. It's the best-kept undirty secret around. So why *is* it secret? It's not rational. It's ritual.

And when you examine it (which is exactly what is not done with rituals), the whole subtext of the celebration *is* sex. Once that veil goes up and you may now kiss the bride, you must keep kissing her whenever a spoon hits crystal. You must dance the first dance to *your* song. You must cut the first slice of cake and take turns smooshing it into each other's waiting mouths. There's the high jinks with the garter and the getaway in the vandalized, shoe-festooned vehicle.

It's a performance—flirting for an audience. It's pretense and foreplay. It's one outdated formality after another, leading to the ultimate climax—sex. Even my ride over the threshold (a vestige of marriage-by-capture) had cheerleaders, though their presence ruled out the very act for which they rooted. Regardless of what the customs or trappings suggested, I'm sure not a single one of them believed I was a virgin. And why should anyone, most of all myself, care? Marriage is a public declaration of love. Sex is a private declaration of marriage. Or should be.

Maybe newlyweds would be better off leaving the sex to their guests. Weddings are, after all, notoriously romantic

for the invited. Maybe once the pressure was off, fresh rituals would evolve. Modern newlyweds would, say, share a
banana split, exchange foot massages . . . talk.

But when I found myself fully dressed the next morning, I wasn't thinking so clearly. Was the marriage off to a
bad start? I fretted. Would our plane crash, our passions
wane, our eyes wander? Were we doomed to a future of
pecklike kisses? Fluorescent-lit dinners? Twin beds? What if
we'd married our fathers, our mothers, our childhood pets?
What if we'd projected or settled? *What if we never had sex
again?*

"Don't be ridiculous," my new husband said as I re-
packed the unused peignoir set—peach thong and bra with
push-up features—I'd so carefully selected. Ridiculous,
exactly. If only I'd known that the lingerie bridal shower
would turn out to be a practical joke, I'd have asked for
appliances. I'd have never paraded around wearing that
paper-plate hat stapled high with bows. If only I'd known
that the rites were expendable, I'd have skipped the embarrassment of the first dance and kept my bouquet. If only I'd
known not to believe the age-old wedding-night hype that
this would be my fantasy night.

"But how could you have known?" my new husband
said. "It's not the kind of thing you read in magazines or
books. Anyway, we have the honeymoon to make up for it,
not to mention the rest of our lives."

And so we did. And so we do.

for better
or
for worse?

survivor honeymoon

amanda eyre ward

I have no memories of a happy marriage. My parents were badly matched from the start, but it took them sixteen years to bitterly divorce. "I didn't know what I was doing," my mother told me. "I chose the wrong one."

I headed into marriage with a list of what didn't work: being naive, having lots of expensive things, quitting your job to stay home with kids, being bored in the suburbs, hoping for the best. From this knowledge, I constructed a weird group of goals: be aware of every possible thing that could go wrong, live cheaply, always have a job and a way to walk out on your own, settle as far as possible from suburban New York, and be ready for the worst.

My husband and I met at a keg party in Missoula, Montana. We were both graduate students—Tip was studying geology, and I was moving toward an MFA in fiction writing. I had dated every creep in my graduate program and was branching out.

The party was thrown by three geology students who

called their home The Fun House. The geologists drank beer instead of wine, had beards instead of sideburns, and none of them quoted Raymond Carver. After two years of *New Yorker* cartoon analysis and deep pronouncements about trout streams, The Fun House was refreshing.

I was telling someone about my dream of having children and traveling with them around Africa. Tip barged right in and said he thought dragging children around Africa was unfair. We talked about this for some time.

Later, I told Tip that there were tunnels underneath my apartment building, tunnels that had once, I'd heard, been used to smuggle opium. Also, I mentioned beer in my fridge. That was that: beer and tunnels. Tip was mine.

On our first official date, we drank whiskey and talked about what had brought us to Montana. Both of us had felt out of place in our previous lives and wanted to make a new sort of life, one filled with adventure, travel, and books.

Our courtship progressed. We argued when Tip went fishing for days without calling me; we made up and went to a George Winston concert. Tip had a bathtub and a bottle of very good Scotch. I spent evenings soaking in his tub and gazing at the picture he had of himself skiing naked in the Colorado mountains. In the mornings, he made breakfast with actual ingredients that he kept in his refrigerator. While I ate SpaghettiOs and Popsicles, Tip had a spice rack. I bought an eggplant to impress him, but I had no idea what to do with it. When Tip pointed out that it was growing moldy, I threw it away.

I worked as a librarian and could order obscure nature films like *Migration of the Wildebeest.* We watched them on his bed, inside his sleeping bag. (Tip had a spice rack, yes, but no sheets.) We fought when Tip made me dinner for my birthday but didn't buy me an actual present. The dinner was the present, he explained. I'm from suburban New York, I told him: a present is supposed to be wrapped.

We broke up for about twelve hours and then met again in a bar called the Rhino. A long night of shouted threats and whispered promises followed. We moved in together. After all the confusion, all the nights I hoped I would meet my love, all the years I had spent trying to make Mr. Right Now into Mr. Right, it was so easy. Tip, there he was, that tall blond boy with the goofy smile and bright eyes. The one made just for me.

Our engagement was complicated. Tip wanted to ask me to marry him in a canoe, rafting the Gooseneck section of the San Juan River in Utah. We packed a canoe with steaks, wine, books, and vegetables. We arranged with a man named Ralph to drive our car to the end of the float in five days. "River's running high," warned Ralph. We ignored him. As we put in, a ranger ambled down to the river to tell us that he'd just rescued a family whose canoe had been wrapped around a rock "like a taco." The water was way too high, and he advised us not to head out.

But we were adventurers. Like John Wesley Powell before us, we wanted to see what was around the bend. We launched our canoe triumphantly, and the water swept us under a bridge, past onlookers who cheered. About ten minutes later, the waves almost swamped the canoe. Tip pulled the canoe over, looked at what was ahead, and said, dejectedly, "We can't do it."

It took about three hours to haul our canoe full of foodstuffs back upriver. When we passed the onlookers, they did not cheer. Ralph gave us our money back.

"Oh, well," I said.

"Oh, well nothing," said Tip. "Tomorrow, we're going to climb a mountain!"

We drove our truck with the canoe strapped on top over rutted roads, and camped in the rain. In the morning, we climbed a damn mountain. At the top, Tip said, "I really, really love you."

"Thanks," I said, and then lightning struck a nearby peak. We ran down the trail to safety.

"Okay then," I said, "time to head on back home."

"Head on back nothing," said Tip, who was beginning to act a bit strange. "We're climbing another mountain tomorrow."

"Fabulous," I said. It rained again that night. At dawn, I poked my head out of the tent to see Tip, wild-eyed, frying eggs.

"Come on! Coffee's ready!" he said. He was shaking, muttering about "early start," and "view from the top."

Now, we call the mountain Proposal Peak. I don't know what it's really called. But we never made it to the top. About halfway, I sat down heavily. "Forget it," I said. "I'm tired. I'm wet. This is it."

"Oh please," said Tip, pushing the sweat from his forehead.

"I can't," I said. "I'm exhausted."

"There's something really great at the top," said Tip.

"A cheeseburger?"

"No," said Tip.

"Then I'm staying right here."

Tip sighed and dropped to one knee. He asked me to marry him halfway up the mountain, and when I accepted, he tied a flower around my finger. We hiked to our campsite, packed up, and headed into town to celebrate. At the True Grit Café, a weary waitress asked if I'd like French fries or onion rings with my burger.

"I'll have both!" I exclaimed. "We just got engaged!"

She shrugged and wrote our order down. She returned with the best onion rings I've ever eaten in my life.

It's hard for me to remember how I felt on my wedding day. Yes, I had the long dress, my mother's lace veil, pearl earrings from a Tiffany's box. Tip and I exchanged vows on the top of another Colorado mountain, and I truly have no recollection about what I was thinking. I certainly look happy in the pictures. (But I stared at my mother's wedding pictures for years, and she looked happy, too.) I do remember, as we fell asleep next to each other that night after a midnight picnic of wedding leftovers, feeling a sense of safety and relief. I had found him, and he was the kind of person who would always take care of me. I cherished Tip—I was amazed and awed by him—and I was his wife. It was a simple happiness, and yet I had never known anything like it before. I feel it still, underneath everything I do: my love is next to me.

My parents had honeymooned in Bermuda. They lay in hammocks and played golf. I guess I thought that if my honeymoon were different, my marriage would be, too. We chose to go to Belize, which, like us, was cheap and edgy. We took three-week vacations and made reservations for only the first night. We stuffed big backpacks with bathing suits, snorkels, and hiking shoes.

We had moved to Texas for Tip's Ph.D. work, and the morning after our wedding, we headed back to Austin, where we planned to catch a flight to Belize City. We spent the night in Amarillo, at the Big Texan Motor Inn. It was the best hotel in Amarillo, our friend told us. Actually, his words were, "Well, if you can eat a seventy-two-ounce steak in an hour, your room is free."

We booked the honeymoon suite.

Unhappily, they had stopped serving beef by the time we arrived. We climbed the stairs to our room, me carrying the straw hat full of strawberries, Tip holding the free bottle of Cold Duck champagne.

The headboard of our marital bed was made of brown antlers bound together with rawhide. And the promised "heart-shaped Jacuzzi" was actually a dingy beige bathtub in the normal oval shape, albeit with some moldy jets. There were cigarette burns in the couch, where other honeymooners must have smoked as they ate their strawberries.

We twisted off the top of our champagne and toasted a new life together under the antler chandelier. My best friend—the only person as strange as me—was now my husband. I remember feeling a bit scared at the prospect of forever. Maybe making our honeymoon as taxing as possible let us both forget about the real challenge: a lifetime of staying in love.

. . .

We made it to Belize by the following day. Belize is an English-speaking country in Central America, located between Mexico and Guatemala. It's known for both its jungles and beaches and is a mecca for serious scuba divers. In July, it's hot.

Under the weight of our enormous backpacks, we trudged to find a bus, which would take us to a ferry, where we could ride a slow boat under the blazing sun to an island called Caye Caulker, where we would keep on slogging until we found our hotel. We had a clean room with a minifridge, which we decided was way too luxurious. By morning, we'd checked into Ignacio's Cabins, where twelve dollars bought us a night in a rickety cabin overlooking the water.

That night, I sidled up to a beachside bar and told the bartender I was on my honeymoon. "Ah," he said lasciviously, "then I will make you a *special* drink."

From one sip I was hooked. Made of coconut rum, pineapple juice, and fresh lime, the cocktail tasted wild and sexy. A drink that tasted the way I wanted to feel. "Order me another," I requested.

Tip went to the bar, and I heard the bartender laugh and say loudly, "Another *Panty Ripper* for the new wife!"

Oh, dear. I had fallen for a cocktail named the Panty Ripper. We were so embarrassed to order them that by our second day, we bought the ingredients and mixed them ourselves. We had cocktails, went for a steak dinner, and sat in hammocks under the moon. In bed, I read *Memoirs of a Geisha* with a headlamp strapped to my head.

Ignacio went crazy the next morning. At least, we think it was Ignacio. A man yelled, roosters crowed, and we realized that our rustic cabin lacked not only electricity, but peace and quiet. Also, drawn no doubt by the fragrance of Panty Rippers, fire ants had arrived in full force. After a day of scuba diving, we ate grilled lobster and discussed the future of our honeymoon. We wanted to do more scuba diving, and we wanted to see a monkey. I knew my parents had not seen a monkey on their honeymoon. In fact, my mother had told me that my father had mostly watched TV in their air-conditioned room.

We headed to San Ignacio, a town near jungle preserves. In a coffee shop, we met a young man named Louis who claimed he could take us into an underground cave system. "Show up here in the morning," he said. "Wear your bathing suit and be brave." The cave was called Actun Tunichil Muknal, "Cave of the Stone Sepulchre."

We couldn't resist. After my morning eggs and Pepto-Bismol, we climbed aboard a van and drove toward the rain forest with Louis. We parked and hiked along a jungle pathway to the mouth of a cave. "Go on and swim then," said Louis, when we hit a river. We put on our headlamps and dove in. When we surfaced, we were inside an amazing cavern. Columns of crystal glimmered from the walls, and Louis led us for three hours, pointing out shards of Mayan pottery. At times, we inched along slick rock walls, and at times we had to swim again, holding our breath. I am scared of heights and almost couldn't climb a rickety ladder to a second-story grotto.

Finally, he told us to stop and close our eyes. We held hands, and when he said, "Now!" we spun around. Illuminated by our headlamps, the skeleton of a young girl shone, partially settled into the dusty ground. She had been killed, Louis explained, as part of a Mayan sacrificial ritual. She had been left in the cave for the gods, and later for adventurous tourists.

At the end of the day I was exhausted, but not exhausted enough to sleep through the music pounding through the walls of our ratty hostel. My husband and I held each other as the theme song from *Friends* played with a thumping techno beat. This was nothing like my parents' honeymoon, I told myself happily.

The next day, I saw an index card tacked to the wall of the hostel:

GLOVER'S REEF

ISLAND GETAWAY

$100 A WEEK

BRING YOUR OWN FOOD

MEET AT MINERVA'S GUEST HOUSE SAT A.M., WAIT FOR BOAT

We had heard that Glover's Reef, a marine reserve in the Caribbean, had some of the best scuba diving in the world. The only resorts we had ever read about on Glover's Reef charged thousands a week. After dinner, we packed our bags and counted our traveler's checks.

We brought our own food: chocolate, rum, various fruit drinks and Coke for mixers. Bread, peanut butter, nasty cheese triangles, fruit. We shouldered our backpacks and hopped a bus that led away, far away from all the lovely beach resorts and vacationers who wanted, well, a vacation. We shared the bus with some Belizean people and some Belizean farm animals. When I smiled wide and told a rotund man in a straw hat that we were headed to Minerva's Guest House, he guffawed and said, "Minerva's! Oh, ho ho!"

I decided to believe that all the people on the bus were laughing with us.

My husband squinted out the bus window, calculating our location. I loved that he read the landscape like a novel and always knew where we were in the world. Before Tip, I had never really used maps. With him, the whole world made more sense.

The bus driver pulled to the side of a dirt road, pointed to the bushes, and said, "Walk awhile that way."

Gamely, we shouldered our packs and bushwhacked. Finally, we came upon a dilapidated dwelling barely held aloft by splintered logs. A hand-painted sign proclaimed, BUNK HOUSE. Dirty tapestries waved from the windows, and a fan hummed hello. The shack had been painted a cheery green and white. "Okay!" I said. We ducked inside.

Lying on bunks were the four other couples who would share our weeklong adventure: Randy, a German man who had married Marisa, a Spanish woman; the Brinkleys, from Columbus, who wouldn't make it the whole week; Sunshine and David, San Franciscans peroxided to platinum blond; and a couple from New Zealand who were biking their way around the world (somehow). We chatted for a while and determined that we had all seen the same index card at the same hostel and none of us had the slightest idea what lay ahead, but for a hundred bucks a week, what the hell.

Minerva arrived, a slight woman in a porkpie hat. She took us down the street to buy eggs and butter, advising that the Frenchman would arrive in the morning to pick us up on his sailboat. When pressed, she explained that he would bring us back in seven days or so.

Mushed into a bunk together, my husband and I slept fitfully.

The Frenchman arrived, as promised, with a young woman who appeared to be either Minerva's daughter, the Frenchman's lover, or both. The Frenchman collected our cash dollars and stood aside as we loaded our gear into the sailboat. Hands on either side of his potbelly, he did not respond to our myriad questions about where we were going and when we would be back. My husband—and I was proud of this, that the handsome geologist in aqua swim shorts was mine—loaded our rum and supplies, donned his DAMN GULLS hat (complete with fake bird dung), and climbed aboard happily. As per my recent vows, I followed him.

We set sail on water as clear and blue as mouthwash. In

English and halting English, we talked about scuba and sunscreen. The Frenchman and the young woman stared stonily ahead, steering the boat toward a tiny island. As we neared, thatched-roof homes became visible. The Frenchman muttered something about *choose a hut* and *pit latrines*. We docked and were met by three more French-speaking people and handed a price list.

The hut and pit latrine, it seemed, were included in our hundred dollars. Everything else—from canoes to water to scuba gear—was priced at a premium. One of the French-speaking people was a dark man with no shirt and mirrored sunglasses. He told me I could call him the Breeze and asked if I wanted to scuba.

"Yes," I said. "We want to scuba." I pointed to my husband and said proudly, "I'm married."

The Breeze was undeterred. "Night dive?" he asked. "How about a night dive tonight?"

We weren't experienced divers, but this was irresistible. We made plans to meet the Breeze on the north beach at sundown. Then we picked our way carefully over the exposed roots of palm trees toward the thatched-roof huts lined up on the beach. We chose one and climbed inside. The view from the hut was amazing, and the structure only swayed a little when the wind blew. We had been given an array of buckets for washing and cooking. We heated up some SpaghettiOs and gulped warm Sprite.

The Breeze was ready to roll when we arrived on the north beach. He piled gear into a boat, and we headed into the waves as the sun set. We perched on the edge of the boat, and I tested my oxygen line. "I don't think . . . ," I said, but the Breeze put a palm in the center of my chest and pushed me into the water. As the weight belt pulled me down, I breathed deeply. Luckily, the oxygen worked.

Being underwater is amazing, but being underwater at night is magical. My flashlight attracted glowing bugs, and moonlight filtered over the fish and plants. The Breeze looked bored as Tip and I swam, hand in hand, through the coral reefs. When I met my husband's eyes, they were also filled with wonder.

We spent a week scuba diving and reading and drinking rum mixed with various juices. We became friends with the other couples, and when Mrs. Brinkley went crackers and insisted she had to "get off this teeny tiny fucking island," we all sympathized. My husband was the only one who knew how to fillet and cook a fish, so evenings were punctuated by visitors bearing gifts of cigarettes or food in exchange for his expertise.

We went a little crackers, too. Tip began recording the actions of various lizards around our hut. I had lengthy daydreams about chlorinated pools and room service. Bugs, as always, were an issue. Walking to a pit latrine became less edgy and more annoying, especially in the middle of the night. But each evening, we watched the sun set over the water. We even threw a party the last day, cooking all our extra food and serving it mixed together. The party was BYOB . . . bring your own bowl.

When we finally sailed back to Minerva's, seven days that felt like seven months later, we decided to take the bus to Guatemala. We had heard that the border crossing was dangerous, but the ruins of Tikal seemed worth the risk.

On the bus, a Belizean woman told me about her honeymoon. "We had a big meal, some dancing, and a nap," she said, patting her pregnant belly. "It was a wonderful nap," she said.

For just a moment, I felt tired. Did I really think that I could ensure a happy marriage by never relaxing? I thought about how wonderful it would feel to slow down. To check into a clean hotel somewhere safe and ease into my new husband's arms. To hope for the best. But I was too afraid of what might happen if I stopped filling my mind with logistics and plans.

We reached the place between Belize and Guatemala, and it felt scary. Shifty-eyed teenagers sidled up to us and offered unbelievable exchange rates. No one could agree on what we needed to pay to get over the border. We were told that Guatemala was filled with armed men who would drive us into countryside, shoot us for our shoes, and leave us to rot.

We pressed on. Over the border, a man approached us and offered to drive us to Tikal. Nervously, we accepted and climbed into his dented pickup truck. We knew this was dangerous. But somehow being in real danger felt good to me. At least when I got into a truck with a shifty-eyed man, a backpack full of expensive items, a passport, and traveler's checks at my side, I knew what to be afraid of.

The man drove us away from the border crossing, into

Guatemala. The road was narrow and deserted. "I want to show you something," said the man. My husband stared straight ahead. I saw that his jaw was clenched. His eyes scanned the road frantically, and I could tell that he was trying to understand where we were.

"What is it?" I said.

"It's a lake," said the man. His voice was hard. My husband swallowed.

But there was a lake, and we stood by it, and the man took our picture. We got back in the car, and the man drove us to Tikal. We saw monkeys and ruins; we flew home and made a life together. We had a son, and my love for him is so fierce I can hardly leave the room much less travel the world without him.

I realize now that our honeymoon was made up of self-imposed dangers: no one made us go scuba diving at night or cross the Guatemalan border. Life—and this was before September 11 and Iraq, and before my son showed me what real fear meant—was safe and simple. Courting thrills in foreign countries seemed more important, somehow, than just taking a nap.

I feel differently now. I want to keep my son safe but not sheltered; I want to write about the world with clarity. I want to sleep heavily at night. These have proved harder tasks than braving ratty guesthouses or scuba dives.

I look at the picture of my husband and me, taken by a Guatemalan lake almost six years ago. My husband told me later that he thought this was the end: the man would take our picture and then pull out a knife or gun. In the picture, he looks tanned and nervous, wearing the aqua shorts that are now hanging on a chair, drying out from yesterday's trip to a local pool to teach our son to swim.

My husband looks straight at the camera. He thought this was the end, and he is holding my hand.

weddings for everyone

amy bloom

I love weddings. I love the tall, blonde bride, curvy and flushed, holding a bouquet of peonies, very much like a peony herself. I love the short, geeky groom, made handsome by his radiant conviction that this pink and perfect girl loves him and smiles for him alone. I love the multi-culti affair: jumping the broom and crushing the glass; the bride in a teal, gold-embroidered sari, the groom in a dashiki; him in a yarmulke and sober suit, her in the traditional barong; two young women in white tuxedoes and leis; dim sum and lasagna at the reception; toasts made by the father from Slovakia and the father from Des Moines and soon multiply pierced teenagers from Ames are doing the czarda.

I love drippy, sentimental toasts made by men who pride themselves on their discipline, and witty, impassioned ones made by demure aunts, who reveal themselves, after a couple of champagne cocktails, to be the offspring of Edna St. Vincent Millay and Sandra Bernhard. I love the older couples. (Although I am disturbed by the bridal business phrase "encore" bride, as if a second or third wedding brings box-office success, the star back by popular demand, which is a brilliant marketing ploy but surely fools no one, least of all the bride, whose fond but wary children and friends gave crystal champagne flutes the first time and teak salad bowls the second and can now be forgiven for contemplating nothing more than a lucky horseshoe. Couldn't we all simply agree that these people represent a fine, shining—or fragile, foolish, but very dear—example of the triumph of hope over experience?) I love the older couples who have been lovers for years, a little complacent in their unconventionality, pleased with their decision to forgo paper and ceremony until there comes a bout of cancer, the death of a dear friend, the birth of a grandchild, and suddenly a wedding and the concomitant piece of paper seem just the ticket. I love long-parted high school sweethearts coming together after twenty or thirty or fifty years, during which whole novels of life (along the lines of *Tess of the d'Urbervilles* and *Middlemarch*) have unfolded, still seeing each other as the handsomest boy in Urbana, the prettiest girl in Eagle County.

I like weddings so much (and having been a bride, a mother of the bride, a bridesmaid, and a guest many times over, I feel that I am, if not an authority, certainly not an amateur) that I think everyone should have one. I think that when I was twenty-six and pregnant with my first daughter, I should have been allowed to take a walk down some aisle. Afterward, we could have had a small party with petits fours and champagne, no dancing, no carrying on. This would not have been a celebration with my husband, the baby's father—with whom I had already *had* a lovely wedding—but with the man who had been my surrogate father, from whom I had been separated for several years by various misunderstandings. We had only recently come back to each other, feeling blessed by possibility (of forgiveness, of family, of his being a grandfather of a sort, at last), and it seems to me now that we were entitled to have had a proper celebration of our eternal love—and a wedding should be the term for what that thing is called. I feel this way about my fifty-year-old neighbor and her three cats; there has never been more touching devotion (on both sides; these cats come when called, lick on request, and sit by her feet until dismissed), and I feel the same about my mother and her best friend of the last fifty years. These ladies deserve a wedding and some presents and some suitable tears and the admiration of friends and family. Why shouldn't we celebrate Jeannie and Dellie as much as (if not more than) marrying-for-money, marrying-for-maid-service, and marrying-for-fear-of-the-future? (I do realize that my particular licensing bureau, which gives licenses only to people who actually love each other and have enough decency and self-awareness to make a go of it, will not be popular. I am prepared.)

Weddings are my astrology charts, my fortune cookies, and my *I Ching*. I learn something from each one, and sure enough, if I don't learn it the first time, another wedding and another marriage will roll along, to remind me that no one under twenty-five should be allowed to marry; that divorced parents who cannot behave at the wedding will get worse, not better, without a firm talking-to; that people who marry out of boredom and fear get more of the same. I was the bridesmaid for my sister when I was sixteen, and learned two things: Do not voice your doubts to the bride or groom as the clergyman is clearing his throat. Also, do not make sixteen-year-old girls wear Minnie Mouse white gloves and dresses that match the tablecloths. (I've been wanting to mention this for some time.)

I was a bride myself with the most perfect wedding weather of all time and can only say that a picture-perfect wedding does not a perfect marriage make. Also, if your mother wants you to wear white, you probably will. (What color is it? I asked her. Oh, she said, cotton color. Beige? I said. Sort of beige, she said. Sort of a beautiful, sun-bleached, very light beige.)

I was a mother of the bride and can speak well for navy silk and false eyelashes. I can also speak to the sense in choosing the squat, stinky citronella candles over the more lovely luminarias (we didn't and the entire bridal party was covered in dime-sized mosquito bites) and to the wisdom of choosing a caterer who knows your world ("Christians?" she said. "Plenty of booze." "Jews?" she said. "Double the hors d'oeuvres.") And although the wedding at which I was a bride did not last, it did give us our daughter, a beautiful bride, and it did give me and her father the chance to shed tears of joy, side by side, and to appreciate each other.

Weddings are not marriages, and I wish they were. Weddings are to marriage as a single bamboo shoot is to a jungle, as a seashell is to the ocean floor: nice enough, not unrepresentative, and almost totally irrelevant. Marriage is all about the long road, about terror and disappointment, about recovery and contentment, about passions of all kinds. Weddings are about a *party*—which is why I think marriage should be approached with blinking yellow lights, orange safety cones, and all other signs of great caution, and weddings should be encouraged as things apart. Why should we expect that looking pretty in white (or the flattering color of your choice) and doing a credible fox-trot has anything to do with staying calm in the face of resentful indifference, selective deafness, Oedipal disorders, or horrible stepchildren? It should be enough, it seems to me, to look as good as one can and enjoy the party. Brides who cannot enjoy their own weddings are either possessed of too much knowledge (the marriage is a mistake) or too much something else (like women who scream when the bouquet has one too many sprigs of baby's breath). I wish that crazy, over-the-top weddings (doves dyed pink, twin elephants, wedding favors from Gucci, and Handel's "Water Music" played by Yo-Yo Ma) led to marriages that were extravagant celebrations of love, that the excess foretold a lifetime of generosity, sensuality, and matching elephants of kindness and loyalty. I wish that simple little weddings, barefoot in a cranberry bog, with ten friends as witnesses, would lead to a life in which less really is more and stays that way. Marriage requires common sense, self-awareness, compatible senses of humor (Jackie Mason will not be happy with Oscar Wilde, although

Bernie Mac might be), compatible sex drives, and enough, but not too much, perseverance. Weddings, on the other hand, offer just a day's happiness, and require only a willingness to dance—even badly—and embrace the world and big love for a short time.

I admire marriages: I puzzle over them, I analyze them, I long to get it right. But I love weddings.

happily ever after

dani shapiro

1. The Proposal. There wasn't one. Not exactly. No
bended knee. No ring buried deep in the whipped-
cream topping of a chocolate mousse. Not even
a candlelit dinner complete with a serenading
violinist. I was thirty-four years old. My future
husband, forty. We had been around the block a few
times. He—with girlfriends on every continent—
had developed a bit of a reputation as a toxic
bachelor. One of those guys who was never going to
settle down. And me? I wasn't exactly a good bet,
myself. Twice married—each marriage had lasted
less than a year. So it would be reasonable to think
that it took many months of dating before the idea
of marriage presented itself. But in fact, we both
knew the second we met each other. The lunatic
thought cascading through my mind the moment I
met him: *There you are.* We were at a Halloween
party, of all things at the home of a couple who has
since divorced. I was not in costume, nor was my
future husband. In fact, if he had been dressed up
as, say, a giant tree (there was indeed a giant tree in

attendance) I never would have made it past hello.
I don't remember what we talked about that night.
A jumble of our histories: our lives as writers, our
suburban childhoods. The people—and there were
many—whom we knew in common. How was it
that we had never met before? Beneath all the words
was a strange knowledge, solid as bedrock. *You're
mine.* We both felt it. *You're mine.* He never asked
me to marry him. I never said yes.

2. **The Engagement.** Having been twice married was
the strangest thing about me, a major glitch on my
C.V. It was very hard to explain, even to myself. I
had had two big white weddings. Two engagement
parties. I had gone shopping for two designer gowns.
I had spent a lot of time dreaming about *the
wedding day* and not nearly enough time thinking
about *the marriage.* And so I didn't want to be
engaged. I wanted to elope. Paris! In the springtime!
I had a vision of old world romance: cobblestone
streets, a magistrate's office (what was a magistrate?)
Vows exchanged in a foreign language, me in a chic
little dress. The two of us—alone—affirming our
future. I couldn't bear the idea of floating down the
aisle in a white confection. A fancy wedding—to
me—equaled *mistake.* All surface and no depth. All
pomp and no circumstance. But my husband—he
who was never going to get married at all—wanted

his parents there. And his siblings. He wanted our union to be witnessed by a few people he loved. And who could blame him? If his parents and siblings were going to be there, then mine had to be, too. And if our families were going to be there, well, then we had to have a few close friends, didn't we? The number swelled to twenty. Twenty people who were sworn to secrecy. It wasn't quite an elopement, but it was the closest we could manage.

3. **The Ring.** I didn't want one of those, either. Not, at least, if by *the ring* you mean *a rock*. I had already experienced the thrill of wearing a rock. The three-carat flawless emerald-cut engagement ring from my previous marriage had wound up on Forty-seventh Street in New York—the jewelry district—a bargain for some bride and groom who didn't care about its messy provenance. So together, Michael and I picked out wedding rings. Delicate platinum flowers and vines studded with tiny diamonds for me. A matte platinum band for him. The process took about half an hour.

4. **The Dress.** A little slip of nothing, a bit of ivory silk, held up by spaghetti straps. Purchased at the same store (Barneys in New York City) as the ring. One-stop shopping! I tried it on for my future husband. No superstition for me. Michael loved it,

but I thought I'd bring my mother to the store to show her, too. My mother could barely contain her horror when she saw me emerge from behind the dressing room curtains. She looked me up and down, confused by the minimalist slip, designed by an intellectual Belgian. *Where's the dress?* So I went down to the main floor and bought a gossamer shawl, as light as air. The shawl cost more than the dress.

5. **The Rabbi.** I found her by calling directory assistance. 1-800-RABBI. I picked out a temple in a good neighborhood. Asked for the rabbi and was told there were five to choose from. I pretty much closed my eyes and pointed. I liked the idea of a woman. And I liked her name. *Amy.* She sounded like someone I might have gone to camp with. And she had a nice, soothing voice, warm and steady, like someone who believed in God. My own feelings about God were complicated. Did He exist? If so, was He micromanaging my life? My husband's beliefs were more straightforward: He had none. But we were both Jewish and each of us had a sentimental attachment to the rituals of our ancestors: the Hebrew blessings, the sound—like no other—of a glass being smashed beneath the groom's heel. I wanted to be married under my dead father's tallis. Even though it had already seen a lot of action, I still believed in the power of its protection.

6. **The Venue.** As they say. Places cease to be restaurants or cafés or small inns in the country and become *venues*. A theatrical backdrop for the main event. We picked a small inn downtown in New York City for the ceremony: a cozy spot where elderly ladies met for tea, and a harpist sometimes played in the afternoons. For the dinner, a private dining room upstairs at La Grenouille, a venerable French restaurant about forty blocks north. The room had a towering ceiling and huge windows. I pictured candlelight, a yellow glow from the sconces lining the old plaster walls. It looked like an elaborate wine cellar. Three round tables, just enough for our number of guests. I tried to choose places that might still exist in fifty years. Places that our kids—if we had kids—might someday point out to their own kids. *That's where your grandparents got married*, they would say. It was permanence I was after. Gravitas. Something that felt real.

7. **The Details.** The food, the champagne toast, the floral arrangements. They were all a lovely blur. Something about pale roses, French double tulips. Filet of beef. Sole veronique. Wilted spinach or haricots verts? A cello for the ceremony. Taped music for the dinner. Cream-colored place cards. The only time in my life I have used the word "boutonniere." Even though I had promised myself I wouldn't get carried away—even though it was a teeny, tiny

wedding—I found myself debating the merits of lemon icing versus mocha. And what about the tablecloths? The tablecloths were important, weren't they?

8. **The Photographer.** I wanted images that would last. Images that would be timeless and classic, yet also somehow casual and carefree. I wanted black-and-white. Nothing posed. And so we found an advertising guy who moonlighted as a wedding photographer. His studio was full of glossy pictures that could easily have been torn from the pages of a J.Crew catalog. No stiffly smiling brides and grooms flanked by their extended families. It was hard—not to mention pricey—work, making everything look simple.

9. **The Guests.** Ah, the guests. *You* try deciding which of your friends make the cut when the number has to stay under twenty. It's much easier to make up a guest list of two hundred! We began with family. My mother, my half sister. Michael's parents. His brother and sister-in-law. His younger sister. That was it for family. We drew the line at aunts and uncles. Certainly no cousins. Our grandparents were all dead—a side effect of getting married so late in life. We started adding the friends. My very best friend, Betsy, and her husband, Ron. My other very dear friend, Helen, and her husband, Bruce. Our

mutual friend Melanie—she who introduced us that very first, fateful night. Esther, my literary agent. Michael's pal Barry. His college friend Eddie, and his girlfriend, Kate. And his other great friend, Scott, and his wife, Becky. That was it. The whole kit and caboodle.

10. **The Honeymoon.** Paris and Provence. A safe bet, to be sure. No Tanzanian safaris for us. No exotic destination requiring malaria pills. We wanted to be alone together in the lap of luxury. Each of us harboring the sneaking suspicion that it might be a very, very long time before our lives involved Frette sheets scattered with fallen flakes from room service croissants, lazy afternoons spent reading whole novels at the prettiest infinity pool along the Cote d'Azur. We were working writers, after all. Working writers (with working writer's salaries) who might one day have children. And so we shopped for faience pottery in tiny hilltop villages. We ate langoustine at midnight. We slept all morning, the *ne pas déranger* sign hanging outside our door. I could go on.

11. **The Marriage.** Here is what I know, and it may be all I know on the subject of being a bride: The ring, the dress, the proposal, the place cards and flowers, the music, the minister or rabbi or justice of the peace—it will all add up to exactly nothing. There

will be a moment when it's all over. A moment
when, in a hungover, happy, bleary state you roll
over and look at the guy next to you and think, *my
husband* for the very first time. *My husband.* The
words will roll over and over in your mouth, in your
mind—until one day, the concept simply becomes a
part of you. You are a wife. You have a husband. The
two of you together make a family of two, of three,
of four, or even—God help you—more. People may,
from time to time, ask how the two of you met.
They may ask how long you've been married. But
here are some questions I've never been asked in the
nine years since my wedding day: *Where was the
wedding? Who was the caterer? What flavor was the
cake? What kind of flowers?*

12. **Happily Ever After.** The dress hangs in its garment
bag in our house in the country. Every once in a
while I think of pulling it out and trying to wear it
to some black-tie event, but after giving birth to our
son, I'm afraid—very afraid—of how it will fit. The
ring—that delicate platinum band of leaves and
flowers—has broken four times and been sent back
to Barneys to be re-soldered. The wedding bouquet
dried and finally crumbled after being subjected
to several moves. Rabbi Amy is a part of our lives.
I called her in despair after a miscarriage. She
officiated at my mother's funeral. The timeless,
black-and-white photographs are still not in an

album. The proofs are in a small box high up on a shelf in my office closet, waiting for me to have a free afternoon to go through them. And the guests? My mother is dead. My half sister and I no longer speak. Two out of three of my invitees—the most important people in my life at the time!—are now people with whom I exchange holiday cards. Ditto for my husband and his friends. The literary agent—let's just say we parted ways. But what I do have—after the crumbled bouquet, the fading proofs, the broken ring, the lost friends and family—is a husband. One whom I roll over and look at first thing in the morning—our middle-aged faces creased by our pillows—and think: *He's a keeper.*

CONTRIBUTORS

Samina Ali was born in Hyderabad, India, and raised both there and in the United States. Her debut novel, *Madras on Rainy Days* (Farrar Straus Giroux), chronicles a young Muslim American woman's journey to freedom and was awarded the Prix Premier du Roman Etranger 2005 Award (Best First Novel in Translation of the Year) by France and was also chosen as the finalist for both the PEN/Hemingway Award in Fiction as well as the California Book Reviewers Award. *Poets & Writers* named *Madras* as one of the Top 5 Best Debut Novels of the Year. The novel has been translated into many different languages and released around the world. Ms. Ali has been invited to lecture on the book extensively, from the University of California, Berkeley, on the West Coast to Harvard and Yale universities on the East. She is the recipient of the Rona Jaffe Foundation and Barbara Deming Memorial awards for fiction. Most recently, essays of hers have been included in *The May Queen* and *Living Islam Out Loud* anthologies. She has also written for publications as diverse as *Self* and *Child* magazines, *The New York Times*, and the *San Francisco Chronicle*. She resides in California with her son.

Jennifer Armstrong is a staff writer at *Entertainment Weekly*, where, after five years, she's still shocked to be getting paid to obsess over TV, books, and pop culture in general. She cofounded and continues to edit the online alternative women's magazine

Sirens (www.SirensMag.com). In her previous lives, she was a daily newspaper reporter and trade magazine editor.

Julianna Baggott is the author of four novels, including *Which Brings Me to You* (cowritten with Steve Almond), and two books of poetry, most recently *Lizzie Borden in Love*. Under the pen name N. E. Bode, she's the author of The Anybodies trilogy, novels for younger readers. She teaches at Florida State University's Creative Writing Program. For more, visit www.juliannabaggott.com.

Amy Bloom is the author of two short-story collections (one a finalist for the National Book Award, one for the National Book Critics Circle Award), two novels, and a collection of essays. She teaches at Yale and lives in Connecticut.

Janelle Brown is a freelance journalist, writing for *The New York Times*, *Vogue*, and *Self*. She was previously a senior writer at *Salon*, covering technology, culture, and the arts; and, in the early days of the Net, worked at *Wired*'s online publications *HotWired* and *Wired News*. She lives in Los Angeles with her husband, Greg Harrison, and their very spoiled Labrador retriever, Guster.

Anne Carle has been writing professionally for seventeen years. Her writing path has led her through various nonprofit organizations, magazines, Internet start-ups, and as of late, a very large financial corporation. Carle currently resides with her partner, three dogs, and two cats in Richmond, Virginia, where they enjoy playing Scrabble, watching bad made-for-television movies, and drumming around a fire pit in the backyard.

Lisa Carver is the author of *Rollerderby*, *Dancing Queen*, *The Lisa Diaries*, and *Drugs Are Nice*. Her love life continues to be a wreck and the wedding proceedings have not gone at all as planned in the essay written for this book, but she is very happy about that, as proceedings that *do* go as planned upset her greatly.

Carina Chocano is a film critic at the *Los Angeles Times*. She has been a staff writer at *Entertainment Weekly* and *Salon* and her work has appeared in *The New Yorker*, *The New York Times*, and *Bust* magazine. She's also done other things, but we don't need to go into them. She lives in Los Angeles with her soon-to-be-husband and her cat, Woofy.

Elizabeth Crane is the author of two collections of short stories, *When the Messenger Is Hot* and *All This Heavenly Glory*. She teaches creative writing at the University of Chicago and Northwestern University and is a regular contributor to *Writer's Block Party* on WBEZ Chicago. She also writes a blog, standBy Bert (www.elizabethcrane.com/blog/), which has at least a dozen readers.

Meghan Daum is a columnist at the *Los Angeles Times* and the author of the novel *The Quality of Life Report* and the essay collection *My Misspent Youth*. Her work has appeared in *The New Yorker*, *Harper's*, *Vogue*, and *Elle*, among other publications. She lives in Los Angeles.

Daisy de Villeneuve was born in London in 1975. Daisy studied Fashion and Fine Art at Parsons School of Design in both New York and Paris. Daisy has written and illustrated two books, *He Said She Said* and *What Goes Around Comes Around*, which draw upon her life experiences, both published by Chronicle Books, featuring her trademark style of felt-tip pen and typewriter text. De Villeneuve has collaborated with Topshop, Nike, and the Victoria and Albert Museum. She regularly contributes to magazines such as *Elle Girl Korea*, *Nylon*, and *British Vogue* as both a writer and illustrator.

Jill Eisenstadt is the author of the novels *From Rockaway* and *Kiss Out* and is cowriter and producer on the 2006 feature film *The Limbo Room*. Her shorter work has appeared extensively in

The New York Times and other places, including *Vogue, Elle, Mademoiselle,* and *Bomb* magazines. She lives in Brooklyn with her husband, the writer Michael Drinkard, and their three daughters.

Rory Evans lives in New York City with her husband, Jamie, and their cat, Cletus P. Savian.

Kathleen Hughes's first novel, *Dear Mrs. Lindbergh,* was published by W. W. Norton in 2003. A graduate of Yale University and the Iowa Writer's Workshop, Kathleen teaches high school English in Rhode Island, where she lives with her husband, daughter, and dog. Kathleen's work has been published in *Pieces: A Collection of New Voices, Talking River Review, Land Grant College Review,* and the *Providence Phoenix* and *Boston Phoenix* newspapers.

Catherine Ingrassia is a professor of English and associate dean for academic affairs at Virginia Commonwealth University. Her books include *Authorship, Commerce and Gender in Early Eighteenth-Century England: A Culture of Paper Credit* (Cambridge, 1998), *More Solid Learning: New Perspectives on Alexander Pope's Dunciad,* coedited with Claudia N. Thomas (Bucknell, 2000), and *A Companion to the Eighteenth-Century English Novel and Culture,* coedited with Paula R. Backscheider (Blackwell, 2005). She is also the editor of Eliza Haywood's *Anti-Pamela* and Henry Fielding's *Shamela* (Broadview, 2004), and a past editor of *Studies in Eighteenth-Century Culture.* She and her husband live with their two children in Richmond, Virginia.

Ruth Davis Konigsberg has been published in *Elle, Glamour,* and *The New York Observer.* She lives in New York City with her husband and son.

Lori Leibovich is the founder of Indiebride.com, and the editor of the anthology *Maybe Baby: 28 Writers Tell the Truth about Skepti-*

cism, Infertility, Baby Lust, Childlessness, Ambivalence, and How They Made the Biggest Decision of Their Lives. She is a contributing editor at *Salon*, and her writing has appeared in *The New York Times, The Washington Post, The New York Observer, Elle, Harper's Bazaar*, and in the anthologies *Mothers Who Think* and *The Real Las Vegas*. She lives in Brooklyn with her husband and son.

Elise Mac Adam writes the "IndieEtiquette" column for Indiebride.com and chronicles the vicissitudes of parenthood in the "IndieMom Blog." She also writes screenplays, including the original script for Cindy Sherman's movie *Office Killer*, and is a filmmaker whose short films are better traveled than she is. Her work has appeared in numerous publications, including the book *City Wedding*, and in *Film Comment, Time Out New York*, and *Condé Nast Traveller* magazines. She is currently writing a book of modern wedding etiquette.

Farah L. Miller lives with her husband in Brooklyn, New York. As the director of new media at Alfred A. Knopf, she produced Web sites for bestselling authors, and has spoken at interactive conferences about reaching niche audiences online. Farah never expected to love being a bride as much as she did. She was so "altared" by the process that in November 2006, she became managing editor at Brides.com, where she is helping other women go bridal without losing their minds.

Jacquelyn Mitchard is the *New York Times* bestselling author of *The Deep End of the Ocean, The Most Wanted, A Theory of Relativity, Twelve Times Blessed*, the novellas *Christmas, Present* and *The Breakdown Lane*, and her newest novel, *Cage of Stars*. She is also the author of *The Rest of Us: Dispatches from the Mother Ship*, a collection of her essays, which are syndicated nationwide by Tribune Media Services. She has published three children's books, including the award-winning *Rosalie, My Rosalie: The Tale of a Duckling*. Her first young adult novel will be published in January 2007. She was a member of the 2002 fiction jury for The National Book Award and speechwriter for former Department of Health and Human Services Secretary Donna Shalala. She lives in Madison, Wisconsin, with her husband and seven children.

Julie Powell is the author of *Julie & Julia* (Little, Brown & Co., 2005). Her work has appeared in *Bon Appetit, Food & Wine, The New York Times Magazine*, and *Archaeology*, among other periodicals, as well as in *The New York Times, The Washington Post*, and *The Boston Globe*. She has reviewed books on *All Things Considered* and appeared as a judge on *Iron Chef America* (the secret ingredient was frozen peas). She is the winner of two James Beard Awards and the first annual Blooker Prize. Julie lives in Queens with her husband, Eric, three cats, a ball python, and Robert the dog.

Dani Shapiro's novel *Black & White* was recently published by Knopf. Other books include the novel *Family History* and the bestselling memoir *Slow Motion*. Her stories and essays have appeared in *The New Yorker, Granta, Elle, Oprah, Ploughshares, Bookforum*, and many other magazines. She is currently Visiting Writer at Wesleyan University. She lives with her family in Litchfield County, Connecticut. Her Web site is www.danishapiro.com.

Curtis Sittenfeld is the author of the bestselling novels *Prep* and *The Man of My Dreams*, which are being translated into more than twenty languages. *Prep* also was chosen as one of the Ten Best Books of 2005 by *The New York Times*, nominated for the UK's Orange Prize, and optioned by Paramount Pictures. Sittenfeld's nonfiction has appeared in *The Atlantic Monthly, Salon, Glamour*, and on public radio's *This American Life*.

Amy Sohn is the author of the novels *Run Catch Kiss* and *My Old Man* and a contributing editor at *New York* magazine. She has also written for *The Nation*, *Harper's Bazaar*, *The New York Times Book Review*, and *Playboy*. She grew up in Brooklyn, New York, where she still lives today.

Lara Vapnyar came to the United States from Russia in 1994. She is the author of a story collection, *There Are Jews in My House*, and a novel, *Memoirs of a Muse*. Her fiction has appeared in *The New Yorker*, *Harper's*, and *Open City*. She lives in New York with her husband and two children.

Amanda Eyre Ward is the author of *Sleep Toward Heaven* and *How to Be Lost*. Her third novel, *Forgive Me*, will be published in the summer of 2007. She lives in Austin, Texas, with her husband and son. They hope to return to Belize very soon, but this time, Amanda would not like to bring her own food.

Gina Zucker's fiction and journalism have appeared in numerous journals and magazines, among them *Tin House*, *Salt Hill*, *Glamour*, *GQ*, *Cosmopolitan*, *Redbook*, and *Rolling Stone*. Her short story "Big People" was chosen for the forthcoming fiction anthology *Fantastic Women* (Tin House Books, 2007), and her story "Punishment" is collected in the anthology *Before: Short Stories About Pregnancy from Our Top Writers* (Overlook Press, 2006). She teaches creative writing at the Pratt Institute in Brooklyn, New York.

ACKNOWLEDGMENTS

Many thanks to my editor, Lisa Weinert, for being a champion of this book and helping it find a home at Vintage Books. To my agent, Eric Simonoff, for shepherding the deal, and to Michael Steger, who was instrumental in permissions and who handled my many questions with grace and kindness. To my family, Marybeth Raff, John Curran, and Maggie Curran, always for your love and support, and for making my wedding one of the best days of my life. To Chase Decker, William Decker, and Annette McGrew for welcoming me into your family with love and laughter. To my good friends Gretchen Comba and Sarah Lese, for listening to my ideas for this book and for the good fortune of your friendship. To my husband, Francis Decker, for being a voice of reason and for always believing in me. And, of course, to the twenty-seven writers who offered their insights, their talents, and their stories of the big day.

CONTRIBUTOR ACKNOWLEDGMENTS

Lori Leibovich: "My So-Called Indie Wedding" by Lori Leibovich, copyright © 2007 by Lori Leibovich.

Elise Mac Adam: "Manners and the Marrying Girl" by Elise Mac Adam, copyright © 2007 by Elise Mac Adam.

Farah L. Miller: "Going Bridal" by Farah L. Miller, copyright © 2007 by Farah L. Miller.

Jacquelyn Mitchard: "First, Reader, I Made Him Up, and Then I Married Him" by Jacquelyn Mitchard, copyright © 2007 by Jacquelyn Mitchard.

Julie Powell: "Rubber Chicken" by Julie Powell, copyright © 2007 by Julie Powell.

Curtis Sittenfeld: "The Wedding Vow" by Curtis Sittenfeld, copyright © 2007 by Curtis Sittenfeld.

Amy Sohn: "Parental Control" by Amy Sohn, copyright © 2007 by Amy Sohn.

Dani Shapiro: "Happily Ever After" by Dani Shapiro, copyright © 2007 by Dani Shapiro.

Lara Vapnyar: "The Girl, the Dress, and the Leap" by Lara Vapnyar, copyright © 2007 by Lara Vapnyar.

Daisy de Villeneuve: "It All Started with Princess Di" by Daisy de Villeneuve, copyright © 2007 by Daisy de Villeneuve.

Amanda Eyre Ward: "Survivor Honeymoon" by Amanda Eyre Ward, copyright © 2007 by Amanda Eyre Ward.

Gina Zucker: "My Mother's Wedding, Myself" by Gina Zucker, copyright © 2007 by Gina Zucker.